Adaptation revisited

MANCHESTER
UNIVERSITY PRESS

For my parents

Adaptation revisited

Television and the classic novel

SARAH CARDWELL

Manchester University Press

MANCHESTER AND NEW YORK

distributed exclusively in the USA by Palgrave

Copyright © Sarah Cardwell 2002

The right of Sarah Cardwell to be identified as the author of this work has been asserted by her in accordance with the Copyright, Designs and Patents Act 1988.

Published by Manchester University Press
Oxford Road, Manchester M13 9NR, UK
and Room 400, 175 Fifth Avenue, New York, NY 10010, USA
http://www.manchesteruniversitypress.co.uk

Distributed exclusively in the USA by
Palgrave, 175 Fifth Avenue, New York, NY 10010, USA

Distributed exclusively in Canada by
UBC Press, University of British Columbia, 2029 West Mall,
Vancouver, BC, Canada V6T 1Z2

British Library Cataloguing-in-Publication Data
A catalogue record for this book is available from the British Library

Library of Congress Cataloging-in-Publication Data applied for

ISBN 0 7190 6045 1 *hardback*
     0 7190 6046 x *paperback*

First published 2002

10 09 08 07 06 05 04 03 02   10 9 8 7 6 5 4 3 2 1

Typeset in Scala with Meta display
by Koinonia, Manchester
Printed in Great Britain
by Bookcraft (Bath) Ltd, Midsomer Norton

Contents

List of figures

The figures can be found between p. 128 and p. 129

Acknowledgements

There are many people who have played a part in seeing this book through to completion. The foremost influence has been Brian McFarlane, whose own work on adaptation is rightfully renowned, and who has valiantly read drafts of this work from the earliest stages and has always been encouraging, incisive and enthusiastic in his responses. I am extremely grateful to have benefited from the input of such a prolific and respected scholar. In addition, Matthew Frost, of Manchester University Press, has taken an ongoing and active interest in the shape of the work, and has helped me become a rather more ruthless editor of my own writing.

Other people have commented, formally or informally, on earlier drafts. The book originated in my doctoral thesis, and thanks are due to my supervisor, Dr Jonathan Bignell, for his hard work and enthusiasm in guiding that earlier work through to completion, and for his continuing interest and support. I must also thank Professor Andrew Higson, who examined my doctoral thesis and made many helpful suggestions regarding publication; I may not have followed all his advice, but I hope to have ironed out some of the flaws to which he drew my attention. In addition, Dr Mary Wood, Adam Mills, Elisabeth Brooke and Deirdre Boleyn have all offered valuable comments on sections of this work.

The Arts and Humanities Research Board funded eighteen months of my doctorate, for which I am grateful. I extend appreciative thanks to Granada Television for the use of the colour still on the cover of this book, and to Matthew Walter, at the University of Kent, for his technical expertise which provided the frame grabs included herein. The librarians at both Royal Holloway College, University of London and the University of Kent have been extremely helpful in finding resources for me. I would like to thank for their support and interest my previous colleagues at Royal Holloway and my current colleagues in the Department of Film at Kent, in particular Professor Murray Smith.

On a more personal note, thanks are due to Charles and Elisabeth Cardwell, and my closest friends, Matthew Brooke and Dr Jon Timmis, for their friendship and loyalty, and to Matthew Frost, for all those things that fall outside his official remit as Editor and which I could not possibly outline here. Finally I must thank my parents, to whom this book is dedicated, for everything.

Introduction

This book arose from a desire to free classic-novel adaptations from the restrictive theoretical and conceptual framework within which they appeared to be imprisoned, and to break away from established interpretative and evaluative paradigms that failed to appreciate these programmes in terms of their particular aesthetic and cultural significance. When this work was first begun (1996), contemporary discourses determined that adaptations be considered almost entirely in comparison with their source novels. For various reasons, this 'comparative' approach is inadequate for the project of interpreting and evaluating adaptations in a careful and rigorous manner. Other theorists clearly felt similarly, for a range of non-comparative studies of adaptations appeared over the next few years. Unfortunately, although newer non-comparative analyses threw up some fascinating interpretations, there was a widespread failure to proffer a solid theoretical justification for the apparent severing of the connection between source text and adaptation. Nor has there been any sustained attempt to distinguish television adaptations from film adaptations, and recognise television adaptations as a distinct form or genre. In Part I, I aim to tackle these problems and provide a convincing, retrospective argument for a firmly non-comparative approach to television classic-novel adaptations. In Part II, four adaptations are considered in detail as I trace the defining traits and extraordinary development of this genre.

Classic-novel adaptations

A brief note regarding the particular group of programmes upon which this book focuses – British television adaptations of classic novels – is imperative here. I have suggested that adaptations of classic novels form a distinct genre; in conceptual terms, this is clearly no straightforward matter, and I return to this problem in Part II. However, preceding the conceptual problems inherent in the notion of 'genre' is a more basic question of categorisation: how does one decide whether or not a programme is a classic-novel adaptation?[1] This label requires some explication, not least because each of its two major qualifying terms – adaptation and classic novel – is also in its own way problematic. This rather cursory account is not intended to explore these terms and the notions that underlie them but simply to clarify the way in which I shall be using them.

Let us begin with the key descriptor: the term 'adaptation'. An adaptation in this particular context, is a film or television programme which is explicitly based on a book. It will be shown later that the seemingly innocuous words 'based on' (a book) actually conceal a minefield of conceptual and theoretical problems, but for now I would like to accept this definition of adaptation – a film or television programme based on a book – as a rudimentary basis for a more detailed definition.

Following this, I restrict the corpus still further by dealing only with adaptations based on 'classic novels'. Here again I am aware of the introduction of a particularly problematic term: 'classic'. The notion of 'classic novels' is hotly-debated, especially within English studies.[2] However, for the purposes of this investigation, I imply by this term that meaning by which it is pre-theoretically understood; that is, I intend 'classic novels' to be descriptive of certain texts which are commonly held by television viewers to be 'classics'. The classic novels under consideration are, of course, limited to those from which television adaptations have been made, and these adaptations tend to draw upon a small (though ever-expanding) number of texts by an even smaller number of 'classic authors'. The authors who are most favoured by the makers of these adaptations – Austen, the Brontës, Dickens, Eliot, Hardy, and so on – tend also to dominate the academic construction and study of English literature (particularly at secondary-school level), and likewise predominate in the catalogue lists of publishers of classic novels.[3] Paul Kerr writes, 'The BBC's conception of literary classics does not differ remarkably from Leavis' Great Tradition, or The Penguin imprints, "Penguin Classics" and "Penguin English Library"' (1982: 9).[4]

There are no simple chains of cause and effect here; the reasons for this convergence are multiple and complex. Books that are adapted for television will sell more copies; books on school syllabuses and those that are most widely read are more likely to be adapted; and so on. There is a circular affirmation of a certain range of books commonly perceived as classics. Consistency across various areas of the public sphere means that certain texts (or, more noticeably, certain authors) are held by the reading and viewing public, programme-makers and educationalists to be classics; in this way the identity of some novels as 'classic novels' is accepted and perpetuated in common parlance. In fact, there are fewer authors whose work is regularly adapted for television than authors whose work is included in undergraduate English courses or the Penguin catalogue; 'adaptations of classic novels' is thus an even more restrictive category than that of 'classic novels'.

The final restriction I have placed upon my choice of texts is that of 'Britishness'. I am concerned only with British (terrestrial) television, which at present includes BBC1, BBC2, ITV, Channel Four and the recently (though not yet fully) instated Channel 5. I have not actively restricted my study to British novels or British-produced adaptations, primarily because such restrictions are unnecessary. The vast majority of classic-novel adaptations broadcast in Britain are based on novels that can be unproblematically termed 'British' (i.e. the authors were born in and lived in, and the novels are set in, Britain), and are made by, and funded wholly or in great part by, British companies or broadcasters. Thus, my concentration upon British television is, in its own way, self-selecting in terms of the broadly British nature of the adaptations themselves.

Most writing about adaptation has tended to focus upon literary adaptations for the screen – the adaptation of a source novel for film or (less frequently) television. The adaptation of 'classic' novels for the screen has, for reasons I shall explore later, provoked more heated discussion than (for example) the adaptation of comic books to film, or television series to novels. The contentious nature of adaptations of classic novels in particular has also stifled the development of new and adventurous approaches to the genre. This is something I wish to ameliorate here.

Taking a new approach

This book may appear rather eclectic in its approach to adaptations, utilising as it does ideas from various fields, some of which have been ignored by television theorists so far. It draws upon notions taken from areas as diverse as cognitive film theory, television studies, aesthetics and postmodern theory. Given the state of play in the fields of film and television studies, this may seem somewhat curious. If it is possible to delimit the underlying methodology or approach of this book it is most easily summed up as both analytical and (broadly) aesthetic.

I aim to explore adaptation in an analytical way, unravelling presumptions and misconceptions, avoiding dogmatic orthodoxies, and exploring both the term 'adaptation' and previous conceptualisations of the process and end-products of adaptation. The approach taken herein is influenced by the analytical approach to film studies,[5] and this book is one of the few instances where this approach has been extended into television studies.[6] Some of its defining features are: a focus on the analytical interrogation of the concepts and beliefs that underlie dominant theories; the asking of particular, 'straightforward' questions as starting points (e.g. 'What is (an) adaptation?'); and the use of theoretical paradigms that are directly suggested by features of the texts themselves.

This approach brings three key benefits to the fields of adaptation and television studies. First, it introduces new material such as Ed S. Tan's and Greg M. Smith's work on film style and mood. Second, it allows me to proffer my arguments as transparently as possible, so that others may directly engage with them. Third, by engaging with the fundamental conceptualisations, beliefs and attitudes that underlie theorists' work, it potentially clarifies, challenges and even revitalises their ideas.

When analysing particular adaptations, I bring to bear pertinent critical and theoretical paradigms as these are suggested by the programmes themselves – that is, I begin from the programmes and move outwards to broader issues, rather than constructing the programmes as 'examples' or 'case studies'. In keeping with my desire to focus on the adaptation as a television programme (not primarily as a literary adaptation), I have selected a few key features of the programmes that seem to me to identify and define them as members of a genre. These are the features that seem particularly important to the affective power of the programmes: they reveal how and why audiences engage with them.

It appears to me that there is a critical contrast between two central aspects of these classic-novel adaptations. On the one hand, it is clear that the programmes' emotive representations of the past and distinctive filmic, slow-paced style are part of their continuing appeal; on the other, the televisual context in which they are situated is characterised by its emphasis on its contemporaneity, presentness and performativity. The classic-novel adaptation thus appears sited in a unique and contradictory position. This position, though implied by writers on adaptation, has never been fully explored. An exploration is begun here.

Above all, this book is concerned with the aesthetics of a particular television genre, and its specific emotional, cognitive and cultural significance as these arise from aesthetic specificities. 'Television aesthetics' have been neglected, brushed aside or reviled in the field of television studies for too long; I hope that if nothing else this book will inspire some readers to (re)consider the importance of an aesthetic approach to television.

Notes

1 One of the most recent books on classic-novel adaptations does not even devote the space I have done to a discussion of what constitutes a 'classic novel'. Erica Sheen, in her introduction to *Classic Novels: From Page to Screen* (2000) merely notes the importance of the educational system in constructing a canon of classics (2000: 3–4). In a sense, her decision strengthens my feeling that one may recognise yet put aside the complexities of a careful, formal definition of 'the classic novel' and proceed upon the understanding of a popular, pre-theoretical conception of a canon of literary classics.

2 For a good overview of this debate, see John Guillery's *Cultural Capital: The Problem of Literary Canon Formation* (1993).

3 Since the rise of the cheap publication of classic novels, culminating in the '£1 classics', the public's perception of novels that are considered 'classic' can only have been strengthened by the huge overlap in the catalogues of all the relevant publishers. The same names and titles crop up again and again; there is little variation between publishers (though this is beginning to change). Thus Paul Kerr's comment of 1982, quoted above, is even more apt today.

4 Kerr's statement avoids the question of whether the BBC and ITV differ in their definition and choice of classic novels. The programmes analysed in Part II suggest that no simplistic distinction can be made between the channels, in this regard.

5 This approach is epitomised in Noel Carroll (1988) *Mystifying Movies: Fads and Fallacies in Contemporary Film Theory*; David Bordwell and Noel Carroll (eds) (1996) *Post-Theory: Reconstructing Film Studies*; Noel Carroll (1996) *Theorising the Moving Image*; Richard Allen and Murray Smith (eds) (1997) *Film Theory and Philosophy: Aesthetics and the Analytical Tradition*; and Carl Plantinga and Greg M. Smith (eds) (1999) *Passionate Views: Film, Cognition and Emotion*.

6 There is an edited collection promisingly entitled *The Aesthetics of Television*, edited by Gunhild Agger and Jens F. Jensen, which is forthcoming from Aalborg University Press; however, publication has been stalled, although the book was first advertised in 1999. There is also a single-authored book, *Television Aesthetics: Perceptual, Cognitive and Compositional Bases*, by Nikos Metallinos (1996), but as the subtitle implies, the emphasis of the book is on psychology and neurophysiology as much as on 'aesthetics', and is based in empirical research in these areas rather than theorising, criticism and interpretation.

(Re)writing adaptations

What is (an) adaptation?

1

> Discussion of a film based on a novel ... arrives sooner or later at a comparison of the film with its source. This kind of criticism may have its advantages. But somehow it leads to the mistaken conclusion that the excellence of the film depends on similarity to the novel ... from which it is adapted. (Fulton, 1977: 151)

A. R. Fulton observes above that 'somehow' and 'sooner or later' discussion of an adaptation arrives first at a comparison between novel and film, and second at an evaluation of the adaptation's fidelity to its source. His 'somehow' is a momentary admission of bemusement, of puzzlement about the manner in which this frequently unintended methodology comes about. Why does writing about adaptation, whether critical or theoretical, and despite concerted efforts to the contrary, tend to end up returning to the methodology of comparison and the related notion of 'fidelity' (faithfulness to the source novel)?

The answer lies in deeply entrenched, pre-theoretical notions of what adaptation is, and what an adaptation is – conceptions which are widely held but mostly unstated and unexplored. The durability of these conceptions is a testament to their instinctive appeal on many levels: emotional, intellectual and 'common-sense'. For this reason, it would be unconvincing to attempt to reject these unspoken tenets out of hand, and simply propose an alternative non-comparative approach.[1] Instead, it is more useful to explore what is commonly meant and understood by the term 'adaptation', in order to expose the fundamental assumptions that have shaped scholars' work. Thus the primary aim of these initial chapters is not so much to provide an 'overview' of work on adaptation as to undertake a similar explorative task to the one that Altman sets himself in his book on genre:

> The purpose here is to highlight the very claims that ... theorists have failed to recognize they were making, the constitutive assumptions that theoreti-

cians have neglected to acknowledge in their own work, the habits and positions that have been silently passed on, often at cross-purposes with official positions and conscious desires. (Altman, 1999: 1)

These initial chapters are concerned therefore not with interpreting adaptations but with conceptualising adaptations as the cultural form and ontological problem they constitute within theories about adaptation and studies of specific instances of adaptation. The focus is on secondary critical, conceptual and theoretical material about adaptation, rather than adaptations themselves. This secondary material reveals a dependence upon pre-theoretical understandings of adaptation, betrayed in the language used to discuss the phenomenon; therefore the aims outlined above are best achieved by an analytical investigation into the language commonly used to discuss adaptation and adaptations.

Going round in circles: defining adaptation

Now feels like a good time to pick a word or a phrase, something short, and go after it, using the available equipment of intellectual retrieval, to see where we get. (Baker, 1996: 207)

The traditional, historically dominant approach to adaptation – the comparative approach, as described above – is above all an exploration of the *process* of adaptation. This does not mean that the focus is on the task of writing and producing a screen version of a novel, but that in concentrating on the different ways in which the adaptation expresses the same basic narrative as its source book, this approach is necessarily concerned with 'what happens when one adapts' – that is, the process of adaptation as it can be perceived in its end-product. Hence, comparisons of source and end-product as textual entities are ultimately observations about adaptation-as-process, not primarily studies of adaptations as artworks in themselves. Most comparative writers on adaptation explicitly foreground their concern with the process of adaptation. Wendell Aycock and Michael Schoenecke's critical survey of various film adaptations 'illustrates the intriguing and complex nature of the process' (1988: 7); Brian McFarlane states that the aim of his book 'is to offer and test a methodology for studying the process of transposition from novel to film' (1996: vii).

There are, of course, two questions incorporated within the question that provides a title for this chapter: 'What is adaptation?' and 'What is *an* adaptation?' For many writers on adaptation (particularly until the late 1990s) these two questions are so closely interrelated that they can almost be, indeed have been, regarded as two parts of the same question. Yet this conflation is conceptually problematic. As suggested above, traditionally, writers on adaptation have been primarily concerned with the issue implied by the first question of this chapter: the process by which an adaptation comes into being, as opposed to the 'end-product', the adaptation itself. Yet this concern, in itself, suggests the answer that would customarily be given in response to the second question, for an adaptation would be defined in terms of its genesis: an adaptation is a text which 'adapts' another text. In positing this definition, comparative theorists allow discussion to return to the topic of what is incorporated within the term 'adapts' – that is, what happens during the progression from source text to adaptation. This reduces the discussion of 'what an adaptation is' to one brief, self-limiting definition.

This self-limiting circularity is due to the equivocatory use of the word adaptation, a result of the homonymic verbal conflation of (the process of) adaptation and (the end-product) adaptation – a conflation which is typically reproduced by comparative writers on adaptation in their work. The *Oxford English Dictionary* offers a series of definitions under the heading 'adaptation', including the following:

1. The action or process of adapting, fitting or suiting one thing to another.
2a. The process of modifying a thing so as to suit new conditions.
3. The condition or state of being adapted ...
4. A special instance of adapting; and hence, *concr.* an adapted form or copy, a reproduction of anything modified to suit new uses.[2]

Support for the traditional comparative approach to adaptation(s) can be found in the above definitions: the process of adaptation is foregrounded, and the process by which the end-product (noted in definitions 3 and 4) is achieved does not just take precedence over this product, but is also regarded as the fundamental defining feature of it. Hence a comparative approach is justified twice over: it seems natural to focus on the process of adaptation, rather than on the end-product and, further, it would seem reasonable to analyse the end-product in terms of its constitutive origins. Therefore, whether our concern rests with the process of adaptation or with adaptations themselves, it would appear that a comparative approach best recognises the generic (genetic) feature which all adaptations share: the very fact of their being adaptations.

This is not to say that alternative conceptualisations of adaptation(s) have not been proffered. Before the 1970s, preceding the rise of the comparative approach to adaptations, several writers, most notably George Bluestone, sketched a very different understanding of adaptations from that outlined above. Bluestone argued that an adaptation and its source text are as fundamentally different as an example of architecture and a classical ballet: 'it is insufficiently recognised that the end products of novel and film represent different aesthetic genera, as different from each other as ballet is from architecture' (1957: 5)[3] – a metaphor later echoed by other writers such as Norman Mailer: 'film and literature are as far apart as, say, cave painting and a song' (in Beja, 1979: 51).

The reason for Bluestone's assertion was to substantiate his argument that the two media are so different that we cannot expect hermeneutic equivalence between them, and that we should therefore abandon 'fidelity criticism', for foregrounding the process of adaptation cannot provide a viable explanatory framework for discussing the end-product itself. Although this does not positively answer the question 'What is an adaptation?', Bluestone's elucidation does implicitly offer an alternative, oppositional view regarding the links between process and end-product, arguing that the process of adaptation, by which an adaptation comes into being (and is thus named) does not provide a sufficient definition of what an adaptation is. That is, a shared, constitutive trait is not necessarily a defining trait.

The two starting points outlined above clearly stand opposed. Bluestone offers us the possibility of asking afresh the question 'What is an adaptation?', by not assuming the genesis of an adaptation to constitute its fundamental identity, yet he fails to ask or answer this question himself, and his forceful and utter destruction of the links between an adaptation and its source text is difficult to justify (even Bluestone failed to maintain the separation of the two in his interpretative analyses of particular adaptations[4]). Comparative writers, on the other hand, offer an insight into the complex relationship between adaptation (process) and adaptation (end-product), yet in doing so deny the conceptual potential of the question 'What is an adaptation?' by conflating the two things, and instituting a vicious definitional circle. In the end, for various reasons explored in the succeeding chapters, the comparative approach proved more appealing to writers on adaptation, and was historically predominant from the early 1970s until the late 1990s.[5]

What is sought in this chapter is the 'adaptation' concealed within the discourses about it. In the spirit of Rick Altman's mission statement quoted on pp. 9–10, this chapter focuses upon distinguishing and answering the two titular questions, not because others have done so, but rather because others have failed to do so, while basing their methodologies upon definite, though unspoken, notions of what (an) adaptation is.

What is adaptation?

Most people are aware of two specific processes that are given the title 'adaptation': biological (genetic) adaptation, without which natural selection and the evolution and perpetuation of species would not occur, and what one could call 'cultural adaptation' (the adaptation of novels into films or programmes, or fairy tales into ballets, and so forth). It is, of course, the latter instance of adaptation with which we are concerned here, but the two processes of adaptation are, to a certain extent, analogous. Neither biological nor 'cultural' adaptation can take place without the existence of a source, an origin(al), and both instances of adaptation serve to perpetuate a more or less recognisable collection of certain 'original' features. Just as a domestic tabby bears a fundamental resemblance to the wildcat from which it 'derives', and is a member of the same genus (*Felis*), one could propose a similar relationship between Ang Lee's *Sense and Sensibility* (1995) and Jane Austen's *Sense and Sensibility* (1811). However, there are obviously substantial differences to be noted between the two modes of adaptation. A brief foray into a comparison of the two is surprisingly illuminating.

Whilst biological (genetic) adaptation is often perceived, outside the scientific *cognoscenti*, as being a gradual process of 'exquisite design' (Gould, 1980: 103), whereby species evolve, gaining stability and strength, 'cultural' adaptation is perceived very differently. Genetic adaptation is understood as a process by which species survive into later generations, and each new adaptation is commonly regarded as an improvement – sometimes even as part of a progressive movement towards perfection.[6] Cultural adaptation, in comparison, is seen as aiding the survival of only the original organism itself; adaptations of Austen's *Emma* or Eliot's *Middlemarch* are valued not for their potential to develop or improve upon the original but for their potential to refer back to and revitalise the source of their geneses. Adaptations can achieve this in two ways: they can aim for textual fidelity, faithfully 'reproducing' elements of their sources on screen, and they can 'send viewers back to the book'. Few would argue that with each further adaptation to the screen *Wuthering Heights* develops – or evolves – towards the creation of a far better *Wuthering Heights* than that penned by Emily Brontë.

Genetic adaptation can be broadly conceived as a linear process of progression, with each new organism in the chain being genetically (causally) linked to its predecessors, but being nonetheless significantly different from them.[7] In comparison, the traditional conceptualisation of 'cultural' adaptation is best imagined as having a base or centre, from which all subsequent adaptations (versions[8]) arise:

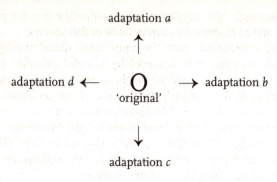

adaptation *a*

↑

adaptation *d* ⟵　O　⟶ adaptation *b*

'original'

↓

adaptation *c*

As can be seen above, each subsequent adaptation is understood to hold a direct relationship with the culturally established original; this is why each adaptation appears to sustain the original, and not to develop and improve it. Unlike genetic adaptations, which exist within a trajectory of linear development, each new cultural adaptation appears to magically cross the chronological gap dividing it from the original text, and is seen as more closely related to that original text than to preceding or contemporaneous adaptations. For example, the 1996 ITV *Emma* would, under traditional comparative analysis, be compared with Jane Austen's source text, just as the 1996 film *Emma* would be.[9] This methodology is rooted in a centre-based conceptualisation of adaptation, which posits a direct relationship between the original source – the 'centre which is the source of life' (Easthope, 1991: 23) – and each new adaptation.

The implication of this approach is that the two screen 'versions' of *Emma* produced in 1996 bear no significant relationship to each other, but are inextricably linked with the text that Jane Austen composed in 1816. Traditional critical or theoretical writing on adaptation thus frequently finds itself undertaking a stubborn project of dehistoricisation on two counts: it denies the linear, textual history of adaptation available to each new adapter, and the relationships through time that an adaptation might bear to other adaptations; at the same time it often fails to appreciate the historical gap that separates the source novel from the adaptation in question, seeing the meanings expressed in both novel and adaptation as somehow transhistorical and unalterable. The consequences of this centre-based conceptualisation for the study of adaptations are manifold; suffice it to say here that this dehistoricisation degrades the critic's understanding of the development of both classic-novel adaptations as a screen genre and the 'meta-text' of which both source and adaptations are part, e.g. the ever-changing, ever-developing *Emma*. In comparison, the common conceptualisation of *genetic* adaptation notes the role that each new 'adaptation' plays within the broader process of evolution, and in shaping the current (state of the) species.

Although conceptually neat, the centre-based model of adaptation is conceptually unsound. It is weakened by its radial structure (the direct links which join each adaptation to the central 'original') and by the pivotal notion of the 'original' itself. Some of the problems inherent within the centre-based model (dehistoricisation and a lack of awareness of generic development) have already come to light. In addition, however, the diagrammatic representation of the traditional conceptualisation of the source text/adaptation relationship exposes the reasons for comparative writers' conflation of the two title questions.

Problems with the centre-based model: the radial structure and pivotal centre

When is an adaptation not an adaptation? This is not intended as a riddle; rather, I seek an answer which is both epistemological and cultural. There are many instances when adaptation (as defined above, and as understood in common parlance) is not recognised as being such, or when adaptation can be seen to have occurred without the end-product being named or defined as an adaptation. These instances undermine the accepted links between process and end-product, throwing into question the explanatory usefulness of a radial model like the one outlined above, which relies upon these links.

The ways in which we use, and do not use, the term 'adaptation' are problematic. As Dudley Andrew points out, 'every representational film *adapts* a prior conception. Indeed the very term "representation" suggests the existence of a model' (1984: 97) (italics in original). Arguably, his definition is excessively broad, though it usefully highlights the similarities between the processes of representation and adaptation, thus placing adaptations more firmly within the context of other films, and not setting them aside for different treatment as if they are special cases. Yet the definition can be narrowed still further, to include only those films or television programmes that draw upon other texts (rather than upon the physical world), and inconsistencies and anomalies can still be found.

Let us take as an example the film *Elizabeth* (1998), directed by Shekhar Kapur. The film is based upon the life of Queen Elizabeth I: it focuses on the first few years of her reign, but provides information in the form of titles at the beginning and end of the film about the years preceding her reign, and about the final years of it. The film can be clearly differentiated from a documentary (though perhaps less clearly from a drama-documentary). A filmmaker making a documentary about Elizabeth's life and reign would use a variety of historical sources – both primary and secondary – and would be likely to quote some written sources verbatim, summarise others and incorporate information from non-written sources into brief dramatic re-presentations. Would we consider this documentary an adaptation? Surely the answer is no; the film is already generically located as a documentary. Therefore, even though the filmmaker has used and reshaped a range of historical sources, 'adapting' them for the documentary in the sense that the *OED* defines above, the film is not typically considered an 'adaptation' of those sources.

But what of Kapur's dramatic 'recreation' of Elizabeth's reign? We are given no indication within the film itself what primary and secondary sources were used by the filmmaker. The film is clearly fictionalised, for the dialogue has been invented and is expressed in a modern, accessible tongue and, unlike many documentaries, there is an emphasis upon Elizabeth's emotional frame of mind and her relationships with those around her. The feuds, treachery and treason that take place are characterised by their personal nature: the Earl of Norfolk's treason is suggested as arising from personal ambition and obstinacy, rather than from the wider Catholic/Protestant troubles; Lord Robert Dudley's treachery is presented as the action of a man driven insane by his love (or obsession) for Elizabeth. Elizabeth's sexual relationship with Dudley, in this film, was a matter of great contention amongst historians:

> In the history books, Dudley was the queen's favourite; in this highly controversial account ... he becomes her lover, deflowering the Virgin Queen. A battery of warning shots has already been fired at the script, including one from Amanda Foreman, a historian at Lady Margaret Hall, Oxford. 'Elizabeth I's virginity is the one thing on which every Tudor historian can agree,' she writes. 'This is ego-driven fiction parading as the truth.' (Anon., *The Sunday Times*, 26 April 1998: 6)

Foreman's response to the film's deviation from historical facts corresponds to the feelings that most filmgoers will have experienced whilst watching this film. Though historical background is provided through intertitles and in dialogue, the film leaves one feeling that one knows and understands much more about the people on whom it is based than the historical and political events that occur between and around them. The film uses history as a basis, as a starting point, but the unknowledgeable viewer is unable to ascertain to what extent the drama is 'historical' and, for the reasons suggested above, accurately senses that the film is more a creation of Kapur's than an adaptation of 'history'. As the star of the film, Cate Blanchett, said, 'Shekhar wasn't interested in historical accuracy' (Anon., *The Sunday Times*, 20 September 1998: 4). In line with common practice, therefore, *Elizabeth* is regarded as a historical drama, not an adaptation.

There is one final variation to consider. Let us suppose, for the sake of argument, that Kapur, during his research, came across a particularly good history book which charted the early years of Elizabeth's reign in detail. With the full permission of the author, whose name appears in the film's credits, he sets about depicting the reign of Elizabeth I. Would this film constitute an adaptation? Certainly it fits the definition of an adaptation suggested above. Yet the audience and critics of the film would be unlikely to name it thus or respond to it as such; they would be more likely to compare the film with their knowledge of the queen's life (or of the Elizabethan period), just as Foreman did in the case of Kapur's film. The film would still be perceived as being a 'historical drama', not an adaptation; despite the use of a singular written source text, the film's primary referent would be perceived as being history itself, and not the history book which so inspired the filmmaker.[10]

Clearly all the examples just discussed have a central feature in common, and one which they share with any dramatic, even fictional, film about Elizabeth I. They are all based upon a real person and the events with which she is known to be connected; in this sense, all such films are adaptations – they are adaptations of history. Yet it is their very basis in history that disallows their inclusion within the genre of 'adaptation' – and it this distinction that is fundamental: a film is commonly understood to be an adaptation not because it adapts but because of *what* it adapts.

Andrew offers a useful explication of this idea: he argues that whilst all representational films function as adaptations – 'as interpretations of a person, place, situation, event, and so forth' – the reason for using the term 'adaptation' only to describe particular instances of this is that 'we reserve a special place for those films which foreground this [adaptive] relation by announcing themselves as versions of some standard whole. A standard whole can only be a text. A version of it is an adaptation in the narrow sense' (1984: 97).

Andrew's delineation of adaptations appears to move the process of defining adaptations forward. It usefully recognises the significance of culture in defining and naming adaptations: adaptations 'announce themselves' as such – this echoes the *OED* definition of an adaptation as 'a special instance of adapting'.[11] Equally pertinent is Andrew's introduction and definition of the concept of the 'standard whole'. This seems to support the traditional centre-based model of adaptation, proposing a centre – a 'standard whole' – and singular radial links from the centre to each version. However, there are two significant conceptual complications concealed within this otherwise useful definition.

First, Andrew's definition fails to recognise the extent to which cultural influence is vital to the constitution and recognition of 'standard wholes' upon which adaptations are based. Adaptations can indeed be said to 'announce themselves', but in some sense so too do 'standard wholes'. Our perception of the cultural status of both source text and adaptation affects the process of classification; as Christopher Orr writes, to understand adaptation 'we need, first of all, to determine the status and function of the literary source within the textual system of the adapted film' (1984: 72).

A case in point is that of Shakespeare, who famously based his plays upon a huge variety of sources: *Macbeth*, for instance, is an adaptation of a Scottish folk-tale; his 'historical plays' draw upon written and oral history.[12] There are reasons that can be offered why these plays are not regarded as adaptations (just as with the hypothetical examples above of films about Elizabeth I), but there are still more problematic examples within Shakespeare's *oeuvre*. Shakespeare's *King Lear*, published in 1608, was based upon a full-text play: *King Leir*, which had been published in 1605 (and performed previously). This earlier text, certainly a standard whole by Andrew's definition, was in turn based upon various renditions of the same story, and Kenneth Muir argues that 'we know from verbal echoes in the text of the play that Shakespeare was acquainted with at least three of these' (1986: 11). And yet we do not refer to Shakespeare's play as an adaptation; indeed, we often use the possessive form of the title which I have used above, as if to assert the independence of the play from any previous, related texts: it is *Shakespeare's King Lear*. Each new theatrical, filmic or televisual re-presentation of *King Lear* is considered an adaptation of Shakespeare's play, not of either the 'original' stories or the previously published play text, despite the latter constituting a 'standard whole' as defined above. Cultural orthodoxy demands that Shakespeare's adaptation be regarded as the 'original', and that other, later adaptations of this culturally established original therefore be regarded as adaptations.[13] Thus the traditional model of adaptation offers a rather simplistic view of a clear distinction between a singular original and separate, subsequent adaptations.

So Andrew fails to recognise the importance of cultural influences in fixing the 'original', the 'standard whole' to which he refers. There is a second issue he leaves untouched, and it is concealed by the last two sentences in his definition: 'A standard whole can only be a text. A version of it is an adaptation in the narrow sense.' There are clear evaluative and ontological implications behind these two statements. A standard whole is a text; an adaptation is a 'version' of a standard whole. Andrew thus implies that the relationship between source text and adaptation is that between text and version. But this in turn implies an evaluation of adaptations – they are just 'versions' of an original – and, more importantly, an ontological distinction between the identities of, say, Jane Austen's *Pride and Prejudice* (1813) and the 1995 television adaptation of *Pride and Prejudice.* If the former is a text, and the latter a version, then can the latter be considered a text? Can the latter claim an ontologically distinct identity as a text separate from the former, or is it to be regarded as some sort of genetic mutation or (in recognition of human influence) genetic modification of the (one-and-only) text: *Pride and Prejudice* (1813)?

Here the importance of the comparative theorist's conflation of the questions 'What is adaptation?' and 'What is an adaptation?' becomes clear. There is an ontologically significant assumption evident in Andrew's description that is shared, though not overtly noted, by all comparative writers. This assumption determines their preoccupation with debates concerning fidelity, their sometimes inaccurate postulations of 'original' or standard-whole source texts, and their assumption that the adaptive roots of an adaptation constitute the major part of its identity. Despite neither asking nor answering the question 'What is an adaptation?', comparative writers nevertheless subscribe to very particular beliefs about what an adaptation is, and these beliefs underlie and support the comparative approach.

Adaptation, according to the traditional comparative model, is the process of adapting one original, culturally defined 'standard whole' in another medium. Each time adaptation takes place, the adapter returns to the same original source and adapts it afresh. The fact of multiple, subsequent adaptation is not of conceptual interest.[14] Therefore an adaptation is a version of a text that has come into being via this process. We are offered again a patent example of conceptual circularity: an adaptation is not quite regarded as a text, but is instead a 'version'; to call something a 'version' is to precipitate the question 'a version of what?' – in this case, an adaptation is a version of the standard whole (text) of which it 'announces' itself to be a version. An adaptation, thus conceptualised, and described within common language terms such as originals, texts and versions, is inescapably linked directly back to the original source and therefore can be justifiably compared with this source.[15]

So the traditional model of adaptation is flawed: it offers a distorted, simplistic understanding of the relationship between source and adaptation, and conceals important links between adaptations. We have seen that adaptation may take place without resulting in an adaptation, thus casting doubt upon the ineluctable nature of the relationship between process and end-product. In addition, the model depends heavily on the notion of an 'original' that is the life-source of all subsequent adaptations; this original is the pivotal point of its structure. Yet there are problems involved in ascertaining such a definite, primary source text.

Further, the language through which adaptations are commonly discussed places limitations on conceptual development. There are several assumptions inherent in this language that must be countered. An adaptation can exist that does not exist *only* because (or *primarily* because) adaptation has taken place. An adaptation cannot simply be defined as an end-product of adaptation; an adaptation is a text in itself, not a 'version' of a standard whole; and the text which an adaptation constitutes cannot simply be classified, explained or interpreted in terms of its being such an end-product or version.

Texts, versions and authorship: 'fidelity to intention twice removed'

> We need to remember ... that a film version of a novel is an independent text and should not be judged ... by how faithful it is to the original: what constitutes an 'original' text anyway? Critics who see film versions of novels largely as adaptations fail to see films as independent texts. (Webster, 1993: 148)

Roger Webster utilises three crucial terms here: version, adaptation and text. He argues that adaptations are 'independent texts' (standard wholes), and that the notion of an 'original' text is somewhat awkward, and he offers a rather different view of 'versions' and 'adaptations'. In his use of these commonplace words he provides the space for a more careful understanding of adaptations. For Webster, a version is 'a particular form in which something is embodied, as a particular way of telling a story' (*Chambers Dictionary*, 1997), whereas an adaptation is a modification of a story to a new medium. Webster's views are supported by several critics of adaptations, including Grahame Smith, in his critique of Christine Edzard's adaptation of *Little Dorrit* (1987).[16] Smith argues that a 'successful' adaptation 'is a version, a reading, a rendering, of the original rather than an adaptation in the strict sense' (1990: 37).

Subtle differences are being drawn here between adaptations and versions. 'Adaptation' implies a continuity between source text and resulting text (analogous to genetic adaptation); it implies that only necessary alterations are made – alterations that cannot be avoided because of the change in medium. On the other hand, a 'version' seems to imply interpretation or variation, reflecting common usage (e.g. 'his version of events differed from hers'). In a similar way, to bring about an adaptation clearly requires (a process of) adaptation – a conscious process of working upon a text in order to suit it to another medium – whilst a 'version' does not imply a process as dependent upon the source text, except for a reliance on salient narrative events. In summary, to call something an adaptation of another text is to highlight the conscious, complex process of implementing changes necessary to re-present the source text under new conditions (in a new medium); to call something a version does not suggest the same, but implies a presentation of a familiar story within the framework of a separate, 'independent' text.

Yet surely there are no adaptations that are not versions? Every adaptation is an authored, conscious response to or interpretation of a source text, one that may or may not be concerned with 'fidelity', but is necessarily concerned with the creation of an independent film or television text. While this subtle distinction between adaptation and version is a useful part of conceptual exploration, to maintain the distinction beyond this seems unnecessary. If 'every adaptation is inevitably an interpretation' (McDougal, 1985: 6), then every adaptation is a version. Clearly, some adaptations aim to 'adapt' more faithfully than others, so it is possible to grade adaptations in terms of fidelity to their source texts, just as Geoffrey Wagner and other theorists have done,[17] but the additional adaptation/version distinction is an unnecessary one.

Moreover, to call an adaptation a 'version' is not necessarily preferable, for the term is commonly used to deny its independence as a text – note the tone of Margaret Harris's comment on *Middlemarch* (1994, BBC): 'for all the good things about Davies's version, it has none of the radicalism of George Eliot's text' (1995: 100). The terms of her criticism are salient: Eliot's book is the original (central) *text*, whilst Davies's programme is merely a *version* (offshoot) of that text. Even in Harris's praise one can see echoes of the centre-based conception of adaptation: 'I think the achievement of this television version of *Middlemarch* is that it develops an authentic reading of the novel' (1995: 97). Note that a version is not a free interpretation but is rather a reading (a revealing use of literary language) that can be either authentic or inauthentic. One assumes an 'authentic' reading is one which remains true to what Harris perceives as being Eliot's intentions for her book; thus Harris also reveals that she feels an adapter's intentions ought to be synonymous with those of the source text's author.[18]

This feeling that the intentions of an adapter should coincide with those of the source text's author is pervasive. Smith's critique of *Little Dorrit*, mentioned above, is critical of Edzard's adaptation for the fundamental reason that her intentions are 'wrong' because they are not the same as Dickens's. Edzard stated her intentions in making her film(s): 'What we wanted to do was to make Dickens come across as real, as a journalist's piece ... Incoherence is unreal. What makes a thing real is making it believable and making it coherent' (Smith, 1990: 40). Smith explicitly criticises Edzard's intentions as a filmmaker, asserting that 'one of Dickens' deepest strengths as a writer is a kind of controlled incoherence, a refusal to render the fictional world into neat and tidy patterns, creating instead a structure that admits mystery, confusion, uncertainty' (1990: 40).

While Smith may be right about Dickens's intentions, one is compelled to ask why Dickens's intentions are relevant here. Surely, if Smith assesses Dickens's achievements in terms of Dickens's intentions, he should assess Edzard's achievements in terms of *her* intentions. Instead Smith offers a damning critique of the film(s) for failing to communicate meanings which the filmmaker never intended to express, but which he personally favours. For example, he argues that Edzard should have made use of 'the wide angle lens ... whose properties are peculiarly suited to the rendering of Dickens' vision in another medium', for 'it is the perfect instrument for the expression of a poetic or symbolic heightening of reality, for caricature, for the "excesses" of satirical indignation' (Smith, 1990: 44, 45). It is noticeable that Smith refuses to acknowledge Edzard's 'vision', subordinating it to Dickens's, and that he ignores her desire for a strongly realistic film as he ruminates upon how the most 'unrealistic' and expressive aspects of Dickens's work could be recreated on screen. Smith's critique reflects Gene D. Phillips's insistence that the adapter should 'preserve the original author's thematic intent and personal vision' (1980: 16).

By elevating the writer of the source book in this way, and by positing a direct relationship between source text and adaptation (version), writers such as these precipitate a strange elision: the author of the source book becomes the implied author of the 'version' of it – the adaptation. Adaptations are therefore often interpreted and evaluated as expressions of the source-text author's intentions, such as in Harris's review of *Middlemarch*, cited above. Harris describes the beginning of the adaptation thus: 'To open the dramatization with Lydgate's arrival is to foreground the novel's concern with *Middlemarch* as a provincial community confronting outsiders' (Harris, 1995: 100). But is it not more accurate to say that this opening foregrounds the *adaptation's* concerns, not those of the novel? Whether the adaptation's concerns are similar to those of the novel, or the programme-maker's intentions are comparable to those of Eliot, is surely a separate issue. Harris also states that 'the commonest criticism I have encountered of the TV *Middlemarch* concerns the absence of a narrating voice, or of George Eliot' (1995: 98). Perhaps one could suggest an alternative issue for discussion: not the 'absence' of George Eliot (her 'voice', style and intentions), but the 'presence' of the programme-maker (and his 'voice', style and intentions), thus renouncing the problematic assumption that George Eliot 'owns', or in any way 'authors', the adaptation.

Smith makes a similar conflation when, discussing the 1980 BBC adaptation of *Pride and Prejudice*, he opines, 'What … does it mean for public knowledge of Jane Austen to experience her work in a form which omits the narrative voice (despite Fay Weldon's attempt to transfer some aspects of it into dialogue in her version of *Pride and Prejudice*) in favour of scenes of tea-drinking and dancing?'[19] (1990: 35). Again, Smith's argument relies upon the awkward notion that this programme is, in some undefined sense, authored by Jane Austen (such that it can be called 'her work'). One is left unclear regarding how the programme can be both Austen's work and Weldon's version – and uncertain as to why the former is elevated in status over the latter.

In this representation of Weldon's adaptation, she is cast merely as a bungling adapter, failing to provide a clear, direct window, unblemished by her own stylistic or imaginative idiosyncracies, onto Austen's *Pride and Prejudice*.[20] Weldon's own intentions are limited to her intention to 'adapt'; to adapt is understood as an intention to render the source-text author's intentions. Intentions are pre-theoretically important – a viewer generally understands texts to express intended meanings, therefore an intentionalist approach to adaptations is arguably acceptable, but intentionality relies upon the existence of a feasible author or authors who can be assumed to be directly responsible for the creation of the text in front of us.[21] It seems both inaccurate and unjust to obviate the intentions of those responsible for 'authoring' the screen text, reducing the adaptation's 'authors' to some kind of transparent medium through which the source-text author expresses his or her intentions. It is reductive to refer the meanings expressed in an adaptation to the intentions of the author of the source text. It is also unfair to assume that the filmmaker's intention to adapt necessarily constitutes a desire to subordinate his or her own artistic aims to the expression of the intentions of the 'first' author, so that the interpretation of adaptations becomes the evaluation of fidelity to intention twice removed.[22]

From the earliest to the most recent writing on adaptation, there has existed a widely shared desire to undermine the tendency for comparison to lapse into fidelity criticism that unfairly assesses an adaptation on the grounds of its fidelity to the book, and to the book's author's intentions, and in literary terms which are unsuited to film interpretation. Yet as A. R. Fulton notes at the beginning of this chapter, this project has been mostly unsuccessful in practice. The reason for this lies in the centre-based, pre-theoretical conception of adaptation subscribed to by many writers. The fundamental assumptions underlying this conception are the reasons comparative writers keep reverting to fidelity criticism: (a) an adaptation as a version is not a text, and therefore has no clear author; (b) the source text is a standard whole, complete with unambiguous author; (c) an adaptation is a mere version of the same standard whole; (d) an adaptation thus shares its author with its source text, and expresses the intentions of this sanctioned author.

'To assign an Author to a text is to impose a brake on it, to furnish it with a final signified, to close writing ... Literary science thus teaches us to respect the manuscript and the author's declared intentions' (Barthes, 1968: 53). These words can be applied to the traditional study of classic novels, but are clearly even more pertinent to the comparative criticism of classic-novel adaptations where, as Orr suggests, many theorists instate 'an Author-God whose message informs the source text as well as the faithful adaptation of that text' (1984: 75). To suggest that an adaptation of *Pride and Prejudice* is in some important sense Jane Austen's work, as Smith does, is to establish the book *Pride and Prejudice* as the 'final signified' of the adaptation, and to 'close writing', for all that needed to be written was written by Austen herself, and Weldon need add nothing of her own. In the same way, the 'respect' for the literary text and for the intentions of its author noted by Barthes take on additional importance when that literary text is adapted for the screen, and lead to the kind of criticism offered by comparative writers like Harris and Smith. Adaptation renders the notion of the 'Author', whose demise Roland Barthes famously proclaimed, even more problematic. It intensifies problems of authorial intention and voice, and complicates the issue of interpretation based upon these factors.

Anthony Easthope describes the practice of traditional literary criticism as offering readings that 'are to be placed on lines "converging on" or "receding from" a vanishing point ..., a centre founded beyond the text' (1991: 34). This centre can be understood as the text's author's intentions. John Caughie, in his introduction to *Theories of Authorship*, writes of contemporary criticism's 'challenge to the concept of the author as source and centre of the text', and notes that 'the result has been a re-consideration of the text or the world as a structured play of forces, relations and discourses, rather than as a site of final, unified meanings, authorised by their source' (1981: 1). His words echo Barthes's: 'the text is a fabric of quotations, resulting from a thousand sources of culture' (1968: 53). The contrast between the traditional, Romantic view of the Authored text (described by Easthope) and contemporary alternative views (outlined by Caughie and Barthes) is comparable to that between the comparative model of adaptation and more recent approaches. In each case, the former insists upon a centralising model sustained by the validating Author of the 'original' text (for to be 'authored' by Austen or Dickens is to be 'authorised' by them); the latter challenges the status, even the validity, of this centre, and insists upon recognising a more open, polysemic and intertextual series of texts which draw upon each other. Contemporary criticism undermines intentionality as a prescriptive basis for interpretation, recognising that we retrospectively assume the author's intentions primarily through our reading and interpretation of his or her work, and instead highlights the impact of other sources upon the text[23] and of 'what is there' as opposed to 'what was intended to be there'.[24] Though the comparative, centralised approach is comfortingly solid, delimited and apprehensible, the strength of later approaches lies in their very decentredness, comprehensiveness and flexibility, in their placing of adaptations within a far wider cultural context than that of an original-version relationship.

An alternative model of adaptation

There is evidently the necessity for a more realistic, complex and nuanced understanding of adaptation. It would be more accurate to view adaptation as the gradual development of a 'meta-text'. This view recognises that a later adaptation may draw upon any earlier adaptations, as well as upon the primary source text. In a sense, this understanding of adaptation draws upon the model of genetic adaptation for its inspiration, in terms of its increased historicity and its recognition of the role that each and every adaptation, as well as the source text, has played in the formation of the most recent adaptation. It allows for generic development, as subsequent film or television adaptations draw upon previous ones, and it does not posit the 'original' source/individual adaptation relationship as a direct, unmediated and ahistorical one.

This alternative model can account for difficult cases such as Shakespeare: it recognises the complex genesis of Shakespeare's plays, the huge range of sources the playwright drew upon for his work, and the pre-existence of, in many cases, numerous versions of the stories he used. Subsequent 'adaptations' can be regarded as points on a continuum, as part of the extended development of a singular, infinite meta-text: a valuable story or myth that is constantly growing and developing, being retold, reinterpreted and reassessed. It might be more accurate to understand each new *Macbeth* (for example) – whether play, film, poem or television programme – as an adaptation of a sort of 'myth', an ur-text that stands outside and before each retelling of the story, and which contains the most fundamental parts of the tale without which an adaptation would lose its identity as that tale. Such an entity is implied in Susan Wilsmore's discussion of the distinction between work and text, wherein she describes a work of art as containing 'a cluster of ... essential properties as is necessary to its very existence' (1987: 311).

John O. Thompson suggests a similar conceptualisation, utilising Roman Ingarden's distinction between the 'work of art' and 'the mode of appearance of the work, the concrete form in which the work itself is apprehended' (Thompson, 1996: 15).[25] Here, the 'work' is comparable to the ur-text, which is expressed within concrete texts; thus adaptations can be regarded as many concretisations of one work.[26] In this conceptualisation, the first 'telling' of a story might be a source of inspiration for other retellings (adaptations), but that which is really being adapted precedes, and is apparent within (but not reducible to) the solid, textual 'source' and its adaptations. The ur-text/work 'Macbeth' is apparent within Shakespeare's text *Macbeth* (ordinarily cited as the 'source'), but can also be appropriated by other texts (adaptations). As Andrew states, 'one must presume the global signified of the original to be separable from its text if one believes it can be approximated by other sign clusters' (1984: 101) – a view which stands in stark contrast to Bluestone's dismissal of 'a separable content which may be detached and reproduced' (1957: 5). Clearly the ur-text or work (or Andrew's 'global signified') consists primarily of the major narrative functions which distinguish the story of (say) *Macbeth* from *King Lear*. The notion of the ur-text or work eases the problem of affixing a true 'original'. In the case of *Macbeth*, it would probably be impossible to discover a definitive 'original', for the first telling of the story was an oral one, and has thus left few traces.

The ur-text or work is missing from the traditional, pre-theoretical understanding of adaptation because although it is manifest in the source and many of its adaptations, it does not exist as a separate, concrete entity outside these texts, a visible part of the system. Yet this lack of specificity, though unfortunate in terms of historiography, could be an advantage in terms of the study of adaptation(s). The ur-text, if neither definite nor finite, if only postulated or implied, extracted from each telling of the story, cannot hold the same sway over adaptations (or retellings) that the standard whole does. The issue of fidelity becomes problematic, for it is hard to assess how faithful a text is to something that does not materially exist. As Walter Benjamin writes, 'the presence of the original is the prerequisite to the concept of authenticity' (1936: 214).[27]

The case of Kenneth Branagh's acclaimed *Hamlet* (1989) reveals that the approach which posits a definite original is simplistic, and demands the recognition of a notional ur-text/work whose location is far less delimited. Branagh considered his full-text film to be one of the most 'faithful' presentations of Shakespeare's text achieved thus far, primarily due to its use of the full play text, but also because of its vivid presentation of the play which 'brought it to life' for the audience. Many critics concurred. Yet despite the fact that 'Branagh claims to restore to texts the authenticity debased in previous cinematic adaptations' (Cartmell, 1996: 3), his presentation is not within the intended medium, and is also set in the Regency period, not in the Middle Ages.[28] How can a filmic presentation, set in a period long after Shakespeare's death, possibly be seen as approximating most accurately the play that Shakespeare envisioned?

Clearly, a sense that the film exhibits fidelity does not refer to the actual play that Shakespeare intended, but to an 'ideal' performance of that text which captures the essence of that which Shakespeare intended to convey and the basic character of the work we call 'Hamlet'. In other words, Branagh is referring to an ur-text/work that lies behind and prior to Shakespeare's conceptualisation of it, and it is this source that (it is claimed) his film most successfully presents. Branagh's film manages to 'capture' *Hamlet* because it represents the 'cluster of its essential properties' cited by Wilsmore (1987: 311). Thus to criticise the film on the basis of lack of fidelity to its culturally affixed source, Shakespeare's *Hamlet*, would be to misunderstand the perception the filmmaker holds of the ideal to which he aims to be faithful.

This approach is not inimical to comparative writers: some have already tried to pinpoint the 'timeless' meanings which cause classic texts to be adapted and reinterpreted for a contemporary audience, and narrative elements have commonly been regarded as key features linking adaptations to their 'sources' and to each other. The notion of a work or ur-text is even suggested by the early comparative understanding of literature and film as 'languages' and adaptation as 'translation'. If the basic events, descriptions of settings and characters (the 'story'), can be translated from language *a* (a written language) into language *b* (a predominantly pictorial language), the story is therefore separate from its telling (presentation) in the sense that it pre-exists its telling; the medium is merely a mode of presentation, the 'language' through which the same basic narrative is expressed. The difference between these past conceptualisations and the one I propose is that comparative theorists have been too eager to 'fix' one culturally lauded source text as the 'original', wherein these meanings are said to lie.[29]

None of what has been stated here disallows the possibility of evaluation. The notion of the 'meta-text' could be employed to evaluate different examples of the same 'work': it is perfectly feasible to defend Shakespeare's *King Lear* or Austen's *Emma* as superior within this framework, should one wish to. Rather than claiming false chronological primacy, or cultural validity based on the status of the 'authors' of these texts, one could argue that Shakespeare and Austen have created the best examples of *King Lear* and *Emma* yet. One must also admit that at some point in the future, someone working in the same or another medium might surpass their achievements. More importantly, an adaptation from literature to the screen necessarily brings into being a separate, autonomous artwork that should be interpreted and evaluated as such. Yet the historical particularities of adaptation criticism and theorising militate against this, as we shall see.

Notes

1 As stated in the Introduction to this book, in recent years there has been a proliferation of non-comparative studies of adaptations, but there has been no sustained attempt to justify the removal of the source novel from the equation. I hope to provide such a justification here.

2 I have omitted definitions 2b and 5, which refer to optical and biological/genetic adaptation. *Oxford English Dictionary*, 2nd edn, 1989.

3 More specifically, Bluestone claims the difference between source text and adaptation to be as substantial as that between 'Johnson's Wax building' and *Swan Lake* (1957: 5, 6). This medium-specific claim is discussed in Chapter 3.

4 Bluestone's critique of the film *Pride and Prejudice* (1940) included many comparisons with Austen's novel, and frequently cited fidelity to the novel as a validation of the film: Bluestone states that a couple of scenes seem at first 'to be mere appendages', but that actually they are 'not so much an addition as a transposition of incidents'. The implication is that the filmmakers have not overstepped the mark, and have thankfully stuck to 'rendering the quality of Jane Austen's intentions' (Bluestone, 1957: 136, 137).

5 Both Bluestone's medium-specific approach and the traditional comparative approach are outlined and discussed in Chapter 3.

6 This inaccurate, yet widely held, understanding of genetic/biological adaptation is revealed in the common misuse of the phrase 'survival of the fittest', where 'fittest' is mistaken to mean 'most healthy/strong/resilient', instead of the intended 'most suitable'.

7 I am obviously oversimplifying in my description of this process, for the sake of conceptual simplicity. My apologies to scientifically minded readers.

8 The term 'version' is explored later in this chapter.

9 *Emma* (ITV) was broadcast in November 1996. It followed a few months after a film adaptation of *Emma* (1996).

10 Another interesting example of the naming or non-naming of adaptation is that of the film *Shadowlands* (1993). The film was based upon a play based upon C. S. Lewis's life. Thus the film is a 'double adaptation' in Andrew's terms, yet was marketed and received in terms of its links with the first term in the series – Lewis's life – not primarily as an adaptation. The book of the film – an adaptation of an adaptation of an adaptation of Lewis's life – was subsequently published.

11 Those adaptations which constitute such 'special instances' are 'announced' through advertisements, trailers, promotional interviews with cast and crew, and other marketing

strategies. Thus the audience cannot fail to realise that the 1995 *Pride and Prejudice* (BBC) is an adaptation of Jane Austen's *Pride and Prejudice* (1813).

12 Shakespeare is known to have drawn heavily on Raphael Holinshed's *Chronicles* (c.1580) for his historical plays and Plutarch's *Lives* for his classical histories, as well as on a variety of published and unpublished stories, plays and poems. The definitive work on Shakespeare's sources is Geoffrey Bullough's eight-volume *Narrative and Dramatic Sources of Shakespeare* (1957–75). Kenneth Muir also provides a good overview of the varied sources of Shakespeare's plays (Muir, 1977).

13 Reciprocally, as Peter Brunette and David Wills point out, 'one never uses the word "original" until there is a copy, which retrospectively creates the "originalness" of the original. There can never be an original until there is a copy of it' (1989: 74). Thus the original and copy can be understood as 'mutually constituting each other' (Brunette and Wills, 1989: 75).

14 Within a comparative approach, the centre-based structure means that the influence of earlier adaptations upon more recent ones is not considered particularly important. The fact of multiple adaptation might, though, be of 'historical' (numerical) interest to writers arguing for the 'timeless appeal' of (for example) Thomas Hardy's or Jane Austen's work.

15 Irrational feelings about the inherent superiority of both the specific source text and the literary medium in which it was created often insinuate themselves into the evaluation of an adaptation at this point.

16 *Little Dorrit* (1987) was written and directed by Christine Edzard. The cinema-release film was six hours long, and was shown in two halves, entitled *Nobody's Fault* and *Little Dorrit's Story*.

17 Various writers, Wagner being one of the most well-recognised examples, proposed a three-category system for ascertaining the 'faithfulness' of an adaptation to its source text. This system is explored in Chapter 3.

18 Harris states in a footnote to her article, 'I recognize that there are unexplored theoretical implications of the privileging of the novel in my discussion' (1995: 97). I hope to flag at least the most important of these here.

19 *Pride and Prejudice* (1979, BBC) was written by Fay Weldon and directed by Cyril Coke.

20 There are clearly echoes here of the 'transparency fallacy', which regards television as a (potentially) unmediated window on the world.

21 For an in-depth and thoughtful discussion of the issues of authorship and intentionality (a discussion which falls outside the scope of this chapter), see Berys Gaut (1997) 'Film Authorship and Collaboration', in R. Allen and M. Smith (eds), *Film Theory and Philosophy*), 149–72, and Paisley Livingston, 'Cinematic Authorship', in the same volume, 132–48.

22 It is important to note that the popular press and film/television critics who write about specific adaptations have frequently resisted the approach to the issue of authorship that academic theorists have adopted. Indeed, writers in the popular press sometimes seem more incisive and 'tuned in' to contemporary adaptations than their academic counterparts, as will be revealed in the analyses of four specific adaptations in Part II.

23 Barthes argues that we should not 'seek out the "sources", the "influences" of a work' (1971: 60) at all, for 'the quotations a text is made of are anonymous, irrecoverable', but here I have to disagree. As many of the writers in *Pulping Fictions* (1996), *Jane Austen in Hollywood* (1998) and *Adaptations: From Text to Screen, Screen to Text* (1999) (see Bibliography for full details) have shown, the 'quotations' of which adaptations are made are in fact recoverable. It is possible to reveal to a significant extent the intertextual 'sources' upon which these films and programmes draw, even though their sources range far beyond the named literary source text.

24 For an even more forthright, and very convincing, rejection of the 'intentional fallacy' see W. K. Wimsatt Jr. and M. C. Beardsley (1995) 'The Intentional Fallacy' in Sean Burke (ed.), *Authorship: From Plato to the Postmodern*, 90–100.

25 Thompson cites for his inspiration *The Literary Work of Art*, by Roman Ingarden (1965), an excellent discussion of these issues.

26 It should be noted that there is no standard, universal use of the terms 'work' and 'text'. There is some variation in the use of these words, particularly since Barthes (1968; 1971) redefined them in order to announce the death of the Author (and his 'work') and the birth of the 'text', and since Nelson Goodman conflated text and work: 'a literary work [is] the text' (1976: 209). A careful discussion of the notion of the literary work, which correlates with my usage of the term, is offered by Wilsmore (1987), who also explores Goodman's arguments. Stein Haugom Olsen (1976) proffers a thorough and useful analysis of common conceptions of the literary work. Barthes's understanding of the term 'work', and his broader arguments, are explored and critiqued by Margit Sutrop (1994) and Peter Lamarque (1990), the latter of whom usefully compares Barthes's assertions with those of Foucault.

27 The replacement of a 'standard whole' original with a more flexible ur-text/work also undermines the power of the definite, authoritative author of the original, for the ur-text/work does not imply such a certain author(ity) behind it. This clearly impacts upon the problems of the authorising power of the 'original's' author, explored earlier in this chapter.

28 *Hamlet* (1996) was written and directed by Kenneth Branagh.

29 The replacement of the 'original' with a source (ur-text or work) is conceptually and interpretatively significant. The differing connotations of 'original' and 'source' reveal the covert attitude to adaptation of the theorist who chooses one term over the other; I refer to the 'source' quite deliberately, as distinct from the 'original'. The label 'original' connotes primacy of chronology and also of status, artistic or aesthetic purity, and uniqueness. 'An' original is ordinarily regarded as 'the' original, thus emphasising its singular precedence as a basis for subsequent copies, adaptations or versions. The term 'source', in contrast, does not imply exclusivity or superiority.

Criticism revisited

Novels are an absolutely untranslatable art form except in the case of the trivial and the second-rate, when it doesn't really matter what happens to them, and in fact being digested into the belly of television is probably the best thing that could have happened to them. (Miller, 1983: 1)

The study of adaptation is politicised both within and outside academe. Academic writer Marion Jordan views her work on adaptation in ideological terms: she refers to being 'left open to attack both from the academic novel-reading right and from the popular front of the cinema-going left' (1981: 199). This image of a field of study torn between two rival camps reflects the situation in the wider critical community. Critics of particular adaptations have long felt the need to situate themselves in one camp or the other: the 'novel-reading right' or the 'cinema-going left', with the former camp historically attracting greater numbers. For a long time, debates about adaptation and critiques of individual instances of adaptation took place within a broader framework of understanding which depended upon maintaining a distinction between 'high art' (literature) and 'mass culture' (television and film). Only recently has the advent of relativist, pluralist approaches to culture begun to challenge this hierarchical structure and validate new aspects of 'popular culture'.

Much early critical work on adaptations was emotionally vivid, even passionate (like Jonathan Miller's polemic above), and this emotional dimension has had a great impact on the field. The shape of 'adaptation studies' has been determined as much by deep-rooted feelings, attitudes and beliefs about adaptation, as by the explicit appropriation and development of conceptualisations, theories and methodologies.[1] The selection of appropriate analytical tools for analysing adaptations was in great part determined by the 'gut feelings', emotional reactions, desires and motivations of the earliest writers. In many cases, thought followed after emotional response. This is not necessarily negative: impassioned, intuitive writing is frequently more engaged and engaging. However, a brief consideration of critical writing on adaptations reveals that some age-old prejudices persist, in defiance of general conceptual and theoretical advances in the field. There is a deep-rooted belief, implied or overtly stated, that literature is an inherently superior medium to television and film, and that this relative superiority ought to be defended. Further, this belief is emotionally 'felt' as much as intellectually 'thought'.

Thus literature–screen adaptations are situated within a variety of often competing discourses; the study of them is apparently inseparable from instinctive feelings about literature, film, television, culture and the process and products of adaptation itself. This applies equally to critical and theoretical writing. Historically, initial attempts to interpret, evaluate and theorise adaptations were inextricably linked to critics' emotional and ideological perspectives on the media involved and on the very notion of adaptation. In a sense, therefore, any consideration of adaptation criticism must begin with an 'emotional' overview that recognises the powerful and continuing importance of these pre-theoretical perspectives. Whilst critical writing on adaptations has progressed significantly beyond early, intuitive responses, later work necessarily reacted to these responses, rejecting them or building upon them. In this way, fundamental beliefs and feelings about literature, film, television, and the process and actuality (in particular the viability and desirability) of adaptation form a trajectory through 'adaptation studies'. The strength of these beliefs explains their perpetuation by critics and theorists today. As Imelda Whelehan wrote in 1999, 'cultural assumptions about the relative worth of the literary versus the film medium are still deeply entrenched enough to be likely to influence our approach to adaptation' (1999: 17).

The impact of a fundamental belief in literature's superiority over film and television, and in the consequently dubious nature of adaptation, has affected not just the 'content' of adaptation studies but also its form. Both critical and theoretical writing on adaptation(s) attempt to obscure the presence and power of these underlying emotions by frequently describing adaptation not in literal terms but through metaphor, analogy and figurative writing (as in Miller's comment that opened this chapter). It is as if the emotional investment of critics and theorists in the subject of adaptation determines a more expressive mode of writing; many writers are writing not so much 'about' adaptations as 'around' them. The powerful emotions elicited by the practice of adaptation bubble under the surface of adaptation criticism; one does not have to dig deep to expose them. But the ways in which writers attempt to conceal or obscure their most irrational responses are intriguing in themselves. It is notable that one of the most common features of critical writing about television adaptations is that critics seem unable to consider the phenomenon without offering some reflections upon television as a medium. Yet a first glance suggests that such critics are surprisingly complimentary about the television genre of classic-novel adaptations.

The 'best' television

It goes without saying that the new series is impeccably made ... The 'classic serial' is perhaps the most prestigious instance of the fusion of the Reithian duty to educate with the need to entertain. ... But what exactly do we get for our money? First of all, we get a seamless patchwork of beautiful images: ... Mrs Cadwallader's outlandish dress steals our attention from what she has to say; every conversation seems to be punctuated by horses trotting across the screen. ... You are tempted to say that you are made to feel just what it must have been like to live in Middlemarch. Then you remember the novel. What, one wonders, will anyone who picks it up after seeing the serial have left to imagine? (Gervais, 1994: 59–60)

David Gervais's discussion of the 1994 BBC adaptation of *Middlemarch* is an emblematic example of adaptation criticism. He makes several notable points: first, that the BBC *Middlemarch* is an example of the best of British television; second, that the programme consists primarily of a sequence of 'beautiful images'; and third, that the programme may 'spoil' the novel for those viewers who come to the novel after watching the serial. These three points are indicative of residual concerns of critics and theorists who come from a literary background, and they echo age-old fears and enmities.

Gervais's first point appears to be highly complimentary: that classic serials are usually the 'best' television, that they are 'impeccably made' and 'politically sound' or, as D. J. Enright puts it, they are 'good, intelligent entertainment' (1988: 8). Before Gervais, other writers had also emphasised the superiority of classic serials over run-of-the-mill television in their reviews of particular classic-novel adaptations. D. Thomson writes of the BBC's 1980 *Pride and Prejudice*, 'it began ... with elegant titles and sprightly music ... We sighed at the picture of rural order and ease, and when the Bennet gaggle was made visible, the screen was a Liberty lawn of fine pastels' (1981: 16). He concludes that the programme exhibits 'the becalmed majesty of a classic novel being poured very carefully into the cathode-ray tube' (1981: 16).

Contemporaries of Gervais continue the theme. Hala Bentley describes the BBC's *Pride and Prejudice* (1995) in even more glowing terms, noting 'the stunning visual impact of this gorgeous, high-budget production' (1996: 143); Rebecca Dickson comments on a cluster of recent Austen adaptations: '*Persuasion, Pride and Prejudice, Sense and Sensibility*, and *Emma* are all delightful visual and audio experiences. Beautiful settings, witty and lively dialogue, lovely costumes, clever irony, and more – overall, they are all well done' (1998: 44).[2]

There are intriguing implications to be found in these comments. First, the best television is, it appears, television which tries to be 'non-televisual'. That is, classic serials tend to under-use, even reject, common television conventions and aim instead to create something that gives the impression of being more serious, reflective, intelligent and thoughtful. One of the main ways in which this is achieved is through the attempt to utilise filmic devices in order to give a sense of artistic 'seriousness' to the programme. Each of the above writers alludes to the aesthetic beauty of these television programmes – they refer to the use of long, slow shots and smooth, 'invisible' editing, to the attention to detail in costume and setting, and to the understated, reserved and 'naturalistic' style of acting most commonly found in these serials. Thus the writers imply that the superior status of classic serials lies in their very rejection of the most common modes of televisual expression – relatively fast editing, a reliance on close-ups, the use of video (as opposed to film), a dependence upon rapidly developed emotional drama (melodrama), and so forth.[3] It could be inferred that in approving as 'the best television' television texts which consciously try to distinguish themselves from what the audience commonly understands to be televisual modes of dramatic represen-tation, the writers reveal their fundamental dislike of television as it is more widely seen and understood.[4]

Metaphors

The above analysis of critical writing presupposes that the praise critics extend to classic-novel adaptations should be taken at face value. How-ever, to do so is to overlook both the tone of their words and the language chosen to express their opinions, language which is overwhelmingly metaphorical. Thomson's considered choice of the words 'a classic novel being poured very carefully into the cathode-ray tube' emphasises the sheer impossibility of such a process – novels cannot be 'poured' into another vessel (medium) in this way; this description therefore exag-gerates the problems of adaptation by offering a metaphor for the process which is clearly so far removed from real possibilities. His description of television as a 'cathode-ray tube' accentuates the technical nature of television over its aesthetic and creative potential, and the complete metaphor has echoes of school science experiments. Thomson thus undermines the value of television as an art, instead implying that it is a rudimentary science, a technology. By constituting television's identity in this way Thomson disallows television's potential and suggests that it is artistically incomparable with the source novel.

Metaphors abound in critical discourse on adaptation, the use of figurative language suggesting its essentially 'emotional', intuitive nature. Enright's use of metaphor is less subtle than Thomson's; he argues that 'the best dramatisations are shadows of the novels they derive from – the BBC's Vanity Fair was a very elegant shadow, a well-dressed skeleton' (1988: 8). Enright's words reveal his belief in the inherent inferiority of television as an artform and in the importance of television 'knowing its place' and not attempting to exceed its own limited capabilities. His use of metaphor is expressively important: classic serials are likened to shadows, to skeletons, suggesting a lack of depth; shadows and skeletons are, to differing degrees 'transparent' and superficial – they consist only of what one can see of them, nothing more. The source book, by extension, remains the living, breathing body; the adaptation is thus consigned to the role of shadow (the shadow of the former self) or skeleton (all that remains after death, after the departure of flesh, spirit and soul). There are interesting resonances here of early perspectives on the film medium: the notion of adaptation as shadow echoes the notion of film as 'shadow play', as a concrete instance of 'Plato's cave'.[5]

Comparably, Gervais implies that there is a superficiality, a lack of depth to the televisual rendering of the novel: the metaphorical 'seamless patchwork of beautiful images' is offered to the audience, he implies, as a substitute for real meaning. This is echoed in his later references to the serial's over-emphasis on surface detail ('the accessories and the settings') in the screen version: 'Could we, for instance, seeing Dorothea on her horse, ask what women like her contributed to the suffragettes and hence to modern feminism? We would not be able to get her horse or her dress out of our mind [sic]' (Gervais, 1994: 62). Although it seems that it is the particular style of these serials that is under attack, it is actually something far greater. The visual image itself, above described variously with words such as 'visually stunning', 'becalmed majesty', 'beautiful images', is condemned. Similarly, Enright makes a damning allegation about the adaptation which he himself described as 'charming': it 'would have succeeded had it been soundless and accompanied only by subtitles in basic English' (1988: 8). And it is this – television's lack of respect for words, rather than images – that precipitates the most vitriolic attacks upon literature–screen adaptations.

Word versus image

> The novelist uses words, the film-maker uses pictures; therein lies the
> simple but major difference between the two art forms. (Murray, 1972: 109)

Theorists from the 1960s onwards have often structured their discourse
on adaptation(s) in terms of an overt distinction between words and
images. William Jinks and Fred Marcus demarcated large sections of
their volumes on adaptation using these very terms: 'The Word and the
Image' and 'From Words to Visual Images', respectively (Jinks, 1971;
Marcus, 1971). Though understandable, this demarcation of novel (words)
from film or television (images) is not only simplistic, for films and
television programmes employ words as well as images (particularly in
classic-novel adaptations), it is also problematised by a cultural and
academic history that favours words over images. Again, instinctive feelings about the two media have guided the study of adaptation(s), setting
up an antagonistic relation between the written word and the screen image.

With regard to adaptation, Enright describes words as 'the first
casualty in this transmutation' (1988: 7). Correspondingly, the second
casualty in this move 'from verbal to visual representation' is the
audience's use of its imagination: 'imagination is starved, for the sake of
an immediately striking and easily digested visual titbit' (Enright, 1988: 7)
(note the junk-food metaphor). Gervais similarly opines, 'What, one
wonders, will anyone who picks [the novel] up after seeing the serial have
left to imagine?' (1994: 60). This is a well-rehearsed complaint – that
'camera-vision cripples the use of the mind's eye ... It is all there for us to
see, not to imagine' (Edel, 1974: 182). However, both Enright's and
Gervais's fears reveal a surprising lack of faith in the novel as imagin-
istically and aesthetically superior. Enright regards adaptations as a threat,
and prefers those that are mere shadows, that do not threaten to equal or
better their source novels. Gervais fears that television, despite its
superficiality and ineffectualness, might imperil the imaginations of
prospective readers of the novel. What is at stake here is the perceived
threat that audio-visual, moving images pose to 'traditional' means of
expression such as words. Again, these writers' fears do not exist in a
vacuum, but echo underlying concerns and issues at stake. In 1964,
Marshall McLuhan noted a widespread feeling that film 'threatens [the]
ancient technology of literacy': the printed word (1964: 82). He observes
the impact of the image not just upon the word but, in line with his wider
arguments, upon literary culture itself, noting common perceptions that
the image, in particular the television image, is 'a "disaster" for a literate,
specialist culture', as it 'blurs many cherished attitudes and procedures'
(1964: 335).

McLuhan's analysis highlights not only a deep-rooted distrust of the visual image as opposed to the written word, but also the academic concerns at stake in this battle between image and word. His comment about the impact of images upon 'cherished attitudes and procedures' denotes the problems literary experts encounter upon attempting to understand and appreciate image-based media like film and television. He thus relates writers' dislike and distrust of the image to their fear of inadequacy and redundancy in the face of 'new' media: the image 'renders literary culture quite helpless to cope with the photograph' (1964: 197).[6] Barthes acknowledges the existence of less self-interested fears about the image in comparison with the word: 'there are those who think that the image is an extremely rudimentary system in comparison with language' – an attitude that is rife (1964: 32). This view is not without some theoretical roots. Notably, Walter Benjamin, in 1936, wrote of how the mechanically produced image destroys the 'aura' that is attached to 'traditional' works of art such as painting.[7]

Some aspects of Barthes's and McLuhan's work open up the possibility of breaking away from rigid prejudices regarding the 'image versus word' stand-off. Barthes proposes an alternative view that the image has an 'ineffable richness' (Barthes, 1964: 32) and attempts to explore with greater care the image and its potential; both Barthes and McLuhan argue for a greater appreciation and understanding of images and their contribution to culture. The views of these authors may sound familiar, even tired, today, but in 1964 discussions of images and words were couched in adversarial terms, and adaptation theorists felt the need to respond by favouring one side over the other (as Marion Jordan suggested). The basis of adaptation studies in literary studies determined a 'pro-words' response from the majority of theorists and critics.

There is however a rather sweeping generalisation underlying both sides of this argument. Fears about (moving) images, and the consequent denigration of film and television in relation to literature, are founded upon a clear understanding of these media as primarily 'visual'. Writers on both sides of the divide imply a belief that in film and television 'the visual occupies a position of primacy with respect to the verbal' (Brunette and Wills, 1989: 62). This assumption – that 'the medium [film] is visual' (Roemer, 1971: 49), and that its visual nature determines its artistic possibilities, is rooted in a tradition that fails to recognise the importance of sound (diegetic sound, music and dialogue) to films and television programmes.[8] And this assumption is long-standing enough to constitute a tradition in adaptation studies. Even recent adaptation critics explicitly note that their 'medium-specific' understanding of film excludes the word, which is regarded as specific to literature. Millicent Marcus, for example, writes of *La voce della luna* (1989):

> in his resolve to make a medium-specific adaptation of Cavazzoni's passage, Fellini scrupulously avoided recourse to verbal solutions. The film therefore excludes all verbal references to Marisa's transformation ... Instead, the metamorphosis takes place audiovisually, with a series of sounds, camera movements, angles and cuts. (1993: 232)

Putting aside the theoretical curiosity of Marcus's notion of filmic medium specificity as something that a filmmaker can either choose to comply with or not,[9] her critique is representative in two ways. First, her reference to 'solutions' configures the process of adaptation as a 'problem'; second, film's use of dialogue, something most filmgoers would regard as an essential part of film texts, is viewed as 'cheating', as resorting to a literary device (words) in a medium that ought to reject the literary. This deliberate rejection of traditional conventions of film for a medium-specific notion of 'ideal filmicness' perpetuates an antagonistic relationship between the word and the image that is not borne out by practice – nor, indeed, by the conceptual work offered by the most advanced comparative theorists of adaptation. Comparative theorist Robert Scholes (1976), for example, reminds us of the simple point that film combines verbal narrative with pictorial representation. In view of Marcus's second observation, one is tempted to wonder whether adaptation is a problem *per se*, or whether adaptation critics have worked to problematise it.

Assimilation to a higher goal

> Education seizes upon the adaptation from the literary classic to serve ... dubious ends. Showing recalcitrant students the film or the television serial is regarded as a way to encourage them to read the original novel. (Ellis, 1982: 5)

An interesting permutation of critics' responses to the perceived threat that adaptations pose to their antecedent novels is that of assimilation into a wider educative goal. Simply, some writers have attempted to engineer a perception of adaptations which places them in a particular relationship with their source texts, namely that of 'study aid' or 'advertisement', thus reconfiguring the presumed 'ethical problem' of adaptation as an advantage. Gervais's essay displays evidence of this alternative attitude to adaptation: that adaptations should send viewers to the book, and should not encroach on the book by creating images that may dull the imagination of prospective readers. As Gervais puts it, 'What matters is what such expensive reproductions tell one about the original and how we think of it' (1994: 63).

The adaptation is thus seen as an addendum, a footnote to the original. Gervais warns against trying to recreate the source text too faithfully and instead recommends considerable alteration and an emphasis on the 'visual sense' (though this seems to fit oddly alongside his criticism of the serial's overly visual emphasis). Ideally, Gervais would like to see the sacred book remain untouched by the dirty hands of mass culture, but if adaptations *must* be made, he proposes a 'useful' task for the programme-makers: to attempt to send new readers to the book. Similarly, Peter Reynolds reassures us that adaptations 'can and do send people out on to the streets to hunt down the original and claim it for themselves' (1993: 10), whilst Thomson grudgingly concedes that classic-novel adaptations 'must be educational even if only a few people are tempted to go back to the books' (1981: 75).[10]

Others have used this approach as a methodology for evaluation: Bentley (1996) assesses the BBC *Pride and Prejudice* (1995) solely in terms of its usefulness in encouraging school students to read and appreciate the source novel; Anthony Bundey undertakes similar assessments in his thesis on the 'educational implications' of adaptations (1986). Even George Linden, who argues that one should recognise an adaptation as 'a work of art in its own right', adds that the film/programme should also '[excite] the reader to go re-experience that work in another medium: the novel' (1971: 169). Charles Eidsvik states the function of adaptations even more unequivocally: 'a movie is a ninety-minute free "ad" circulated to millions of people' (1977: 32).

The ramifications of this approach are clear: a return to fidelity criticism. The educational usefulness of classic-novel adaptations depends upon the adaptations' fidelity to their source novels (upon 'advertising standards') and upon the role of adaptations in conveying the story, ideas, themes and opinions of the source text's author.

Academe

> The field of adaptations has in the past been dominated by scholars working primarily from an 'English lit.' perspective, who may be inclined to privilege the originary literary text above its adaptations. (Whelehan, 1999: 17)

As Whelehan observes, most early adaptation criticism was written by film critics (in journals and magazines) or by academics working within the field of English literature, unlike more recent work on adaptation, which has been produced mainly by film or television theorists. This is because of the historical development of film studies out of English studies, both in the UK and the US. Many of the writers discussed above, such as Bentley, Enright and Gervais, were trained and are situated within English, not film, television or media, departments, and their literary perspective has had implications for their work on adaptations.

> All too often, readers with a great deal of literary sophistication bring a [particular] attitude to film adaptations: that is, whether or not a film based on a cherished novel succeeds *as a film* – as a cinematic work of art – is a matter of not the slightest interest compared to the question of whether it is 'faithful'. (Beja, 1979: 88) (italics in original)

As Morris Beja suggests, the historical influence of literary concerns and literary models of interpretation has affected writers' conceptualisations, interpretations and evaluations of adaptations in very distinctive ways. To a certain degree, the influence of literary models has restricted the development of a coherent model of the adaptive process and an effective methodology for interpreting and evaluating adaptations. As Gerald Peary and Roger Shatzkin noted in 1977, 'many younger film critics [examine film] in a different way than the person trained only in literature' (1977: 4). The development of film and television studies as independent disciplines increases the potential to move the study of literature–screen adaptations beyond simplistic, instinctive responses. As John G. Blair writes, 'One side benefit of the growing credibility of film studies is that now differences between media need not be freighted with reflex judgments in favor of one or the other' (1996: 5).

However, to represent contemporary adaptation studies as a field in which literary studies have gracefully given way to screen studies would be rather inaccurate. Just as long-held emotional responses to literature, film, television and adaptation have shaped the field, underlying feelings within academia continue to influence writing about adaptations. English is itself a relatively recent field of study in higher education (in comparison with theology, philosophy, and so on) and, having now become an established part of the university curriculum, it appears to be under threat from film, television and media studies, as the latter have become subject areas in their own right. Whelehan and Cartmell, in the introduction to their first edited volume on adaptation, *Pulping Fictions* (1996), note that film and media studies 'continue to seduce students away from' English, and that 'horrified defenders of traditional English studies lament the fated take-over by media studies of English, with courses in Star Trek and Batman replacing those in Milton and Shakespeare' (1996: 1). In this way the decision to study screen adaptations, and the choice of methodology for doing so, again become politicised within academia.

From criticism to theory

Historically, then, writers of adaptation criticism were comfortable with offering opinions, frequently unsubstantiated by any conceptual or theoretical understanding of the nature of adaptation or of television's (or film's) potential. As McLuhan put it, 'the favorite stance of literary man has long been "to view with alarm" or "to point with pride" while scrupulously ignoring what's going on' (1964: 199).

Writers of adaptation 'theories' have long aimed to resist the intuitive, untheorised positions exemplified in much critical writing, and to establish firm conceptual, theoretical and methodological bases for their work. Theoretical writing was in part, therefore, a response to the critical writing discussed in this chapter, and attempted to answer – implicitly or otherwise – the kind of questions Morris Beja raises:

> What relationship should a film have to the original source? Should it be faithful? Can it be? To what? Which should be uppermost in the film-maker's mind: the integrity of the original work, or the integrity of the film to be based on that work? ... What types of changes are permissible? Desirable? Inevitable? (1976: 81)

The very vocalising of these questions aided the progression of the field, as the most irrational feelings, attitudes and prejudices about adaptation were exposed. The theoretical and conceptual work that resulted is revisited in the next chapter.

Notes

1　The term 'adaptation studies' is used as a shorthand here. Adaptation and adaptations are studied in various fields: English literature, English language, film studies, television studies, comparative literature and so on. 'Adaptation studies', then, does not constitute a formally recognised field of study; my use of the term conceals a plethora of approaches from theorists in many different areas. I refer, broadly, to writing which addresses literature–film or literature–television adaptation(s), whether it be primarily interpretative or 'theoretical'.

2　For fuller details please see the Filmography.

3　This apparent 'rejection' of the televisual by the traditional classic-novel adaptation is explored more fully in Part II. My focus here is not on the validity of these critics' notions of the televisual, but on the attitude to the medium of television betrayed in their writing.

4　The term 'televisual' is used cautiously here to refer only to notions of conventional television presentation. A far more detailed conceptualisation of the televisual and a discussion of its medium-specificity are offered in Chapter 4.

5 Metaphor has also played a central role in conceptualising and theorising adaptation. Metaphor in these contexts is not necessarily detrimental, of course; strong arguments have been made in the fields of cognitive studies and knowledge representation for the value of metaphor in developing knowledge and understanding (MacCormac, 1985; Way, 1994). Rather, it is the particular metaphors being employed here, and the ends to which they are being employed, that are dubious.

6 The problems of thinking about 'visual' media from within a literary framework have arisen frequently throughout the development of adaptation studies, as will be seen later in this chapter and in Chapter 3.

7 It should be noted that Benjamin did not regard this loss of 'aura' as a wholly negative event; rather he foresaw radical potential in this movement away from the traditional, revered art object.

8 I consider the way in which the soundtrack is frequently overlooked in favour of the image track in film and television theory – and especially in adaptation studies – elsewhere (Cardwell, 2000a).

9 See Chapter 3 for a discussion of medium specificity.

10 The repeated emphasis on 'returning to the book', of 're-finding' the original, corresponds with the comparative centre-based conceptualisation of adaptation discussed in the previous chapter.

Theory revisited

The criticism of adaptations has existed for as long as adaptations have been made. However, it was not until fairly recently that 'adaptation theory' came into being.[1] Very little was written during the early years of film with the aim of addressing conceptual questions about adaptations or proposing viable theoretical frameworks and methodologies for the study of adaptation. It was in 1957 that George Bluestone wrote his seminal, and highly influential, work *Novels into Film*. Until then, much of what was written about adaptation was critical, concerning specific films of specific books, and most of this textual criticism rested upon unquestioned assumptions regarding the phenomenon of novel-to-film adaptation and theoretically undeveloped expectations concerning what could (and should) be achieved in terms of the 'transferral' of a text from one medium to another.[2]

So adaptation 'theory' is a relatively young field. However, it is possible to identify salient trajectories, developments and changes of direction within this subject area. The necessity to engage with large theoretical issues, such as the nature of a 'medium', has led adaptation theorists to employ a variety of existing conceptual paradigms in their attempts to create a suitable theoretical framework for understanding the process of adaptation.

There have been three paradigmatic approaches to adaptation that have marked out the terrain of adaptation studies, each of which I shall deal with in turn. These approaches are: the medium-specific approach, the comparative approach and the pluralist approach.

The medium-specific approach

Medium-specific theories have influenced the development of adaptation theories, in one way or another, from the beginning, though each theory of adaptation differs in its understanding of and degree of reliance upon, or rejection of, concepts of medium specificity. The traditional tenets of medium-specific theories can be broadly summarised thus: a) each separate medium (in this case, novel, film or television) is unique; and b) its unique nature gives rise to forms of artistic expression distinct from those in other media, shaping as it does the medium's conventions and setting limitations regarding the possible forms of representation available in that medium. As Noël Carroll summarises, the medium-specific theorist believes that 'each art form has its own domain of expression and exploration ... determined by the nature of the medium' (1996: 26).

It is clear that the essential element of this type of theory is its causal implication: not only does a medium-specific approach make the common-sense claim that the texts produced in one medium are different from those produced in another medium, it also advances a claim regarding the fundamental (ontological) source of this difference. It is also apparent why such theories are of particular interest to adaptation theorists, who have traditionally been concerned with the process of adapting a text from one medium to another very different medium. Medium-specificity theories offer an explanation for the perceived differences between media, and so would seem to offer a viable framework for understanding the phenomenon of adaptation. Indeed, some of the earliest theorists did subscribe to medium-specific notions, a conceptual commitment which consequently created methodological and interpretative problems (as I shall signal later).

A medium-specific approach, highly dependent as it is on the notion of differentiated, unique and incompatible media, clearly complicates the study of a particular television/film genre which appears to ignore medium-specific restrictions and which has always been popular with both filmmakers and audiences. A medium-specific approach thus problematises the study of adaptation and consequently would appear to contain the potential to engender a variety of divergent and rigorous analyses. Although a study of adaptation that uses medium-specific beliefs as a point of departure could encourage conclusions which postulate the 'natural' (intrinsic) superiority of the literary text over its visual adaptation (the impossibility of adaptation and the valorisation of one medium over another), it could equally instill open-mindedness and a willingness to appreciate the film/television text as a work of art in its own right. Thus a medium-specific approach has the potential to inspire a resulting collection of interesting and salient analyses of film and television adaptations.

By the same token, the study of adaptations, from the point of view of the medium-specificity theorist, is potentially fascinating in that it would seem to provide an opportunity to test the parameters and limitations of a particular understanding of medium-specific theory. Carroll argues that

the development of a medium-specific thesis relies upon two components: the 'internal component [that] considers what a medium does best of
all the things it does' and the 'comparative component [that] considers
what a medium does best compared to other media' (1996: 8). As Carroll
implies, it is often through comparison between media that the specificities of a medium are seen in relief, and thus it seems reasonable that
the development and maintenance of medium-specific notions are evident
within the corpus of work on adaptation.

Bluestone implies exactly this process of evaluation when he states
that 'a comparative study which begins by finding resemblances between
novel and film ends by loudly proclaiming their differences' (1957: ix).
Bluestone implies that he sees adaptation study as a chance to test (and
affirm) his own notions of medium specificity. Beja, similarly, introduces
his book with its aim to 'get a sense of all that they [literature and film]
share, to be sure, but also of all the traits that they do not, so that one may
grasp as well what is unique about each form' (1979: xii). And McDougal
states that a 'comparative analysis of film and literature ... helps to define
the unique properties of each medium by probing its relative strengths
and weaknesses' (1985: 7).

Bluestone's book *Novels into Film* is one of the earliest and most
influential books written within the field of adaptation theory. Many of his
ideas and observations have been extended and elaborated in later work.
What differentiates his approach from later theorists, though, is his overt
belief in medium-specific arguments, and in the importance of these to
the study of film, and of adaptations in particular.

Bluestone's proposed theory of adaptation offers an archetypal example
of a strong medium-specific approach to this subject. In his preface and
first chapter he states his laudable commitment to an unbiased, fair
approach to (film) adaptations, making clear his intentions not to favour
the source text over the adaptation – a direct response to the dominant
tendency at that time, described by Lester Asheim a few years earlier:
'personal preferences, snap judgments, isolated instances, and random
impressions ... characterize most of the writing in the field' (1951: 289).
Bluestone's attitude to adaptations is founded upon a fundamental
understanding of film as a totally separate and different medium from the
novel. Thus he begins with a declaration of belief in medium-specific
arguments: 'In the last analysis [of the two media – novel and film], each
is autonomous, and each is characterised by unique and specific
properties' (1957: 6). Further, 'It is insufficiently recognised that the end
products of novel and film represent different aesthetic genera, as
different from each other as ballet is from architecture' (1957: 5).

Bluestone asserts that each medium is autonomous and is characterised by unique and specific properties; that these differences between media give rise to textual differences in form and theme; and that the resulting texts in one medium are therefore necessarily different to the resulting texts in another medium: 'Because novel and film are both organic – in the sense that aesthetic judgments are based on total ensembles which include both formal and thematic conventions – we may expect to find that differences in form and theme are inseparable from differences in media' (1957: 2). Bluestone therefore reasons that differences of form and theme between the texts of different media are determined by ('inseparable from') the unique, inherent technological and ontological properties of each medium. Jean Mitry expresses a similar argument in a compressed form when he states that 'the means of expression *in being different* would express different things – not the same things in different ways' (1971: 1) (italics in original). This set of assumptions validates Bluestone's attitude that film adaptations must be judged not in comparison with their source book but on their own merits. The key question that he would propose we ask of each adaptation is, 'Is it a good *film*?'

As regards film's ontological specificity, Bluestone outlines those technological features of filmmaking which result in unique textual characteristics. Following Eisenstein, editing is of central importance:

> In cinematic terms, then, the method of connecting the film strips becomes the basic formative function. For the two strips, joined together, become a *tertium quid*, a third thing which neither of the strips has been independently. This is the essence of that much abused concept of Eisenstein's which we have come to know as montage. (1957: 25)

> If the film is ... severely restricted in rendering linguistic tropes (despite dialogue which will be discussed presently), it has, through the process of editing, discovered a metaphoric quality all its own. (1957: 24)

Thus Bluestone argues that the particular components of film (film strips, which can be cut and joined) give rise to particular and unique textual forms (editing). Similarly, Beja begins from the 'physical and technical aspects' of film (1979: 20), comparing it with language, which is composed of words and constructed using grammar and syntax (1979: 54);[3] Mailer also emphasises his belief in medium specificity with his statement that 'you have little bits of film strips, each the equivalent of words' (in Jinks, 1971: 5). Clearly this categorisation of literature and film in terms of their physical or technical constituent parts echoes the distinction made by other writers between words and images respectively (Jinks, 1971; Marcus, 1971), building a medium-specific conceptualisation that is technologically determinist.

On this understanding, textual features are *secondary*: they are 'caused by' the ontological specificities of each medium; the ontological/technical nature of film is '[the component] which sets in motion, and gives direction to, the relationship of all the other components' (Garvin, 1964: 23). In terms of adaptation, then, Bluestone commits himself to the traditional medium-specific argument that most (if not all) of the textual characteristics of the novel cannot be recreated on film or television, because these characteristics arise from the verbal form of the written text. Literary textual characteristics cannot be reproduced from the completely different technical foundations of film; this consequently disallows almost any similarity between novel and film texts, and, of course, between novel and adaptation.

This conclusion is endorsed by Bluestone himself: 'changes are inevitable the moment one abandons the linguistic for the visual medium' (1957: 5); only basic 'events' in a novel can be re-presented on screen, and this re-presentation constitutes a completely new, incomparable artistic representation which is an essentially different artistic entity, its features arising from the technology of the film/television medium itself and (almost entirely) the medium alone. What is most surprising about Bluestone's book, then, is his methodology for analysing actual, specific adaptations: 'The method calls for viewing the film with a shooting-script at hand. During the viewing, notations of any final changes in the editing were entered on the script. After the script had become an accurate account of the movie's final print, it was then superimposed on the novel' (1957: xi). All differences between the two written texts were then noted in the source novel, with the following result: 'Before each critical evaluation, I was able to hold before me an accurate and reasonably objective record of how the film differed from its model' (1957: xi).

In this methodology, based on Asheim's methods (1949), one can see a quite astounding evidence of a 'lack of fit' between Bluestone's conceptual principles and intentions, and his attempts to apply his theories to real case studies. In view of Bluestone's fundamental belief in the specificity, and incomparability, of the two media, the incongruity of his methodology as outlined above is manifestly apparent. How can one reconcile his strongly expressed belief in medium specificity with his apparent belief that one can offer an 'accurate account' and 'reasonably objective record' of a film through the *written word* (in the shape of a modified shooting script)? If, as Bluestone has argued at length, it is impossible for a novel to be simply 'transposed' onto film, due to the fundamentally different nature of films and novels, i.e. the technical basis of production of each, how can it be possible to 'transpose' in the other direction – to transfer a film into a written account of itself?

Of course, one must consider the historical context of Bluestone's methodology. Without the advantage of video recorders, he would have had to find another way to record his memories of the film. However, even if his written summary is thus justified, his careful 'literary' comparison is not. If, as Bluestone states, the texts arising from the two media are fundamentally distinct, what is the usefulness of attempting to compare them in this way? Surely he is employing a methodology which, metaphorically, attempts to compare two things as different as (to use his own example) 'Wright's Johnson's Wax Building [and] Tchaikowsky's *Swan Lake*' (Bluestone, 1957: 6)?

Perhaps we have been too hasty in classifying Bluestone's work as a 'theory' of adaptation. He presents us with a conceptual discussion of medium specificity and a proposed methodology for studying adaptations, but as his methodology for analysing adaptations does not arise in any way from the conceptual framework that he constructs for us, it is unrealistic to see his book as a text that offers a considered and complete 'theory' of adaptation.

The limits of medium specificity: equivalence between novel and film

Later theorists of adaptation noted the problems that Bluestone's strict medium-specific approach raised for the study of adaptation(s): the very existence of adapted texts seems to defy the laws of medium specificity. As Andrew says, Bluestone takes 'pleasure in scrutinizing this practice even while ultimately condemning it to the realm of the impossible' (1984: 101). Bluestone himself says of one screen adaptation (*Pride and Prejudice*, MGM, 1940) that it 'render[s] the quality of Jane Austen's intentions' and 'do[es] not alter the meanings of Jane Austen's novel' (1957: 136), and, as Andrew writes, if one accepts the possibility that meaning can be reproduced in a medium different to that in which it was produced originally,

> one would have to hold that while the material of literature (graphemes, words, and sentences) may be of a different nature from the materials of cinema (projected light and shadows, identifiable sounds and forms, and represented actions), both systems may construct in their own way, and at higher levels, scenes and narratives that are indeed commensurable. (1984: 101)

The potential for intermedia textual similarities, something for which Bluestone offers evidence but does not appear to offer a theoretical explanation, is highlighted by Eisenstein's much earlier work – 'Dickens,

Griffith and The Film Today' (Eisenstein, 1949). As we have seen, Bluestone drew upon Eisenstein's famed writing about editing and montage, two specifically filmic characteristics. However, Eisenstein saw many more textual similarities between film and literature than Bluestone did, even proposing, through the employment of convincingly drawn comparisons of adapted texts, that Charles Dickens, in particular, offered 'film-indications'. These 'film-indications', created through the structure of Dickens's stories and his use of language, constituted 'precursors' to specific film techniques such as close-ups (1949: 211–12), montage (213–14), dissolves (198–9) and parallel editing (205). Eisenstein was not alone in drawing this comparison. George H. Ford, writing about Dickens's *Hard Times*, offers a comparison of an extract from the book and from the shooting script for Granada's adaptation (1977) and concludes convincingly that:

> What is noteworthy about this example is not just that the script follows Dickens' text word for word but that *his* text seems to have been set up for direct transcription into the screen version. Dickens does not say that the girl hates the old bully; he *shows* it by gesture. ... The gestures are thus spelled out explicitly and appear in the film exactly as Dickens has specified. (1987: 324) (italics in original)

Grahame Smith draws a similar comparison, rejecting Robert Giddings *et al.*'s medium-specific argument that Dickens cannot be adequately recreated on screen because 'his stock in trade is words' (Giddings *et al.*, 1990: 46) with the argument that 'this is hardly a helpful comment on a difficult problem. If the gap between the media concerned is "totally unbridgeable" then there seems to be absolutely no way forward' (Smith, 1990: 61). Other writers have been subject to similar observations of correlation between their work and adaptations of it – Thomas Hardy, for example (Lodge, 1981: 95–105; Sinyard, 1986: 45–50; Webster, 1993: 147–8).[4] Through attention to actual instances of source/adaptation correlation, the problematic nature of medium-specific concepts in the study of adaptation is foregrounded.

This raises significant doubts regarding Bluestone's medium-specific theory. If we accept such examples of correlative characteristics in film and novel, then it becomes much harder to argue that textual characteristics within the end-products of different media arise from the unique properties of the media themselves. Indeed, Eisenstein and the other writers *do* fall short of arguing for this.[5] The lack of explanation and discussion in Bluestone's work regarding the many similar conventions and forms of representation that appear in literature and film (and that have been noted by Eisenstein *et al.*) is of great import to his theory of adaptation. Is it really reasonable to state that many characteristics of film arise from the unique properties of the medium, when the very characteristics that are usually considered the most typically 'filmic' seem to be equally abundant in some examples of literature? Does this mean that Bluestone's position is untenable?

Bluestone apparently foresaw (and pre-empted) the problems inherent within his strictly technologically determinist approach. He argued that both audience and censors affect the conventions of filmic representation:[6] 'Differences in the raw materials of novel and film cannot fully explain differences in content. For each medium presupposes a special, though often heterogeneous and overlapping, audience whose demands condition and shape artistic content' (Bluestone, 1957: 31). So, moving away from technological determinism, Bluestone argued that close similarities between literature and film could be explained because they arise from the expectations of similar audiences, and within comparable contexts. One could cite the similarity between the social context of Dickens's novels – serialised, and written with a wide public audience in mind – and that of films and, even more obviously, television programmes. According to Bluestone, shared conventions of literature and film are audience-determined. Eisenstein makes a related observation but, unlike Bluestone, does not commit himself to any causal connection between audience and conventions:

> What were the novels of Dickens for his contemporaries, for his readers? There is one answer: they bore the same relation to them that the film bears to the same strata in our time. They compelled the reader to live with the same passions. They appealed to the same good and sentimental elements as does the film ... they alike mill the extraordinary, the unusual, the fantastic, from boring, prosaic and everyday existence. (Eisenstein, 1949: 206)

Eisenstein does not go as far as Bluestone does and suggest that the audience and the general social context within which films are made play a part in determining the 'unique properties' of film. Eisenstein contents himself with exploring the similarities between Dickens's popularity with his readers and that of the cinema with its audience. Following this line of argument it is not unreasonable to propose that conventions of artistic representation, initiated in various ways, become predominant because they appeal (for whatever reason) to a contemporary audience and thus to a majority of contemporary writers and filmmakers, who work in a commercial environment, and whose success is strongly dependent upon procuring large audiences for their work.

Evidence that adaptations from novel to screen display many similarities raise significant problems for medium-specific theories in general. As Andrew articulates, 'it is at this point that the specificity of these two signifying systems is at stake' (1984: 101). Yet there is still some space for medium-specific explanations. Eisenstein's non-medium-specific approach explains why certain forms of representation persist both within artforms and across the arts, but not why some conventions remain unique to particular media and are not taken up in others. In these cases the salience of a very 'diluted' technologically determined (medium-specific) model is apparent; the ontological basis of a medium places limits upon what can be done within that medium.[7]

The theoretical and methodological consequences of commencing a study of adaptation based upon notions of medium specificity, and the limitations of such an approach, are apparent. Bluestone clearly spotted some of these problems himself, and then attempted rather unsuccessfully to construct a 'get-out clause' to relieve himself of the commitment he had made to medium-specific concepts (in the form of his 'audience-determined' arguments). However, although flawed, Bluestone's arguments have had great influence over later adaptation theorists, even when they ostensibly reject medium specificity. Even the most recent summaries of the field are incomplete without him (Giddings *et al.*, 1990; McFarlane, 1996; Cartmell and Whelehan, 1999), and many theorists accept at least some of his central claims.

The comparative approach

> When we contemplate all the obstacles to adaptation, we may feel certain that it cannot be done; yet when we place less emphasis on some abstract sense of theoretical proprieties and consider the real world, we cannot avoid the recognition that important filmmakers have in fact adapted novels into films which are themselves valuable and distinguished, and occasionally masterpieces. (Beja, 1979: 79)

Subsequent writers recognised the truth of Beja's common-sense approach. They aimed to overcome this contradiction between theory and the actualities of filmmaking practice. They established what can be termed the 'comparative' approach to adaptation and, although in the 1990s the field of adaptation studies diversified into a plurality of approaches, the comparative approach has been historically predominant in the field from the 1970s onwards.

Lofty aims

The comparative approach had, at its incipience, two substantial problems to overcome within contemporary work on adaptation. On the one hand, the field was riddled with an overwhelming distaste for adaptations, and the prevailing assumption was that screen texts could never be as good as their source texts. Existing comparison of an adaptation with its source consisted mostly of a critical listing of failings of the latter, and rested upon an assumption that fidelity was a filmmaker's only reasonable intention and a film's only proper outcome. On the other hand, fierce defenders of films and cinema, like Bluestone, relied at that time upon notions of medium specificity, which had problematic consequences when applied to the study of adaptation.

By rejecting notions of medium specificity, the comparative approach solved, in one quick move, the central problem which concerned medium-specific theorists of adaptation. As Dudley Andrew pointed out, strict adherence to notions of medium specificity disallows even the possibility of 'adaptation' in any sense in which the term is commonly understood. Once the truism that 'adaptation can happen' was accepted, comparative theorists were free to concentrate on *how* adaptation happens, to explain equivalence in novel and film and to explain failures to attain equivalence; the particularities of this process then became adaptation theorists' central concern. The chosen methodology, which involved narrative and (later) semiotic analysis of both novel and film texts, offered a fairer and more realistic approach to adaptation than the derogatory comparison that was already in place. Narrative deconstruction offered an analysis of both film and book, not (as previously) an analysis of the book followed by references to the film, thus creating a more equal relationship between the two, instead of a hierarchical relationship between 'original' and 'version'; semiotic analysis offered an even more suitable method for studying filmic elements that are non-linguistic, such as lighting, mise-en-scène, etc. This approach can explain instances of apparent 'fidelity' but can also explain the rarity of such instances, for it makes manifest the sheer profusion of factors which make up a narrative text and which make one narrative text so different from another. Whilst acknowledging fundamental differences between the two media, this approach also allows for the possibility of 'faithful' adaptation.

As with the medium-specific approach, the comparative approach responded to early objections levelled at film, television and adaptation by pro-literature theorists. The key goals of the comparative tradition of adaptation study, and the sentiments that underlie it, are openly expressed by most of the writers working firmly within the comparative tradition. Brian McFarlane, in his exemplary book *Novel to Film*, argues that 'the study of adaptation has been inhibited and blurred by three chief approaches':

(a) the near-fixation with the issue of fidelity
(b) the reliance on an individual, impressionistic sense of what the two texts are like; and
(c) the implied sense of the novel's supremacy or, the other side of this particular coin, the sense that a film is a film and there is no point in considering it as an adaptation. (1996: 194)

Having staked out his ground in contrast to both early critics of adaptation and medium-specific theorists like Bluestone, McFarlane distances himself from previous critics of adaptation by stating that, 'The aim of this book is to offer and test a methodology for studying the process of transposition from novel to film, with a view not to evaluating one in relation to the other but to establishing the kind of relation a film might bear to the novel it is based on' (1996: vii).

This manifest rejection of an 'evaluative', value-based judgement of screen adaptations in comparison with their source texts clearly echoes the sentiments of preceding medium-specificity theorists, and is found widely throughout the corpus of texts advancing a comparative approach to adaptation. Gerald Peary and Roger Shatzkin, in 1977, were already identifying the work contained in their volume in relation to the background McFarlane refers to:

> Perhaps a tiny minority of the writers herein serve one medium to the detriment of the other: they are visual junkies ... or they are proudly out-of-fashion literati, who think almost any transformation from print to celluloid inherently sinister. Most contributors, however, are tempered in their judgments. ... Such catholicity and common sense, obvious as they might appear, are more rare than typical. (1977: 1)

Michael Klein and Gillian Parker, in 1981, expressed a similar argument:

> Too often discussions about adaptations from literature to film have for some reason been clouded by categorical claims for the superiority of one of the two art forms. ... Because of this general assumption ... some balancing of the scales seems called for here, in this brief survey of the issues surrounding the metamorphosis of literature into film. (1981: 2)

Wendell Aycock and Michael Schoenecke, in their book *Film and Literature: A Comparative Approach*, make manifest similar sentiments through the selection of work included: the variety of essays chosen, when read as a collection, offers a balanced range of criticisms of individual adaptations – criticisms that sometimes favour the film adaptation over the source text, and sometimes the source over its screen version, as evidenced by the examples given by Aycock and Schoenecke in the introduction to their volume:

> Robert Murray Davis, [in his discussion of the] novel and film of *All the King's Men*, points out not only the failures in the attempt to adapt this literary classic, but also some of the reasons for the failures. ... In '*One Flew Over the Cuckoo's Nest*: A Tale of Two Decades', Thomas J. Slater points out that 'Milos Forman remains true to the spirit of Kesey's novel by keeping his basic message but renovating the story to make it relevant to a mid-seventies audience'. (1988: 2)

Though taking the same open-minded stance on adaptation as previous medium-specificity theorists, comparative theorists start from a very different fundamental understanding of what adaptation actually *is*, and this understanding plays a determining role in the methodology proposed by such theorists for studying adaptation. As a result, comparative theory is more theoretically sound than earlier medium-specific theory, because there is a strong link between the theoretical conception of what adaptation is and the methodology proposed for studying it, whereas medium-specific theory, as we have seen, cannot adequately explain convergence between novel and film and would seem to negate even the very possibility of 'adaptation' in the sense in which it is pre-theoretically understood.

Film language, narrative and semiotics

A comparative approach is one that regards adaptation as an attempt to retell the same narrative in a medium (film or television) different from the one in which it was originally told (literature or, more specifically, the novel). Clarification is needed regarding the terms 'medium' and 'narrative' in this statement, as the comparative approach is centred on a particular understanding of these two concepts.

Let us begin with the term 'medium'. In contrast with the medium-specificity theorist, who proffers a causal link between the technical and ontological structures of film or literature and their possibilities for expression, comparative theorists regard the media of film and literature as two different 'languages' or, later, two distinct 'signifying systems' (drawing on semiotics), following Metz (1974, 1977).[8] The term 'film language' or 'language of film' is widely used: Klein and Parker describe most adaptations as being 'literal translations of the [written] text into the language of film' (1981: 9); Robert Richardson offers an extended comparison of the 'verbal and visual languages' of literature and film

(1971); and Monica Rector discusses 'television language' (1991). Some writers have attempted to draw very close parallels between verbal language and 'film language', so that 'just as the word is seen as the equivalent of the frame, the sentence is compared to the shot, the paragraph to the scene, and the chapter to the sequence' (Beja, 1979: 34), and 'grammar and syntax [is equated with] the editing' (Murray, 1972: 110) (see also Richardson, 1971; Mailer in Jinks, 1971). However, most theorists understand film as a language only in the loosest sense – that is, as a communicative or signifying medium.

Comparative theorists recognise that the notion of medium-as-language (and consequently adaptation-as-translation) needs careful elaboration, for all verbal languages share the same basic constituents and the same basic structures – letters, words, sentences – but verbal language differs in an elemental way from film, because film is also pictorial, and, furthermore, film's pictorial capabilities are a central component of its storytelling process. Thus, although the term 'language' is applied to an audio-visual medium, because a medium is seen as that through which meaning is expressed, it must also be noted that comparative theory generally takes into account the terminological inadequacies inherent in calling the film (or television) medium a language. For example, Geoffrey Wagner qualifies his use of the term 'the grammar of film' with the words 'insofar as [this] may obtain in this field' (1975: 19); Stuart McDougal (1985) and Brian McFarlane (1996) make similar qualifications. However, comparative theorists (like many film theorists) feel the correspondence between verbal language and film are sufficient that 'the methodology of literary analysis [is] equally applicable to the study of film' (Jinks, 1971: x).

The comparative approach recognises formal, textual differences that are most commonly found between different media, but does not insist on the technologically determinist, causal links made by proponents of medium specificity. This lack of direct causality between the technological or ontological aspects of a medium and the formal characteristics of its texts means that there is the possibility of convergence between two different media, no matter how infrequent or aesthetically unsuccessful this convergence may be. A comparative approach, that is to say, is less concerned with the technical, and thus formal, capabilities of each medium and more concerned with the specific conventions that constitute its system of signification. This is often overtly stated: Jordan, working broadly in the comparative tradition, distances herself from medium specificity, arguing that the majority of technical and ontological differences 'do not have either prescriptive or proscriptive force', and that formal differences between films and novels are 'largely differences dictated by convention rather than by technology' (1981: 26); P. C. Mayer argues more forcefully that an ontologically essentialist view is 'ultimately untenable' (1980: 208).

Within the traditions of the comparative approach there is an emphasis on looking for the ways in which the same narrative is told using different conventions. This means that there is a reliance on theories concerned not with technologies, but with storytelling and signification. This explains why comparative theorists seized upon semiotics, already fairly well-developed in film theory, to supplement structuralist narrative theory. Thus we come to their use of the second term to which attention is drawn above: narrative. Comparative theorists complicated the concept of 'narrative' (in the sense that they acknowledged the complexity of this concept) in order to provide a more reasonable, judicious framework for assessing specific adaptations. By using narrative theory to discover which elements of a written narrative could feasibly be transferred to screen, and conversely which elements could not, a fair assessment could be offered of what the screen adaptation of that narrative could reasonably be expected to achieve in terms of being a 'recreation' of the source text. In addition, to prevent this exercise turning into computation of all the things that film 'cannot do', semiotic theory is employed to assess how non-transferable aspects of a novel's narrative can be expressed through the use of different signs, within a different sign system.

The comparative approach has undergone considerable refinement since its inception, culminating in a theoretically grounded, clear methodology for studying adaptations. A discernible progression towards more rigorous theoretical analysis, and a more consistent application of this to specific adaptations, can be seen if we compare theorists of adaptation writing in the late 1970s and early 1980s with those writing later on, into the mid-1990s.

Early comparative theorists utilised a variety of fairly simple models drawn from narrative theory to theorise the process of adaptation; in particular, texts were understood in terms of narrative, story and plot. Beja delineated these thus: 'a narrative is any work which recounts a story'; 'a story: a sequence of events in time'; a 'plot' is the way in which the story is structured – for example, the order of events, the themes which guide their organisation, etc. (1979: 4). Wagner, in 1975, drew a further distinction between story, plot and discourse (the 'tone' in which the story is told).[9] And Klein and Parker, in 1981, were already employing a limited amount of film theory and narrative theory in order to analyse more productively the differences between the two media and the possibilities for convergence between them, respectively. Klein and Parker assumed the transferability of story (plot) and distinguished this from discourse. They discussed the medium-based (but not medium-specific) nature of discourse in film and novel:

> Both the formal and semiotic qualities of film are an inherent part of the background or secondary field of a cinematic image and thus of the discourse of the work. In a sense, we may regard the total visual and aural configuration of a film (camera position and movement, lighting, editing, and music, as well as cultural or semiological material) as background, analogous to the novelist's devices of description or metaphoric and tonal language in prose fiction. (Klein and Parker, 1981: 4)

This use of elemental narrative theory (with its structuralist leanings) could certainly help to explain how one film may be judged to have captured the 'spirit' of its source novel, whilst another that more faithfully reproduces the plot of its source text may be considered to have failed in this respect; the former can be said to have recreated the *discourse* of the original text through the specific 'formal and semiotic qualities of film', whilst the latter, it can be proposed, has managed to re-present the *story*, but has failed to use film's 'visual and aural configuration[s]' to recreate the book's discourse. This important development in adaptation theory offers an explanation for the interpretation Bluestone put forward regarding MGM's production of *Pride and Prejudice*: that it captured the spirit of Jane Austen's novel (1957: 115–46) – an interpretation inexplicable within the terms of Bluestone's own theoretical framework of medium specificity.

Klein and Parker's mention of semiotics is justified through their description of filmic representation:

> In addition to its distinct formal and expressive aspects, film also conveys a range of cultural signs – the facial expressions, gestures, dialects, dress, and style of its characters; the architecture, advertising, landscape, and common artifacts of its setting; the semiotic expression of a culture in a particular historical period. (1981: 3)

Their reference to semiotics signals the wider integration of semiotic theories into the broadly narrative-based approach of comparative theorists. Two years previously, Beja had suggested that an approach to adaptation that regarded film as a 'language' was flawed, and that 'a much more fruitful approach has been the newer one associated with semiotics, the study of systems of signs and meanings, which has sought to describe cinematic language' (1979: 54–5). Andrew, in 1984, utilises a similar (structuralist-influenced) approach to adaptation study to that of his peers, deconstructing novel and film and analysing them in terms of their constituent parts. Andrew relies more heavily upon semiotic theories and terminology, perhaps reflecting the fact that he is writing as a film theorist and not primarily as a literary or adaptation theorist.

As Beja recommended, Andrew's approach not only recognises that the notion of 'film language' is a problematic one but also tries to avoid the pitfalls arising from this notion by utilising semiotic concepts and terminology. Semiotics is perhaps a more straightforward and reasonable way to approach the signifying system of film as, unlike broader narrative theory with its roots in literary criticism, semiotics does not favour verbal signification over non-verbal/pictorial signification, yet still offers a valid theoretical vantage point for the study of literature. Early comparative theorists employed narrative theory (specifically, the distinction between story and discourse) to explain the ability of particular adaptations to recreate the 'spirit' of their source novels, but these theorists did not (or could not) explain how, *specifically*, this discourse could be recreated on screen, in a 'language' so fundamentally different from that of literature.

The semiotic conception of the two media that Andrew offers us not only appears better suited to the features of film but also seems to imply a greater possibility of intermedia convergence. Hence Andrew states that 'the analysis of adaptation then must point to the achievement of equivalent narrative units in the absolutely different semiotic systems of film and language' (1984: 103). He emphasises the transferability of plot and the possibility of the re-presentation of the source novel's discourse through the use of 'the same codes [that] may reappear in more than one system' (Andrew, 1984: 103). Andrew therefore employs semiotics to conceive the capabilities for representation in novel and in film as being the sum of the possible signs which each of these systems can utilise.

McFarlane's study, written in 1996, represents a peak in the progression of the comparative approach, incorporating laudable aims, coherent theoretical grounding (narrative and semiotic theories) and a transparent methodological structure for the study of adaptations. In order to make a clear distinction between the theoretically inadequate approaches that had previously characterised adaptation study and his own work, he takes great pains to elaborate the theoretical basis of his work and to comprehend his approach in a reflexive way and in the context of various theoretical traditions; for example, he terms his approach to adaptation a 'modified structuralist approach', thus acknowledging what he perceives to be the major theoretical influence apparent in his work (McFarlane, 1996: 201). As McFarlane states, 'It has been the modest aim of this study to see if any apparatus might be found to replace the reliance on one's subjective response to the two texts as a basis for establishing similarities and differences between them' (1996: 195).

In pursuit of this goal, McFarlane greatly extends the inclusion of narrative and semiotic theories, offering a detailed outline of both of these, upon which he bases his theory of adaptation and his analyses of case studies. Therefore McFarlane outlines his conception of the constituent parts of 'narrative', a conception arising primarily from Barthes's and Chatman's work on this subject, and shows how this structuralist-based understanding of narrative can be used to ascertain which elements of a novel can readily be transposed to film and which elements cannot.[10]

The crucial distinction between the comparative approach and earlier medium-specific ones is that discourse is no longer understood as being necessarily determined by, or inextricably tied to, the language/system through which it is expressed; rather, discourse is created through a huge variety of signifying conventions. These conventions may be predominant in one signifying system rather than another, and may indeed be better suited to one signifying system rather than another (i.e. may be more readily accepted by the reader/audience as successful in expressing meaning). However, such an understanding of the creation (and re-creation) of discourse does, significantly, offer a feasible explanation for the success of some 'faithful' adaptations, thus avoiding the absurd negation of the possibility of adaptation implied by some of the earliest theorists in the field.

Categorisation

> The assumed aim of the process of adaptation is ... to reproduce the contents of the novel on the screen. Hence the habitual reaction of conventional criticism to a literary adaptation: a judgement as to whether the adaptation has kept faith with the novel. (Ellis, 1982: 3)

In order to combat the tendency that Ellis notes, comparative theorists recommend that the fairest, most objective way to study adaptation is to implement a systematic categorisation of the kind of adaptation being studied, in order to ascertain each adaptation's intended relationship with its source text. This categorisation can be accomplished through determining which of the elements that *can* be transposed from novel to film *have* been so transposed and, equally importantly, how the adapter has chosen to 'properly adapt' the discourse that characterises the novel.[11] If the adapter has transposed as much as possible from the novel and has also attempted to find filmic equivalents for the untransferable elements then the adaptation in question can be fairly examined in terms of one whose primary aim is fidelity. If, on the other hand, the adaptation reveals considerable alterations to the transferable elements of the novel, and also appears to use the signifying system of film to create a discernibly different discourse (for example, if the film appears to offer a critical commentary on the story being re-presented), then the adaptation should be judged on its own terms and not in terms of fidelity to the source novel.

Many comparative theorists have divided adaptations into 'groups' according to the extent to which the screened text resembles the novel, proffering a 'classification of films adapted from novels from the point of view of their use of their source material' (McFarlane, 1996: 198). Klein and Parker divide adaptations into three main groups, according to how 'faithful' to the original novel the screen adaptation seems to be:

> most films of classic novels attempt to give the impression of being faithful, that is, literal, translations of the text into the language of film. ... A second and different approach to adaptation is one that retains the core of the structure of the narrative while significantly reinterpreting or, in some cases, deconstructing the source text. ... A third approach is one that regards the source merely as raw material, as simply the occasion for an original work. (1981: 10)

In corresponding order to the categories described by Klein and Parker, above, Wagner uses the following group headings: 'transposition, commentary and analogy' (1975: 222–31) and Andrew employs the corresponding category headings of 'borrowing, intersection and trans-formation' (1984: 98–104).[12] The retention (and fine-tuning) of this system of categorisation as a starting point for evaluating particular adaptations is vital to the comparative approach as one rooted in the motivation to be 'fair' in its expectation of what an adaptation 'should be'; this system of categorisation asserts the artistic validity of adaptations that deliberately deviate from the book, whether the result is to offer an 'in-built critique' of the source text or to create an original artwork that merely extracts the bare bones of the novel. For example, Wagner groups his case-study analyses and assesses each group in terms of the relationship the adaptations actually bear to their sources – he does not presuppose that each adaptation aims for fidelity to its source text.

Categorisation serves to propel adaptation studies forward, away from subjective value-judgements and age-old prejudices, and towards a more conceptually coherent, theoretically grounded and methodologically rigorous state. Giddings *et al.* ask, 'Why don't we enjoy and judge films of Dickens, Thackeray, Jane Austen and company *as films or television drama?*' (1990: xix) (italics in original). One might like to argue that we ought to – that adaptations should be judged according to their own virtues, and not in relation to their source novels. But particularly at the time that most comparative theorists were writing – from the 1970s to the mid-1990s – the reality of common discourse was that an adaptation could simply not be regarded in the same way as any other film or television programme. The cultural baggage that adaptations have traditionally shouldered has worked to negate the possibility of their being valued in terms of artistic qualities in the same way as other films or television programmes; this is particularly true of adaptations of classic novels. As Andrew so neatly puts it, 'Adaptation delimits representation by insisting on the cultural status of the model. ... In the case of those texts explicitly termed "adaptations", the cultural model which the cinema represents is already treasured as a representation in another sign system' (1984: 97).

As we have seen, the 'treasured' status of the source book has had a huge impact on the study of adaptation. Thus, a methodology which destabilises this preoccupation should be valued for its contribution to a more balanced and thoughtful view of adaptation. As McFarlane argues, 'these attempts at classification ... represent some heartening challenges to the primacy of fidelity as a critical criterion. Further, they imply that, unless the kind of adaptation is identified, critical evaluation may well be wide of the mark' (1996: 11). Unfortunately, the system of categorisation – that vital element which constitutes an attempt to evaluate adaptations on their own terms – is methodologically flawed by circularity and vagueness.

Problems with categorisation

In order to judge the extent to which a filmmaker intended to be 'faithful' to the source novel, we must first undertake narrative analysis to discover to what extent the adaptation offers narrative equivalencies to the novel's narrative.[13] This done, we can decide whether the adaptation is a faithful 'transposition', a 'commentary' or an 'analogy' (Wagner, 1975).[14] So far, so methodologically clear. But then what?

Let us take adaptation x. If, through the above procedure, it is decided that adaptation x is one that aims to be a faithful transposition, then our next task will be to discover the extent to which it is faithful – i.e. the extent to which the filmmaker has succeeded in finding filmic equivalencies for elements of the written narrative; we will then judge the filmmaker's success in these terms. But we have already undertaken such a procedure, in order to decide to which category the adaptation belongs. To repeat this process will offer few new insights into the adaptation and its merits as a film. If the adaptation was found to contain enough equivalencies to be considered a 'faithful' adaptation, then we already know that, to a certain extent, the filmmaker has succeeded in finding such equivalencies and thus in producing a relatively 'faithful' adaptation. All that can be done then is to pinpoint the failures of the filmmaker to find *other* equivalencies (though in a 'faithful' adaptation, by definition, these failures will not outnumber his or her successes). Here methodological circularity results in the production of the kind of critique to which the majority of comparative theorists claim they are opposed – a list of the ways in which the film fails to 'live up to' the book.

Let us suppose, instead, that we determine adaptation *y* to be of the type 'commentary' or 'analogy' – that the primary aim of the film or television programme is *not* fidelity to the source novel. What, then, does the comparative approach offer us in terms of a methodology for studying and evaluating adaptation *y*? In short, very little. If the basis of analysis is comparison between film and novel, then only those elements in the film that are also present in the book will be highlighted in the resulting analysis. As these elements have already been sought out and noted, we are left with a considerable proportion of filmic text that is not explicable in terms of the source book and is therefore (within the comparative mode of approach) left uninterpreted. Furthermore, the comparative theorist's use of semiotics within a 'modified structuralist' framework restricts the possibility of a full commentary on broader aesthetic aspects of the screen text. Even a detailed semiotic deconstruction of an adaptation runs the risk of being limited to a breakdown of components, thus losing sight of the text as a complete artwork.

Problems with the comparative approach

The comparative approach is not ideal: its central tenets, in which its strength lies, also contain weaknesses which give rise to the potential for misappropriation. The fundamental aims of this school of thought, as overtly stated by McFarlane and others, are not the only ones which the comparative methodology can be used to achieve. Comparative theorists' work exists on the continuum established by the earliest writers on adaptations, and it can be (mis)appropriated by writers unsympathetic to their ideals. For example, a declaration of belief in the possibility of convergence can easily be co-opted into *expectations* of convergence; that is, knowing that the story, plot and discourse of a source novel can potentially be 'recreated' on screen can lead theorists and critics to assume fidelity as a responsibility of adapters.

This tendency can be seen even in the best comparative work. Jordan, for example, at first offers a thoughtful, incisive and theoretically sound discussion of adaptation, but then goes on, in her 'case studies' of Henry James's novels on screen, to review the adaptations in terms of 'losses' from the original and, even more specifically, makes exactly the conflation of potential with expectation I describe above: 'there are moments [in the novel] perfectly easy of inclusion which the film seems *wantonly* to suppress' (my emphasis) (1981: 106). Beja, too, warns against 'wanton' disregard for the source novel, asking us to distinguish 'which changes are arbitrary, or in any case not necessary, and which ones seem inherent in the differences in the media' (1979: 84), the latter being acceptable, the former not. This attitude is apparent in Deborah Kaplan's essay on 'Mass Marketing Jane Austen', where she argues that she is not critical 'of film alterations per se – but of alterations made in the service, I presume, of broad commercial appeal' (1998: 179). Clearly there are acceptable (medium-determined) reasons for alterations, and unacceptable reasons, which include the artistic whims of the individual adapter, and the compulsions of the marketplace.

Further, recognition of the existence of different types of adaptation (transposition, commentary and analogy, to use Wagner's terms) can in turn induce a proclivity towards favouring one type of adaptation over another. Much praise, for example, is reserved for the last category of adaptation – analogy – a 'mode [that] refutes the commonplace that adaptations support only a conservative film aesthetics' (Andrews, 1984: 100). This could be because this type of adaptation best reinforces film as an autonomous art form, for the adaptation is regarded as an independent, 'original' art work: 'an original is allowed its life, its own life, in the cinema' (Andrew, 1984: 100).

It is interesting though, that stalwart defenders of literature state a similar preference. Wagner argues that of his three categories, 'transposition' (a faithful adaptation) is 'typically puerile' (1975: 223), and 'commentary' is 'an infringement on the work of another' (223), but analogy produces 'another work of art [that] cannot be indicated as a violation of a literary original since it has not attempted (or has only minimally attempted) to reproduce the original' (227). I would submit that such theorists' motivations are dubious; these writers feel that the best adaptations are the ones that leave the sacred book well alone. Recall, for example, Miller's insistence at the beginning of Chapter 2 that adaptations were only acceptable if based on 'trivial and second-rate' novels. Thus categorisation, designed to bring greater objectivity and fairness to the study of adaptations and to reduce the influence of 'the near fixation with the issue of fidelity' (McFarlane, 1996: 194), can be used not to further understanding of filmmakers' choices, styles and creativity but to make the case for adaptations that are 'culturally correct' in terms of their respect for the source novel (where 'respect' is understood as 'leaving the novel alone' and not encroaching on it). Once again the same subjective responses to adaptation texts bubble to the surface.

Comparative analysis can also unintentionally perpetuate the valorisation of traditional literary approaches over innovative film and television theory, and thus literature over film and television. The use of concepts extracted from narrative theory, and the focus on the process of novel-to-screen adaptation, mean that writers within the comparative tradition sometimes end up proposing a list of television's or film's potential forms of representation in terms of the forms of representation possible in the novel, and thus implicitly postulating the written, novelistic form as the 'original', established form, superior to that of the visual text. This tendency to regard film in literary terms is summarised neatly by Karen Kline, who says that such critics 'privilege traditionally literary elements while minimizing specifically cinematic elements, and they value similarities rather than differences between the written and cinematic texts' (1996: 71). Echoes of the incorporation of film within literary structures are present in Ghislaine Gelion's comment that 'It is as if the cinema had to discover its own language in someone else's language, that of the novel. It is in this constant imitation – and confrontation – with literary forms and structures that film has gradually evolved from a dramatic art and slowly matured as narrative art' (1988: 143).

Again, as in the critical writing explored in Chapter 2, film is damned through the faint praise of metaphor. Film is said to have 'evolved' and 'matured' from a dramatic art to a narrative art through adaptation. Film's maturation, its coming-of-age, is due to the beneficial influence of its predecessor and mentor – literature; film has finally 'grown up', and is nearing equality with its worthy forebear as it moves from dramatic representation towards a more literary form. (See also Richardson, 1969, for an argument couched in similar terms.) Screen adaptations remain imprisoned within a literary framework.

Contextuality and intertextuality

McFarlane himself has expressed doubts concerning the flexibility and scope of the approach he propounds, suggesting that there are aspects of adaptations themselves that remain unaccounted for and undiscussed if film theorists adhere strictly to a comparative approach (1996: 200–2). McFarlane's misgivings are justified.

Theorists from the mid-1990s onwards, drawing upon an increased diversity of approaches to film and television, have attempted to release adaptation from its enclosure within literary discourse. These theorists noted that an emphasis on comparison means that the comparative theorists' analyses of adaptations did not fully consider very influential contextual factors that leave traces within the television or film text (see

Andrew, 1984; Giddings *et al.*, 1990). These factors include socio-historical, institutional and intertextual contexts. Comparative theorists were aware of this 'hole' in their approach, and tried to fill it by including a discussion of the context of adaptations in their exposition and analyses. However, this aspect of their writing has historically been somewhat half-hearted.

Comparative theorists tended to focus on the socio-historical and institutional contexts of adaptations. Thomas J. Slater, in his analysis of *One Flew Over the Cuckoo's Nest*, insists that the film reflects the time of its production (the 1970s) – its social mores, conventions and beliefs – as much as it reflects the period in which the source book was written (1988: 45–58). This is a move away from a simple comparative approach and towards a recognition that the medium is constituted as much by its context, uses and social status as by its technical attributes. Slater's essay is in a small minority in Aycock and Schoenecke's volume – most of the analyses employ a simple (though not necessarily simplistic) 'compare and contrast' methodology.

Similar accounts that attempt to incorporate an understanding of adaptations' social contexts tend to state their case in terms of ideological analysis, arguing that the novels' narratives are re-presented in order to serve ideological purposes. For example Elizabeth Atkins, in '*Jane Eyre* Transformed', claims that 20th Century Fox's adaptation of 1943 destroyed the feminist aspects of the source novel by changing the narrative so that Jane became less independent and more reliant upon Rochester (1993: 54–60), whilst Arthur Lindley, in 'Raj as Romance, Raj as Parody', argues that Lean's film *Passage to India* (1984) subverts Forster's political message by turning the story into a romance (1992: 61–7).[15] The tradition of ideological criticism has gathered momentum. The pluralist collection *Pulping Fictions*, edited by Deborah Cartmell *et al.* (1996), offers a range of essays written in a similar vein: essays which propose that adaptations subvert the original meanings of the novels in order to perpetuate particular, contemporary ideologies through the films.

Writers in the comparative tradition who have considered the institutional contexts of adaptations have done so with altogether less success than those dealing with social contexts. Despite emphasising the importance of institutional factors, these writers seem to encounter difficulties in the application of their understanding of such factors to actual adaptations. Wagner spends some time outlining and comparing the institutional characters of both film and literature (1975: 40–6), but fails to incorporate this comparison successfully into his analyses of film texts, instead concentrating on narrative elements. The same problem arises in Giddings *et al.*: we are presented with a summary of the conditions of television production, but these conditions are again passed over in favour of narrative analysis in the ensuing case studies; this is not really surprising since, despite the discussion of the very different institutional contexts of film and television, Giddings *et al.* state that 'the majority of the issues discussed refer equally to film and television, since the concern is generally with the "visualization" of the prose text' (1990: 1). In another instance, Julian Moynahan says of *Great Expectations*, 'By hitching the cinema wagon to all this Dickensian visual richness, subtlety, and amplitude should it be easy, *crass commercial pressures apart*, to make a classic film out of a classic novel?' (1981: 144) (my emphasis).

One might infer that Moynahan intends to show how 'crass commercial pressures' have affected the adaptation and to take this into account in his analysis of David Lean's film of 1946. However, he does no such thing, instead criticising Lean's adaptation because too much of the narrative was 'cut' or altered. Bundey (1986) devotes an inordinate amount of space to a discussion of the historical development and current cultural contexts of both novel and film, none of which is actually utilised in his discussion of specific adaptations. Generally, the reliance on studying narrative transferral seems to prevent a satisfactory consideration of the institutional contexts of adaptations. Although the presentation of (social and institutional) contextual factors encourages comparative study towards a broader appreciation of adaptations in general, the failure to successfully mobilise this contextual knowledge within case-study analyses is disappointing.

Within the comparative tradition, few writers have grappled with the complexities of the *intertextual* nature of television and film and the place of adaptations within this context. Notably, however, two writers suggest that this is a crucial area for development in the field. Andrew calls for adaptation studies to take us

> into the complex interchange among eras, styles, nations and subjects. This is as it should be, for adaptation, while a tantalising keyhole for theorists, nevertheless partakes of the universal situation of film practice, dependent as it is on the aesthetic system of cinema in a particular era and on that era's cultural needs and pressures. (1984: 16)

McFarlane is even more progressive in his recognition of the importance of adaptations' intertextual contextuality. He writes, in his conclusion, of 'extra-novelistic influences', under two sub-headings: 'Prevailing cinematic practices' and 'Other elements of intertextuality' (1996: 200–1). McFarlane stresses the importance of recognising that 'any narrative film – adaptation or not – will be made within the prevailing parameters of the cinema, within certain cinematic traditions', and that

'The critic who fails adequately to address the [adaptation's intertextuality] is guilty of undervaluing the film's cultural autonomy as well as failing to understand the processes by which the novel has been transposed to film' (McFarlane, 1996: 200).

Importantly, McFarlane also recognises that the 'modified structuralist', comparative approach he proffers is not the best way to achieve a satisfactory analysis of the above factors: these factors are 'not readily susceptible to the quantifying possibilities referred to above' (1996: 210). Thus McFarlane, who proffers one of the most advanced and coherent examples of comparative theory, lends support to the assertion that this highly influential and dominant mode of adaptation study is not the best choice for studying adaptations as film or television texts in themselves.

The importance of intertextuality

Adaptations are also films or television programmes. Through their manipulation of content, style and mood, they refer not just to the novel as a source text, but also to other texts, other films and programmes made using similar conventions. Classic-novel adaptations, for example, draw upon a whole range of generic features in order to establish their identity: features of content (lavish costumes and sets, long shots of country houses and landscapes, restrained action, large amounts of dialogue), and features of style and mood (slow-paced filming and editing, a 'nostalgic' mood).[16] These intertextual references, constituting defining character-istics of a genre as they do, may prove to be even more relevant to a film's or programme's meanings and effects than its novelistic source text. A careful and responsive analysis needs to recognise such intertextual nuances in order to comprehend fully the film or programme and all its shades of meaning.

Even excluding intertextual references that exist as indicators of a generic identity, there are additional overt and specific intertextual references present in classic-novel adaptations, which are so often interpreted in comparative terms due to the texts' presumed concern with fidelity to the respective source novels. There is an archery scene involving Emma and Mr Knightley in the 1996 film *Emma* that a comparative approach would dismiss as pure invention: it does not appear in the source book. Yet the scene is not without textual historical resonance – a very similar scene was included in MGM's *Pride and Prejudice* in 1940. The repeated scene is evidence of historical intertextual reference across different classic-novel adaptations, the reference drawing entirely upon broad generic development rather than either of the two different source novels. Similar examples of intertextuality exist across genres: in *The Tenant of Wildfell Hall* (1996, BBC), there are shot sequences which overtly call to mind alike sequences from *The Piano* (1993). *Wildfell Hall* utilises the intertextual reference as a filmic 'short-cut', relying on the viewer's awareness of *The Piano* for additional meaning. Though a comparative approach might note the thoughtful, understated 'feminist' tone of *Wildfell Hall*, by relating it only to the source book it would fail to appreciate the subtleties of the screen text, which draws upon a broader frame of reference to establish its mood. The ways in which the film utilises imagery from sources other than the source book in order to convey specific meanings frequently pass unremarked.[17]

In summary, there are aspects of filmic and televisual adaptations which do not have equivalents in a literary source. Therefore, if we study adaptations by looking for equivalencies we will overlook elements of the film or programme that are vital to its own, particular aesthetic appeal, and its meaning as an artwork. This is particularly important as contemporary texts are so often the 'tissue of quotations' to which Barthes (1968) referred – quotations abstracted from other adaptations, films or television programmes. It makes sense to reject a centre-based, comparative understanding and accept a more flexible conceptualisation. Evidence of generic development and nuanced intertextual references in contemporary adaptations also validates an approach that regards adaptations in terms of an ever-developing meta-text.[18]

Losing – and finding – adaptations

The most unsatisfactory and disappointing aspect of the dominant comparative tradition is that, somewhere along the line, adaptation theorists seem to have lost sight of the adaptations themselves. The comparative approach proffers a 'theory of (the process of) adaptation', yet fails to provide a full framework for the analysis of adaptations – the film or television texts. In the comparative tradition of adaptation studies, adaptations are simply 'case studies', textual resources for the comparative study of literature and film and the study of narrative.[19] In short, the main body of work in the field of adaptation studies has in fact been within the sub-field of 'process-of-adaptation' studies. Key questions have included: Can we adapt? How can we adapt? How should we adapt? What happens, during this process, to the book's narrative?

This is clearly a valid area of study in its own right. But the fact that this area of study constitutes the greater proportion of writing on adaptations is worrying; it can only impoverish our understanding of adaptations as films and television programmes. Comparative theorists have used adaptation(s) to facilitate discussions of other theoretical issues in which they are interested. Perhaps it is time to ask what the study of adaptation is for: to illuminate theories of narrative or medium specificity; to engage in a debate about the cultural values and statuses of literature, film and television; or to investigate continuities and change in cultural production? Adaptations are rarely studied for themselves – rarely is interpretation valued as much as theorising; broader theoretical issues take precedence over local aesthetic concerns.[20]

Other genres have fared better in comparison. Consider the academic study of Westerns and documentaries. In the study of Westerns, theoreticians have carefully examined generic traits, looking at a wide range of films in order to form a broad conceptualisation of the Western genre, not just in terms of narrative structure but also in terms of shot types, lighting, key motifs, etc. – this despite the (pulp) literary basis of many Westerns. In the study of documentary there is theorising on the use of source material: how faithful to its sources the documentary is; how well these sources are structured; how the intentions of the maker have been realised through his or her manipulation of the material, and so on. However, equal weight, especially in more recent work, is given to a discussion of aesthetics – lighting, sound, visual organisation, style, etc. In each of these examples, the film or television text is the basis for conceptualisation – it is the reason for the study and is therefore foregrounded in any subsequent theorisation. The central concerns of theoreticians arise from the key characteristics of the genre itself – not just its source material but also distinctive aspects of its style, form and content.

The study of adaptations, then, requires a core of different questions. These might include: Can we conceptualise a 'genre' called 'classic-novel adaptations'? If so, what are the key generic traits of this genre, and how have these altered over time? What other filmic/televisual[21] conventions and generic traits do adaptations employ, and to what effect? Which innovative or underused paradigms in television or film theory might adaptation theorists usefully employ (e.g. cognitive film theory or medium specificity)?

The pluralist approach

How else might we regard an adaptation, apart from as a text that draws upon a source novel? This is a question that film and television theorists have begun to tackle. In the 1990s, some theorists realised that the traditional comparative methodology fell short in some way. They began to distinguish the process of adaptation from the end-product adaptation.

They analysed particular adaptations, bringing to their interpretations a more explicit awareness of film and television conventions, and cultural and historical contexts. This recent work reveals a broader engagement with a wide range of actual adaptations and an interesting collection of resultant interpretations, and frequently offers a radical departure from the methodology that relies on sustained comparison between novel and screen text. The theoretical framework adopted draws upon concepts developed in film, television and cultural studies, and utilises traditions of ideological criticism and theories about identity, culture and history.

Three edited collections epitomise the pluralist approach although, appropriately, they differ from each other in various ways: *Pulping Fictions: Consuming Culture Across the Literature/Media Divide* (Cartmell, Hunter, Kaye and Whelehan (eds) 1996); *Adaptations: From Text to Screen, Screen to Text* (Cartmell and Whelehan (eds), 1999); and *The Classic Novel: From Page to Screen* (Giddings and Sheen (eds), 2000). As the title of the first volume implies, the influence of cultural studies and media studies is apparent in the essays included therein. The study of adaptation has been taken up with interest by theorists in these fields, with both positive and negative consequences, as the two most recent collections reveal.

Cartmell and Whelehan's edited collection *Adaptations* displays continuities with the earlier *Pulping Fictions*. Again, a wide range of adaptations is covered, from *Sense and Sensibility* and *Little Women* to *Trainspotting, Batman* and *101 Dalmations*. The writers' commitment to considering the role of adaptations within cultural terms is revealed in references to work like Henry Jenkins's on fandom and Pierre Bourdieu's on cultural capital. The editors explicitly locate the collection within the tradition of cultural studies, and offer the following justification: 'A cultural studies approach foregrounds the activities of reception and consumption, and shelves – forever perhaps – considerations of the aesthetic or cultural worthiness of the object of study' (Whelehan, 1999: 18). Instead of engaging with issues of 'aesthetic or cultural worthiness', the writers aim to judge 'the " success" or "failure" of the film or TV version' (Whelehan, 1999: 17).

One might wonder on what criteria adaptations are to be judged, as it appears that the writers wish to exclude questions of aesthetic or cultural value. However, across all contributors, there is a high level of consistency in this regard: adaptations are to be judged in ideological terms (one might uncharitably characterise this as a judgement about a work's 'political correctness').[22] So the analysis of individual adaptations is framed within an evaluation of the ideological implications of the text as a whole: *Sense and Sensibility* is found lacking in its representations of gender – it 'dulls the radical edges of Austen's novel' and 'smoothes [*sic*] over ideological conflicts in the novel' (North, 1999: 46, 48); and *Clueless*, despite its popular culture credentials, is assessed by Esther Sonnet as 'a symptom of a popular cultural anti-feminist desire for an unchallenged patriarchal order' (Cartmell, 1999: 25). Continuing the theme, and displaying the importance of cultural theory and continental philosophy to this volume, Roger Bromley writes of the film *The Scarlet Letter*:

> My problem with this adaptation is not that it desecrates a canonical text, or even is 'unfaithful' to it, but that it produces meanings which give credence to the ideology of the 'imperial self' and ignores the fact that, in a political culture, the self that narrates speaks from a position of *having been narrated and edited by others* – by political institutions, by concepts of historical causality and by 'allegorical master narratives'. (Bromley, 1999: 79) (italics in original)

In recent work, adaptation is again politicised. Writers within the pluralist approach reject sustained comparative criticism and the elevation of the source novel and its author over the adaptation, as I have proposed we should do. However, whilst I wish to move away from the traditional comparative approach because of its conceptual and methodological flaws, and the limitations it places upon interpretation and evaluation, these writers reject it for ideological reasons. They wish to challenge and overthrow 'reverence for the text and the author' (Cartmell, 1999: 37) because such reverence is regarded as ideologically – rather than conceptually or methodologically – dubious, and dependent upon the maintenance of an outdated and elitist hierarchy. Laudable though these motives are, the result is to negate the range of possibilities opened up by a non-comparative approach. Questions of aesthetics and generic development are subordinated to questions of ideology; the close analysis of style, tone, narrative structure, performance and so on is employed only in the service of making a wider political point. The impact of a plethora of theories from cultural studies, continental philosophy, traditional film theory[23] and English literature is that sometimes the analysis of the films and programmes themselves loses its proper place at the centre of discussion.

Perhaps another reason for the marginalisation of the aesthetic particularities of adaptations is the persistence of a long-lived trend in adaptation studies. Despite Whelehan's criticism that 'the field of adaptations has in the past been dominated by scholars working primarily from an "English lit." perspective' (Whelehan, 1999: 17), the majority of contributors to *Adaptations* are academics working in English departments.[24] The same is true of the edited collection *The Classic Novel: From*

Page to Screen. Though the editors of the latter book bravely state that 'all the essays in this volume take the question of fidelity as their primary critical point of reference' (Sheen, 2000: 2), the essays are by no means an exercise in old-fashioned fidelity criticism. Consciously eclectic in the range of adaptations considered, this book exhibits a considerable variety in the approaches taken to the films and programmes discussed. There are examples of fidelity criticism (MacKillop and Platt, Sinyard), but there is also evidence of feminist criticism (Dennett), close analysis (Lee), psycho-analytic criticism (Sheen, Bignell) and historicist criticism (Giddings, Selby, Bignell). The volume is true to the pluralist project, offering a plethora of very different analyses. Unfortunately, though, familiar problems recur. The emphasis on 'fidelity' is not conceptually justified or theorised, as with the rejection of fidelity criticism in *Adaptations* – in each case the approaches chosen are simply asserted. This is particularly disappointing in the light of McFarlane's meticulous justification of his comparative approach; conceptually and methodologically, the pluralist approach is a poor response to the challenges raised by McFarlane. In addition, *The Classic Novel* promises an emphasis on close analysis (Sheen, 2000: 11), and some contributors consider the use of editing and framing, but there is very little work included that refers to details of music, sound, pace and timing, gesture and performance.

It is a welcome development that the study of adaptations is beginning to be undertaken by theorists from disciplines other than traditional literary studies. This reduces the risk of losing the adaptations themselves within a mire of discussion about other tangential issues. The input of cultural studies and continental philosophy has been valuable in drawing attention away from the comparative approach. The pluralist approach recognises that an adaptation's relationship to, and equivalence with, its source novel is not necessarily more salient than its relation to other 'resources' such as other adaptations, and film and television conventions; its institutional context as a marketed, audience-targeted, contemporary media text; and its particular historical, social and cultural context. However, it still does not offer us a focus on the adaptations themselves as independent artworks.

New directions

Throughout its history, adaptation studies has taken up a series of new directions, influenced from the start by fundamental attitudes to, prejudices and assumptions about, and conceptualisations of, literature, film, television and adaptation(s). The study of adaptation arose in an environment that valued literature over the newer arts of film and television, and that steered its investigations in directions that would validate and valorise literary art over audio-visual arts. The growth of medium-specific theories (such as those extolled by Bluestone) worked to counter-balance the field, promoting film as a unique and valued artform in its own right; however, medium-specific beliefs proved extremely problematic for theorists eager to explore the possibilities for 'equivalence' in adaptation.

Responding to both the flaws of essentialist medium-specific approaches and lingering prejudices regarding the superiority of the literary medium over film and television, the comparative approach drew upon established theories of narrative and semiotics to offer a coherent understanding of the process of adaptation and the relation of an adaptation to its source. Developed from the 1970s onwards, the comparative approach was refined and polished, until McFarlane's work (in the 1990s) offered a more rational, theoretically sound and methodologically consistent model for comprehending adaptation than had ever been proposed before. Yet, as McFarlane himself admitted, the comparative approach is limited, especially in terms of considering the influence of factors other than the source novel upon adaptations. Notably, the comparative approach, because of its preoccupation with the source novel/adaptation relationship, neglects issues of social and institutional contexts, intertextuality and genre.

In order to address these issues, another new direction was sought and taken: the pluralist approach. But as I suggest above, this approach is still unsatisfactory, both conceptually and methodologically. Each of these approaches to adaptation brought something of value to the field, but each was in some way lacking. Part II develops from extant concerns and questions raised by medium-specific, comparative and pluralist theorists of adaptation. A novel, alternative approach is needed, yet inspiration can be found in some of the oldest ideas. Medium specificity has been too readily dismissed as it fell out of fashion. Appropriately modified, and combined with other paradigms, a medium-specific understanding of television can in fact provide us with a valuable framework for considering television programmes including classic-novel adaptations. Equally, attention to aesthetic questions is overdue in the field, and the recent renewed interest in close textual analysis suggests a potentially rewarding methodology.[25] Most importantly, the approach taken to each adaptation ought to be suggested by the adaptation itself; similarly, any account of the 'genre' of classic-novel adaptations ought to foreground the defining traits of that genre. Finally, television adaptations must be distinguished from film adaptations – an understanding of the specificity of this televisual form is long overdue.

Notes

1 Like 'adaptation studies', 'adaptation theory' is in a sense my own retrospective construction. By 'adaptation theory' I mean writing about adaptation – the process and the end-product – that attempts to apply theoretical tools in order to illuminate adaptation(s), conceptualise adaptation(s) and/or proffer a methodology for the analysis of adaptations.

2 Although critics have always reviewed both film and television adaptations, most theoretical and conceptual writing about adaptations has focused on film adaptations. For the purposes of this chapter, I shall not distinguish unless necessary between theories concerning adaptations on film and those concerning television.

3 It is worth noting that Beja, unlike Bluestone, warns that a conceptualisation of film cannot be based only upon an awareness of its technical and ontological features – that to reduce film to celluloid is like saying a novel is just a book (1979: 22).

4 The correlations noted between film and literature can, of course, be incorporated into a discourse that subjugates film to literature, as theorists can insist on claiming that 'literature did everything first'. Beja offers a more balanced response: 'in such realms literature and film meet so intimately that it is difficult or impossible – and perhaps ultimately unimportant – to discern which art "originates" an idea or a technique and which one immediately takes it up for its own ends' (1979: 76).

5 Eisenstein outlines the unique processes of filming and editing, and emphasises the considerable differences between the production of film and literature, but he does not suggest a causal link between the inherent features of a medium and its predominant forms of representation. Rather, his examples of similarities between the conventions of representation in literature and film seem to contradict such a notion.

6 It is clear that Bluestone's views on audience and context cannot be properly assimilated into his medium-specific argument. However, he regards these views as crucial to his theorising, so it is important to consider them.

7 The value of a diluted medium-specific model will be illustrated in Chapter 4, where adaptations are examined in relation to the 'televisual'.

8 Most comparative theory is concerned with film, not television, adaptations. However, the narrative/semiotic approach depends primarily upon an understanding of film as an audio-visual medium, so to this extent television and film can be considered together.

9 Wagner makes these distinctions implicitly, through his system of categorisation. Although his third category of adaptations – 'analogy' – is composed of films which radically alter the *story* of the source text, the second category – 'commentary' – is constituted by films which, whilst retaining the basic story, alter the way in which this story is expressed, thus changing the 'tone' or 'spirit' of the narrative. His method of analysing adaptations relies on a distinction, then, between story and discourse – the latter being understood as the way in which the story is expressed and as separate from the story itself. Klein and Parker, and Andrew, used a similar system to Wagner's.

10 Utilising established concepts, McFarlane begins by differentiating story, plot and discourse as previous scholars have done. He defines 'story' as the list of key events that take place and 'plot' as the way in which these events are ordered or, in the case of adaptation, re-ordered; he groups story and plot together under 'narrative'. He calls that which we have previously designated discourse 'enunciation'. Whilst story is, according to McFarlane, potentially transferable from novel to film, plot is not, for films lay emphases upon different aspects of a story from those which novels highlight, due to film and novel being 'two separate systems of signification' (1996: 23).

　　McFarlane's summary of transferable elements correlates to the categorisation of narrative elements proposed by Barthes. He argues that the constituents of narrative that Barthes terms *functions proper* can feasibly be subjected to direct (straightforward) transposition to screen; these 'functions' are further subdivided into *cardinal functions* and *catalysers*, both of which are events included in the narrative (the former being events central to the story ('hinge-points of narrative') and the latter being smaller events which are simply 'details' within the narrative – moments which add to the clarity of the story and aid its telling but which are not pertinent, in themselves, to the development of the story) (McFarlane, 1996: 13–14). In comparison, those elements of the novel which Barthes terms *indices* are more closely linked to *language* (their original mode of expression, in the case of adaptation) than functions proper and thus complicate the process of adaptation to a non-verbal medium. Indices can be sub-divided into *informants* and *indices proper*, the former consisting of pieces of information such as names, dates, and so forth and the latter being composed of more abstract elements such as mood, tone and character (those elements we customarily include within our conception of 'discourse').

Whilst informants are readily available for transfer, indices proper require what McFarlane terms 'adaptation proper', for these elements are heavily dependent upon language and cannot be reproduced on film in a directly comparable way. McFarlane offers an example: our conception of the meaning or 'spirit' of a novel is dependent upon the style in which the novel is written but this, in turn, is also dependent upon the 'linearity' of the novelistic form, whereas our conception of these things whilst watching a film is dependent upon the 'spatiality' of the filmic form. That is, we take in 'information' or 'meaning' from a novel by reading sequentially, comprehending the meaning of the text bit by bit as we read, whereas many different pieces of information in a film can be presented on the screen at the same time, thus requiring us to understand the text in a different way and at a pace more greatly determined by the text itself.

11 The phrase 'to properly adapt' used here is drawn from McFarlane, who delineates 'transfer' from 'adaptation proper'.

12 McFarlane avoids employing a category system. Instead, he argues that one can designate different processes occurring within any given adaptation. These processes include 'transferral' from the novel and 'adaptation proper' (complete adaptation to a new medium) (see McFarlane, 1996, 22–30).

13 Here, following McFarlane, the term 'narrative' refers to the novel's story and discourse – its 'letter and spirit', if you like.

14 I am leaving aside the problems involved in ascertaining the intentions of the filmmaker, which must, in the main, be garnered through viewing the text itself. If, for example, a screen adaptation is closely comparable with its source text in plot, but not in spirit (discourse), should we deduce that the filmmaker was trying unsuccessfully to be 'faithful' to the book (one category) or successfully to alter the spirit and substitute a discourse that offers a commentary on the book (a different category)? If we are to judge a work's success or failure in terms of these intentions, our uncertainty regarding them is surely a considerable obstacle to fair judgement. However, for the sake of argument, I shall allow that we can, utilising additional sources such as interviews with the filmmaker, ascertain his/her intentions in terms of fidelity.

15 *Jane Eyre* (1943) was written by John Houseman and Aldous Huxley, and directed by Robert Stevenson; *A Passage to India* (1984) was written and directed by David Lean.

16 These matters are explored fully in Part II.

17 The intertexuality of *Wildfell Hall* is discussed in Part II.

18 The idea of the meta-text is raised in Chapter 1.

19 In McFarlane's book, and in his PhD thesis upon which it was based, the analyses of films are actually separated from the 'theory' and entitled 'The Case Studies' (McFarlane, 1996; 1987).

20 One of the key reasons for this tendency towards wider theorising, rather than very specific, close analyses of a particular genre, might be the preference that publishers and journals have for broader work that will appeal to a wider audience. Another, more fundamental, reason is that theoretical debates are a continuing source of fascination for

the theorist. Neither of these reasons seems to constitute adequate justification for allowing 'theory' to drown the text under discussion.

21 Here, 'televisual' should be understood merely as an adjective of the root word 'television'. However, it is possible to elucidate a wider conceptualisation of 'the televisual' which attempts to isolate medium-specific features (see Part II).

22 The phrase 'political correctness' here is not meant to imply that the writers seek some kind of simplistic, fashionable 'correctness' in an adaptation's representations of gender, race, sexuality, and so on. Instead I mean that the writers are keen to ascertain how politically aware and developed the adaptations appear to be.

23 The term 'traditional film theory' here denotes the paradigm of film theory dominant from the 1970s to the mid-1990s – a paradigm based in semiotics, psychoanalysis, continental philosophy and ideological criticism. This is opposed to more recent film theory based in analytical philosophy, cognitive psychology and close textual analysis, the turning point probably being marked by the publication of *Post Theory: Reconstructing Film Studies* (Bordwell and Carroll, 1996).

24 The location of a writer within an English department does not, of course, necessarily determine the kind of criticism he or she will produce. However, it does suggest a familiarity with certain theoretical paradigms, and perhaps slower responses to new developments in film and television studies. These edited collections substantiate such assumptions.

25 The increased interest in close textual analysis was evident in the call for papers for the conference 'Style and Meaning', held at Reading University in March 2000. Contributors were asked to explicitly employ close analysis, or to reflect upon its usefulness in interpretation and theorising.

Television adaptations in the televisual context

4

It is crucial that we begin to develop an understanding of the television classic-novel adaptation that recognises the importance of its televisual context; to this end this chapter considers the genre in question, its locus and the interplay between them.

Genre

In order to pursue a non-comparative, 'generic' approach, it is necessary to delimit the scope of study. This book offers a particularised study of a television genre: British classic-novel adaptations (as broadly defined in the Introduction). As Altman's recent, careful interrogation has shown, the notion of genre is extremely complex. It is perhaps somewhat of a simplification to propose that classic-novel adaptations constitute a genre in a strict sense of the term, particularly as Part II reveals dramatic generic development within this set of programmes, leading to an eclectic range of very different texts.[1] Altman observes that 'in current practice, the very act of identifying a genre requires that generic texts be lifted out of time and placed in a timeless holding area as if they were all contemporaries' (1999: 19). I hope to avoid such a simplification. The model of adaptation proffered in Chapter 1 aims to rescue adaptations from their direct, ahistorical relationship with the source novel, recognising the specificities of their historical contexts and their place in a trajectory of generic development; it would be self-defeating to re-imprison them within a rigid generic framework that did not recognise each one as an individual artwork.

While remaining aware of these problems, however, for the sake of verbal conciseness I shall use the terms 'genre' and 'generic traits', the latter being a useful shorthand referring to expected conventions.[2] After all, as Higson argues, these texts 'share a particularly strong group style'

(1993: 114); classic-novel adaptations 'look and feel like chapters of a single interminable Classic Serial' (Brownstein, 1998: 16). Indeed, the words 'look and feel' are most apt, for it is a particular combination of conventional *content*, *style* and *mood* which maintains classic-novel adaptations' generic identity; each of these facets will be explored in Part II.

Definitions and descriptions

Paul Kerr was one of the first writers to treat television adaptations of classic novels primarily as television programmes, and to analyse them accordingly. He set out his objectives thus:

> Articles about specific film and television genres generally start out with some sort of definition, but neither Raymond Williams' 'dramatisation of well-known works', nor the more tortuously tautological 'classic serials are serialised classics' seems to get us very far. Indeed, after more than 30 years of classic serials on British television such definitions seem all but superfluous. Both the term 'the classic serial' and the television form it describes are so familiar to programme makers, critics and viewers alike that it is perhaps less urgent to ask *what* classic serials are than to ask *why*. (Kerr, 1982: 7) (italics in original)

Kerr's analysis is essentially an ideological critique of the genre: he argues that classic-novel adaptations operate as part of an ideological project to elevate and perpetuate an elite literary culture, to maintain the distinctions between 'good' (BBC) television and 'trash' popular culture, and to build reactionary nostalgia for a mythologised 'ideal' era in Britain's colonial past.

Kerr's attitude and approach are indicative of many television and film theorists' beliefs about the importance of ideological criticism. Unfortunately this preoccupation leads to a significant gap in his description, which bodes ill for the value and accuracy of his ensuing ideological analysis. There is an epistemological slippage evident in Kerr's use of the word 'definition'; his narrow understanding of this word borders on semantic obfuscation. The inclusion of the six words 'and the television form it describes' allows Kerr to gloss over the vital difference between a dictionary definition and a close analysis of televisual form, by conflating the two under the term 'definition' and suggesting that a dictionary definition approximates a statement about 'what classic serials *are*' (my emphasis). Clearly no simple semantic analysis of the words 'classic serials' will offer a coherent account of what these programmes are, just as we do not assume that a 'dictionary definition' of the word 'Western' (e.g. a film set in the American West) is an adequate answer to the question 'What is a Western?' In both cases we would expect some reference to details of texts from within each genre, and a general summary of recurring motifs, etc.

The reason for this epistemological gap is fairly obvious – it allows Kerr to move swiftly on to the issues that are close to his heart: the institutional, social and ideological pertinence of these serials. This preoccupation is understandable not only because of its political import but also because it maintains a long-held tradition in film and television studies, where ideological analysis has predominated over alternative approaches. In a rather covert way, Kerr tries to gloss over the importance of an aesthetic understanding of adaptations and conceal his lack of appreciation of the significance of aesthetic features. In order to make the kind of judgements about adaptations he wishes to make, one would expect him to have to look very closely at adaptations' aesthetics: their style, common motifs, conventions – and then move to show how these defining features can be further theorised. While his subsequent outline of the institutional status of classic serials is useful, Kerr's failure to refer to the specific defining characteristics of these programmes leaves his comments about 'history' and 'culture' looking somewhat under-substantiated and tendentious.

Kerr proffered his argument in 1982. Since then, non-comparative approaches to adaptations have gathered momentum, frequently conflating the question 'What are classic-novel adaptations?' with the question 'What is the ideological nature of these adaptations?' In the most successful analyses we find a proposed answer to the latter developing out of a far clearer understanding of the former than had been offered before. Analyses since the early 1990s do not generally contain the explanatory and evidential gap present in Kerr's piece, but instead look closely at the 'genre' of classic-novel adaptations and then attempt to move from its characteristics to its import in cultural or political terms.[3]

In a sense, then, Part II is concerned with generic identity. What traits of style and content do classic-novel adaptations share? How do we recognise one of these programmes when we see it? Is there an underlying identity shared by these programmes other than that they all have literary sources? Common experience tells us that as we channel-hop from one programme to the next we can, in the majority of cases, ascertain what type (genre) of programme each one is within a couple of seconds. Though there will be some exceptions, classic-novel adaptations tend to share a distinctive 'look'. As Kerr notes, 'Careful comparison between [classic novels] and their tele-versions reveals the tendency towards homogenisation in television adaptation. The very profound formal differences that [exist] between novels become all but invisible on television' (1982: 11).

The 'strong group style' of classic-novel adaptations has been widely noted, especially since its contemporary style was consolidated in the 1980s and early 1990s.[4] Bentley, Gervais and Thomson, despite their condescending tone, were united in picking out the central stylistic features of the adaptations which were the targets of their criticisms, though they focused almost entirely on the visual nature of the texts and paid little attention to the use of sound: 'a seamless patchwork of beautiful images'; 'elegant titles and sprightly music'; 'pictures to "sigh" at'; 'immediately striking'; 'stunning visual impact'.[5] What is evident here is a fundamental agreement between these writers on several defining features of classic-novel adaptations: their sumptuous, beautiful, pictorial images, strung together smoothly, slowly and carefully, resulting in an identifiable, distinctive style.

The way adaptations look (their visual style, recurring motifs, generic traits and stylistic conventions – all those things that, in combination, set them apart from other programmes enough to constitute a set or genre), and indeed their use of a certain type of elegant, decorous or wistful orchestral music on their soundtracks, cannot be explained in literary terms. Such is the pervasiveness of these features that we accept this generic style with little awareness of its lack of literary origins – what feature can be found in virtually every nineteenth-century novel to explain, for example, the use of long-take, extreme long shots of grand buildings, or the preference for slow, smooth tracking shots over alternative shots which are more quickly and painlessly achieved? We must look elsewhere to explain the presence of this distinctive style to which these adaptations tend to adhere; the source novels do not help us.

The style described can be explained partly as a amalgamation of markers of 'quality' which confirm adaptations as examples of 'bourgeois' television, claiming a certain cultural status not just through their extra-textual links with 'great literature' ('the idea that the more what is seen on television is "like" literature, the "better" it is' (Giddings, 1983: 42)), but also through their use of a 'cinematic' style – in particular, through their aesthetic links with the stylistic qualities of 'highbrow' films. As John Hill argues, 'such devices do not … indicate cinematic self-consciousness, or the director's signature, so much as a certain kind of "artistry" and cultural worth which helps to distinguish such films from more popular genres' (1999: 81). Classic-novel adaptations are thus differentiated from other television programmes – even from those that share some 'generic' characteristics, such as costume dramas based on pulp fiction (e.g. Catherine Cookson adaptations). In addition, the emphasis placed upon high production values and other markers of quality works to differentiate these programmes from the 'debased culture' of everyday life in the present time.

Classic-novel adaptations are also said to announce their generic identity through their claims to be part of a literary, rather than a televisual tradition, achieving validation through their adaptation of the 'plot, setting, characters, dialogue and, of course, cultural status' of a classic novel (Kerr, 1982: 11). Whilst many scholarly writers have argued that a classic-novel adaptation announces itself as an 'adaptation of a Great Literary Classic' (McArthur, 1978: 40) (i.e. in terms of its claim upon its literary source), this is an unnecessarily limited view. Within popular discourse, conceptions of 'what a classic-novel adaptation is' have frequently been extended beyond a 'genetic' explanation.[6] Fay Weldon argues unequivocally for a non-comparative approach that appreciates the television text for its own achievements:

> If you want to read the book, say I, read the book! If you want to see a good show, see it. And if it reminds you vaguely of the book, or vice versa, that's a bonus but it's hardly any longer the point. And it's perverse and meaningless to make invidious comparisons. If you can't stand the pain don't turn on the telly. (Weldon, source unknown)

The most interesting aspect of Kerr's work is the way in which he characterises the genre as one that differentiates itself from both the televisual and the present contexts. He comments on the special position accorded to the genre within television:

> for the BBC at least, the classic serial has been institutionalised to the extent that it has become a kind of anthology series slot, appearing on certain days (the accustomed Sunday slot in particular involves a secularisation of religious awe into a kind of cultural humility), garnishing the schedule at important moments in the television year. (1982: 8)

Thus classic-novel adaptations are portrayed as distinct from other television programmes, characterised in terms of a 'haven' within the televisual. Over Christmas 1999, viewers were treated to two serialised Dickens adaptations: *Oliver Twist* (ITV) in December, and *David Copperfield* (BBC) on Christmas Day and Boxing Day; they were also offered an adaptation of Henry James's *The Turn of the Screw* (ITV) and Mrs Gaskell's *Wives and Daughters* (BBC). The television schedules thus depended upon 'heritage' pieces, in terms both of the programmes' content and of their links with long-standing televisual traditions: the traditional Christmas Dickens adaptation, the Christmas ghost story, and other quality family viewing. In comparison, there was little science fiction, the season apparently inducing collective nostalgia rather than a shared look forward to the future and the twenty-first century. It is thus apparent that the scheduling of classic-novel adaptations has altered little. All three 1990s adaptations discussed in Part II (*Pride and Prejudice* (1995), *Moll Flanders* (1996) and *The Tenant of Wildfell Hall* (1996)) were broadcast on Sunday evenings, although alternate episodes of *Moll Flanders* were transmitted on Monday evenings, allowing a rare escape from the traditional slot.

However, although Kerr's arguments were extremely accurate at the time, and are still useful to some degree, in wider terms generic development has outrun his analyses. Textually, 1970s adaptations, with which Kerr would have been familiar, exhibit an overt 'literariness' through an excessive reliance upon language and a downplaying of the pictorial or visually impressive or expressive. They are understated, slow-paced and somewhat prosaic by today's standards, but these features worked to mark them out as quality pieces, as different from other television. There is, as Kerr suggests, an air of 'worthiness' about them. But we need only look at the differences between the 1971 (ITV) and the 1995 (BBC) adaptations of *Persuasion* to see how dramatically the genre has been transformed. The 1971 attempt offered us a wooden, dialogue-based presentation against a background of unimpressive, rather featureless sets, filmed with an almost static camera and betraying all the claustrophobic features of a small studio production. The few location shots depicted rather dull, grassy countryside that was framed as background rather than as 'landscape'. In contrast, the 1995 *Persuasion* pitches us straight into the action; utilises the camera's potential for movement and variable shot size, depth and focus; restructures the narrative, using parallel action, to create momentum (if not suspense); and offers aesthetic pleasures as well as diegetic ones. Far from seeming 'literary', the 1995 adaptation is positively televisual, and is less afraid to tamper with its source in order to create gripping television. It is vital to recognise the increasingly powerful influence of the televisual context in which contemporary classic-novel adaptations exist.

The televisual

A more detailed understanding of the televisual context is now essential. I argue here for a cautious medium-specific understanding of television.[7] Several key features of the medium are noted – its presentness, performativity and intertextuality, and its capacity for integration into the wider socio-cultural context of our daily lives – and I argue that these features, in combination, not only serve to distinguish television from other media, such as film, but also result in specific textual characteristics, which are exhibited and utilised in television texts (programmes, advertisements, continuity announcements, etc.). Part II contains references to the model of the televisual proffered in this chapter, as it traces the influence of the televisual in textual features of particular classic-novel adaptations.

Temporality and 'presentness'

Television images can, like film images, be understood as tenseless – as having the potential to be co-opted into a variety of tenses through their placement within a narrative and the addition of sound and dialogue.[8] Like the film image, though, the television image has been historically characterised as present. In the case of television, additional evidence is offered for this description:

> While in film each frame is actually a static image, the television image is continually moving, very much in the manner of the Bergsonian *durée*. The scanning beam is constantly trying to complete an always incomplete image. Even if the image on the screen seems at rest, it is structurally in motion. Each television frame is always in a state of becoming. While the film frame is a concrete record of the past, the television frame (when live) is a reflection of the living, constantly changing present. (Zettl, 1978: 7)[9]

Zettl argues for television's 'presentness'. He observes the presentness of the television image, and suggests a difference between the 'past' film image and the 'present' television image through a description of the television image as always 'becoming'. Even when a programme was shot on film (as, for example, most classic-novel adaptations are), the programme's film images themselves undergo the same transmission process as other programmes' images. For Zettl, the technological differences between film projection and television broadcast determine television's eternal presentness, for its images are never completed, always becoming.

This ontological aspect of the television image bears wider implications for television's presentness. There is a sense in which the television image is unique because it is not solid, complete and extractable, in contrast with the photographic (and film) image, which McLuhan argues 'isolates moments in time' (1964: 188). Yet television images are commonly perceived as being exactly that. Unlike films shown in the cinema, television texts often use freeze frames: at the end of individual advertisements and advert breaks, at the conclusion of episodes of some dramas (e.g. soap operas), and so on. In addition, television viewers can use video recorders to pause texts at specific points. Therefore television viewers, even more than film audiences, perceive television as made up of a series of separate images that can be captured and held. Indeed, our (and Zettl's) use of the term 'television image' (or television frame) implies the possibility of pinpointing one complete 'picture', however briefly.

The development of more advanced home video recorders, and the advent and wider dissemination of new media, however, encourage viewers to perceive television images as on a continuum, in the way that Zettl suggests. As viewers are able to manipulate television texts that are recorded on video, slowing them down and speeding them up, editing and altering the video image, the notion of individual frames, regular in form and duration, is undermined. The television images themselves, far from being understood as 'present', become detached from their regular temporal flow, and take on a more uncertain temporality: they appear tenseless.

This change is, however, more obvious in video images than in television ones. Moreover, the curious tenseless nature of the television image is reconfigured and asserted as present through other ontological and conventional features of television. John Ellis argues that 'the TV image has further distinct qualities of its own ... that mark it decisively as different from the cinema image with its photo effect' (1992: 132). Without digressing into a discussion of television's 'photo effect', one can note the general perception of television's connection with realism and, through this, reality.[10] Most significant is the *temporality* of this connection with reality. Zettl notes that 'the television frame (when live) is a reflection of the living, constantly changing present' (Zettl, 1978: 7), whilst Mary Ann Doane observes television's 'persistent reference' to an eternal 'present-ness' (1990: 222). Both emphasise the importance of (the potential of) live television as a medium-specific feature that affirms television as 'eternally present', and note that this potential for liveness is implicated in the texts that television presents to us. I shall return to this feature of television shortly.

Television requires that we address questions of temporality even more than film does. The issue here is not how television texts represent tense and the passing of time. A discussion of such matters involves identifying 'television' as a collection of representational texts, just as when we 'watch television' we are actually watching texts. To consider television's temporality is to refer to a different entity, or a different aspect of television; it is to talk about television in terms of another of its features through which we commonly define it: its role as 'a system for reproducing on a screen visual images transmitted (usually with sound) by radio signals' (*OED Concise*, 1995). This definition of television is clearly concerned not with what we watch but with how television as a medium brings what we watch to us; it defines television as a transmitting device.[11]

The transmission process fundamentally differentiates television from film. As Richard Dienst writes:

> A televisual image has to be established and sustained onscreen moment by moment. With transmission, images and sets of images pass the time and fill out the current: in this sense television is always 'live'. On film, on the other hand, the image appears in a here-and-now necessarily separate from the then-and-there of its production. (1994: 20)

Of course, in the case of television that is not broadcast live, its images, like those of film, are also separated from their place and time of production. However, Dienst's foci are significant: the centrality of transmission, the live nature of this constant flow of images, and television's resultant potential for live broadcasting. As Dienst says, 'the transmission is essentially instantaneous (moving at the speed of electricity): hence the technical basis for "immediate" or "live" visibility' (1994: 18). In a live broadcast, television uniquely not only broadcasts across space,[12] but also creates a relationship in time between what is being broadcast (the actual performance) and those who are watching the broadcast; the actual performance is simultaneous with the viewing of it.[13] Obviously, adaptations and other dramas are hardly ever broadcast live, but television's transmitted nature forms the basis of an extra-textual presentness unique to the televisual medium. Transmission engenders an 'absolutely mechanical present tense, always occurring elsewhere first – a temporality that is, precisely, the metaphysical center of television understood as communication, representation, and visibility' (Dienst, 1994: 164).

Television's particular characteristics as a medium therefore include a peculiar actual or perceived relationship with real-life time. This feature of television's temporality explains, as Roger Silverstone terms it, television's 'spatial and temporal significance, ingrained as it is into the routines of daily life' (1993: 575).[14] The specific nature of television's mode of communication – transmission – means that television connects with our own perception of real-life time, because we are aware that the broadcast of programmes is constant, and that the programme schedule fits within the same real-life time structures as we do; as Stephen Heath puts it, television has a 'seamless equivalence with social life' (1990: 267).

Lawrence Grossberg extends this notion still further: 'Television viewing is a large temporal part of our lives ... its power to restructure the temporal and spatial aspects of our lives remains unquestionable' (1987: 34–5). The transmission, the screening of each programme, is live, and television's transmission of texts is continuous: 'TV continues whether a particular set is turned on or not' (Ellis, 1992: 138). This constant audio-visual transmission is a unique characteristic of television, and thus constitutes a primary building block in a medium-specific conceptualisation of 'televisuality', for it affects both the way in which we engage with television and the characteristics of many television texts.

While television's ontological feature of constant transmission means that the medium is 'eternally present' (now), the same feature determines that television is always present in a spatial sense (here). In terms of viewer engagement with television, television therefore manifests a 'veritable dailiness' (Silverstone, 1993: 574). This dailiness – the quotidian nature of television (unlike film, for example) – means that 'broadcast TV is also intimate and everyday, a part of home life rather than any kind of special event' (Ellis, 1992: 113). As Feuer argues, 'the set is in the home, as part of the furniture of one's daily life; it is always available; one may intercept the flow at any point. Indeed, the "central fact" of television may be that it is designed to be watched intermittently, casually, and without full concentration' (1983: 15).

At a textual level, the impact of these medium-specific characteristics is considerable. On the one hand, television often utilises its eternal presentness/presence by emphasising the 'live' (or pseudo-live) nature of its texts: in news programmes, coverage of sporting events, continuity announcements, and so forth. In these instances, the perceived present-ness of the televisual image is accentuated by an emphasis on its liveness (presentness in the sense of both here and now), which increases the excitement of the televised event. Similarly, the widespread use of direct address accentuates the present-to-us nature of television, its continual presence within our daily lives.

On the other hand, television texts must fight to overcome the sense that they are quotidian, to grab the attention of the 'casual' viewer, in a way that film does not need to do. Therefore, as John Ellis notes, 'the role that sound plays in TV is extremely important' (1992: 128), for sound and music can work to draw the errant viewer's eyes back to the screen – thus the increase in volume during advertisement breaks, and the use of continuity announcements and direct address that overtly calls out to the viewer. The use of sound is not the only way in which specific television texts attempt to distance themselves from run-of-the-mill television and mark themselves out as special events. Classic-novel adaptations have historically been preoccupied with exactly this process, and Part II will reveal the techniques they use to distinguish themselves from quotidian television – to elicit concentrated attention from the distracted television viewer.

Television therefore interacts with our present lives in a way that film does not. The transmission (or, as I shall argue below, the 'performance') of each text is perceived as being 'present', due to its locus in television's continuous flow. Added to this, our interpretation of the tenseless televisual image is that it is of the present tense, as described above. Thus, our mode of television viewing is always in some sense present, triggered by both extra-textual factors and textual elements. 'Television is ... constantly present. It is eternal' (Silverstone, 1993: 575).

It may appear that we have reached a conclusion that is not entirely new. After all, it was in 1975 that Raymond Williams first conceptualised 'the central television experience: the fact of flow' (1975: 95), and the televisual arena elaborated here bears a strong resemblance to that which he then proposed. However, it is vital to address directly the niggling sense, shared by so many theorists, that the 'presentness' of televisual flow is of fundamental importance to our understanding of the medium. An understanding of the extra-textual televisual presentness of classic-novel adaptations can shed light upon the ways in which they are marketed, artistically constructed, watched and critically appraised; to appreciate the importance of this medium-specific feature of television is to more fully understand the nature of the programmes in question.

It is worth flagging here the wider reliance on notions of medium specificity amongst television, as opposed to film, theorists. Ellis summarises his own arguments about television form:

> broadcast TV has developed distinctive aesthetic forms to suit the circumstances within which it is used. These forms are distinct to broadcast TV as a phenomenon, rather than to video as a phenomenon. They have as much to do with the fact that broadcasting presents a continuous set of signals that are either received or missed by their potential audience. (1992: 111).

In effect, Ellis is assuming there to be textual ramifications arising from television's ontological features. There are indeed such ramifications, a number of which are explored below.

Television and performance

A key feature arising from television's transmitted nature and our awareness of this is that television programmes are very often 'performative'. The term 'performative' is awkward in the sense that it has been used differently in different fields of study, so I shall delineate what is intended by my use of the term.[15] Simply, to say that a television programme is performative is to suggest that we watch the programme at the level of performance. Television, like a cabaret or a music-hall recital, and unlike conventional cinema, offers us a continuous stream of texts; it offers us a series of performances, each programme, advertisement and promotional slot constituting a new performance. Television's flow 'assembles disparate items, placing them within the same experience, but does not organise them to produce an overall meaning' (Ellis, 1992: 117). One can distinguish two performances: the original, actual performance by the actors, recorded by the camera(s), and the performance which is the transmission – the playing – of the particular text.[16]

Some television texts highlight the first type of performance as an aspect of their appeal: they constantly draw our attention to the perform-ance being offered by the performers (and recorded by the crew), as opposed to persuading us to immerse ourselves in imagining the actuality of the events in the text before us. Live shows like *TFI Friday* and *Ruby Wax* are prime examples of these highly performative texts. Many comedy or 'spoof' films and television shows (the *Naked Gun* and *Carry On* films, for example, or comedy programmes like *Smith and Jones* or *The Two Ronnies*) increase the audience's propensity or inclination to read them as performances.

In addition, the audience understands all television and film texts to be transmitted, or 'performed', for their pleasure. Thus we watch these programmes in a similar way to that in which we watch a *theatrical* performance, slipping between an awareness that we are watching a group of actors pretending to be a certain set of characters, and a closer engagement with ('immersion in') the text itself. This is not the moment to digress into a discussion of the nature of this 'closer engagement' with the text; suffice it to say that it takes the form of a sort of 'imagining' inspired by what we are seeing performed – a 'partial loss of touch with the here and now', as Margaret Morse puts it (1990: 193). We are, however, always aware of television texts as performances within the continuous stream of transmitted texts, because of television's above-described unique relationship with our real-life time, arising from transmission.

Our perception of television texts as performative affects our reception of even the most realistic or naturalistic fictional programmes, such as classic-novel adaptations. The actors' performances here, for example, serve to highlight the contemporaneity and televisuality of the programmes in which they exist. As Part II will show, classic-novel adaptations rely upon the deployment of realistic, historically accurate props and costumes in order to present representations of the past that are a focus for audience engagement. The audience is aware of the fact that the props are rarely 'real', and that the costumes are modified to fit the body shapes of 1990s' actors, not 1800s' people. Yet these factors do not adversely affect the audience's imaginative engagement with the 'past' that is being presented to them, for they know that it is not *really* the past but a truthful, careful re-presentation of it – a performance. In addition, the actors' performances are often crucial in dispelling any 'illusion'[17] that it is not a performance we are watching; our 'imaginings' are disrupted, irrevocably undermined.

When we watch actors performing, they can never wholly disappear beneath their roles, for each actor/character inhabits the same body and physical space. Actors, especially well-known ones, which in classic-novel adaptations is often the case, can never simply be viewed as the characters they play. 'When we watch any fictional film, we are to some degree aware that the performances on the screen are the result of the actors' skills and decisions' (Bordwell and Thompson, 1993: 159); the same is true of television programmes. Alex Kingston as Moll Flanders (1996), Tara Fitzgerald as Helen Hunter and Rupert Graves as Arthur Huntingdon (both in *The Tenant of Wildfell Hall*, 1996) are never viewed simply as Moll, Helen or Arthur, but as Alex-as-Moll, Tara-as-Helen, Rupert-as-Arthur. These actors are too well known for the viewers to imagine, for an hour or so, that they are not Kingston, Fitzgerald and Graves; indeed, they were cast because of who they are, because the viewers know them.

Whilst the re-use of the same few actors in classic-novel adaptations and 'heritage films' functions on the one hand to assert the existence of a distinct generic microcosm – the 'world' of the classic-novel adaptation – it also functions to import additional and particular resonances to the parts the actors play, and to accentuate the programmes' links with other texts and with the outside world. 'Our responses to a new film [or programme] are affected by everything we know about its actors' (McDougal, 1985: 6). Actors are associated with previous roles they have played, interviews they have given, and scandals they have been involved in, as much as the part they are currently playing. Television's constant, present performance is even less conducive to such an engagement as will allow the audience to 'forget' the actor performing the character, but even in the cinema, the slightest break in the audience's concentration brings them back to full awareness of whom they are watching.

This 'break' can often be provided (deliberately or inadvertently) by the film itself, as most viewers can verify through personal experience. Deborah Kaplan notes that 'incidents in the private lives of public persons may ... become ghosts that haunt a particular production' (1998: 18). On watching *Sirens* (WMG, 1994) in a half-full cinema with a quiet, well-behaved audience, any 'imagining' that Hugh Grant was not Hugh Grant-as-Anthony Campion but actually Anthony Campion was shattered by a combination of audience knowledge of recent gossip concerning his private life and an unfortunate piece of scripted dialogue (written before the scandal broke). Grant had recently been caught by Los Angeles police, receiving the attentions of a prostitute called Divine Brown; the story had been splashed all over the papers and he was photographed, looking sheepish in the police file records, and grovelling to his partner, Elizabeth Hurley, and interviewed, expressing his sincere embarrassment and regret about the whole affair. His dialogue in *Sirens*, as he spoke with his diegetic wife about unnamed past transgressions, included the lines: 'I don't by any means regard either of us as saints … Yes, I've done plenty of things I'm ashamed of'. As his wife Estella (Tara Fitzgerald) enquired 'What sort of things?', the audience's titters became laughter. The readiness with which the audience laughed at this unintended extra-textual reference (existing within a diegesis already weighed down with sexual overtones) emphasises how consciously aware they were that it was Hugh Grant, not Anthony Campion, who was speaking. The audience quickly and eagerly extended Grant's words beyond their intended referential meaning, relating them extra-diegetically, and thus adding to their somewhat limited enjoyment of a relatively feeble film.

In a similar way, my own close engagement with the film *Maurice* (1987) was considerably attenuated during the scene at a cricket match, near the end of the film. Watching it on video, with a friend, I spotted a young woman in a walk-on part who looked strikingly like Helena Bonham-Carter. So convinced was I, and so unconvinced my friend, that we spent several minutes rewinding and replaying the shots of her, studying carefully the rather fuzzy picture produced by a worn videotape. At that point, the only 'representation of the past' which concerned us was that of Bonham-Carter's early career, and our interest was in the performer, not the performed.[18]

It is not just the distinction between actor and character that foregrounds a text as performance. Props and locations, too, when deployed within a text, 'stand in' for fictional places, and the audience's awareness of the difference between a concrete object existing in the real world and the fictional object it is meant to represent can also draw attention to the performative nature of the text. During my second viewing (on videotape) of *Howards End* (1992), the poignant scene of Ruth Wilcox's death failed to capture my emotional attention when I realised that the building used for the 'sanatorium' was in fact Founder's Building, Royal Holloway College (with which I had been unacquainted upon my first viewing of the film, in the cinema). The result of my excitement at discovering this was that I paid no attention to the dialogue and had to rewind the tape to discover what I had missed. Suddenly, the scene presented not Ruth Wilcox, dying in a sanatorium, but an actress pretending to die in a converted administrative office at Royal Holloway College. Failing to look past the performance to engage imaginatively with the diegesis, I perceived the text only on a performative level.

These were unintended extra-diegetic incidents, textual references unwittingly directing the viewer's attention away from the role the actor was playing to the actor playing the role, or from the 'fictional' building to the 'real' one, and disrupting any sense that the text had closed boundaries separating it from the outside world (and, in the case of the classic-novel adaptation, its 'past' world from the present world in which the audience views the text). Yet many recent television adaptations *encourage* this kind of extra-textual relation: in particular, they often appeal to the viewers to use their knowledge of the actors in order to supplement their perceptions of the actor's performance-in-role. Jordan describes the impact of our knowledge of the earlier performances of an actor upon our viewing as a 'background resonance' that is 'added' to our perception of a character (1981: 197–8); Kaplan writes 'some of the actors' past roles also "haunt" their characters in these films [and programmes]' (1998: 181).

The audience's knowledge of characters in television texts is therefore informed by their performative dimension. Resonances of previous roles and real-life incidents encourage the viewers to build up their perceptions of the characters actors are playing in a complex layering process. Those adaptation theorists who argue that film and television characters are less complex, less 'three dimensional' than those in novels sometimes fail to consider this 'layering process' of characterisation to which the individual actor effortlessly contributes so much, and to which the knowledgeable audience responds.

The performative nature of television texts also reasserts their contemporaneity, through their use of actors and props that exist in the present. In addition, actors' appearances outside programmes assert their existence as contemporary, real people, whose job it is to 'act' as if they were other people. In the case of classic-novel adaptations, the fore-grounding of the text as performative does not halt our imagining of the past that is instigated by our viewing of these programmes. Only if we subscribe to a concept of 'false belief' or 'suspended disbelief' to explain audience engagement with screen texts does the above discussion of the actors' presence severely problematise these programmes.[19] However, if we reject the 'belief' paradigm, and accept instead that the audience responds to the text by engaging in 'imaginings' based on the situations played out on the screen, then it becomes clear that the programmes' performativity can complicate our reading of the text and increase our insight into its meanings. The active mental negotiation of our perceptions of the contemporaneity of the performance, and our imaginings of the 'past' that are inextricably tied to the text's representations of it, augments our viewing experience. Far from simply submerging ourselves into the text, submitting to our 'belief' in the past we see recreated on the screen, we are aware of both the 'pastness' of the text (a vital component, constituted by its manipulation of historically accurate settings, props, costumes, etc.) and the 'presentness' of the text (its performance: the manipulation of these things by cast and crew). The importance of this past/present dichotomy is revealed in the programme analyses in Part II.

Intertextuality

Television's performativity depends upon both extra- and inter-textual references, to the real world (where actors and props exist) and to other texts (where actors' other characters exist). Yet many television texts depend upon a far greater level of intertextuality. Jim Collins argues that 'the all-pervasiveness of different strategies of rearticulation and appropriation is one of most widely discussed features of postmodern cultural production' (1992: 333); television, as the 'quintessence of postmodern culture' (1992: 327), utilises intertextuality to a large degree. Television is full of parody, of pastiche, of overt references that link one television text with another. Many comedy programmes are based on sketches parodying other television programmes; advertisements 'tend to make oblique and punning references to each other's advertising campaigns. The audience is expected to understand these references' (Ellis, 1992: 134).

Clearly, intertextuality (the making of references to other artworks) has existed in, and been vital to, artworks for hundreds of years, but it has been proposed that television's use of intertextuality is different in that it is specifically postmodern. Broadly, postmodernists argue that the difference between traditional intertextuality and postmodern inter-textuality is that the former aims to express or enhance meaning, whereas the latter is merely a superficial pastiche of images and references, where 'pastiche appropriates styles and looks from other periods and times for its own textual use' (Caldwell, 1995: 218), and where 'a sign is not an index of an underlying reality, but merely of other signs' (Barry, 1995: 87). That is, the intertextual referentiality of television programmes is understood to refer not to any aspect of concrete reality but merely to other signs.[20] Jameson implies that the difference between traditional and postmodern intertextuality is rooted in the latter's playful depthlessness: 'depth is replaced by surface, or by multiple surfaces (what is often called intertextuality is in that sense no longer a matter of depth)' (1991: 12).[21]

Both types of intertextuality are evident in classic-novel adaptations; in fact these programmes depend upon intertextuality for their efficacy. As is the case with any 'genre', classic-novel adaptations utilise a range of standard generic motifs of content, style and mood which 'refer' to other previous and contemporary classic-novel adaptations and 'heritage programmes' in order to establish their generic identity and emphasise their place within a wider generic context. In a sense, such 'generic intertextuality' is firmly postmodern, in that its referents are merely other representations, not real life, and in that they are often used with little or no critical distance from or reflection upon their sources. Indeed, Jameson regards programmes like these as part of an extended 'pastiche' of the past they so often aim to represent – based only on previous representations of the past, they offer only representations of representations, a huge tapestry of intertextual references divorced from historical 'reality': 'the history of aesthetic styles displaces "real" history' (1991: 20). However, Collins allows for a postmodern intertextuality less dissimilar from traditional intertextuality, arguing that 'the "already said" is constantly being recirculated, but from very different perspectives ranging from nostalgic reverence to vehement attack or a mixture of these strategies' (1992: 333). Collins's more flexible postmodern intertextuality more accurately describes that which is employed in classic-novel adaptations, as revealed in Part II, for other texts are 'cited' within nostalgic, historicist, reflective, critical or playful frameworks. In turn, varied uses of intertextuality demand various modes of engagement with the text – all of them 'knowing' (as Ellis implies, above). As Rachel M. Brownstein argues, 'you are invited and assumed to be in the know' by recent classic-novel adaptations (1998: 18); intertextual referentiality depends upon the viewers' capacity and willingness (their desire, even) to engage with the text as active readers.

The televisual context

Above, the specificity of the televisual medium has been considered in terms of its textual, intertextual and extra-textual characteristics. Classic-novel adaptations exist within a televisual context that incorporates more than the actual broadcasting of the programmes. For this reason, an analysis of the wider field of discourse about these programmes should be included in any discussion purporting to illuminate the genre. It is through this discourse that adaptations are 'announced' as described in Part I.[22]

Though some elements of this discourse are clearly textually televisual (trailers shown on television, for example), some appear to be extra-televisual – outside the bounds of the medium itself, simply referring to it. These include advertisements, promotions, and critiques and discussions in magazines, newspapers and the *Radio Times*, as well as on websites. Yet such a simplistic division is inaccurate. The conception of the televisual elaborated thus far can be extended still further. Tony Fry suggests that

> television is not only more than its technology but also more than its cultural form – it has become what we will call the televisual, and as such is definable as an ontological domain. Which is to say television has become something with its own phenomenological qualities that cannot be reduced to one thing, to one being. (1993a: 11–12)

This is an exciting extension of the term 'television', developing as it does the concept of the 'televisual'.[23] Previously, television has been characterised as a technology (as a system for broadcasting images) and as a cultural form (as a medium of representation), yet what is fascinating about the televisual is the scale of its affective influence. Its interaction with our everyday lives, and its spatial and temporal specificities, cause it to be greater than the sum of its parts. Fry continues: 'what the televisual names then is the end of the medium, in a context, and the arrival of television as the context' (1993a: 13). Not only does this characterisation of the televisual emphasise its fluid and elusive nature – the difficulty of conceptualising it in its entirety, in technological, cultural and metaphysical terms – it also describes the spreading of television's sphere of affective influence to form an immense 'web' (or 'world') that is the televisual. Thus seemingly extra-televisual artefacts such as the *Radio Times*, critical previews, reviews and letters are actually not outside television, separated from it, but are instead part of the televisual web that weaves itself into so many aspects of our daily lives. There are both formal and informal links that bind these artefacts to television: the *Radio Times* is historically linked to the BBC; there is a social network of programme makers and critics; and the television audience is connected with the medium through the very fact of their viewing.

On a less tangible level, television's complex interplay between texts in turn extends the televisual into other areas of art and life. Television now extends beyond the box that appears to contain it, in the corner of our living room; it is pervasive, 'its transmissions are no longer controlled by the flick of a switch' (Fry, 1993a: 13). It is no longer a part of our culture, but constitutes a culture in itself. Thus, programmes exist as the central core of television, but the televisual incorporates other texts, too, which are as much a part of the televisual context as the programmes are. The televisual (as opposed to television) is simultaneously textual, intertextual and extra-textual, constituting a 'televisual world'. To understand this vast context is to come closer to fully appreciating the genre of classic-novel adaptations, for these programmes increasingly utilise their locus within this context, skilfully creating for themselves a unique, yet distinctively televisual and contemporary cultural identity.

Postmodernism – a note

> All of those formal and narrative traits once thought to be unique and defining properties of postmodernism – intertextuality, pastiche, multiple and collaged presentational forms – have also been defining properties of television from its inception. (Caldwell, 1995: 23)

This is not the place for an extended discussion of the postmodern and its relevance to both television and the televisual. It is pertinent, however, to flag briefly the many connections that exist between the above conceptualisation of the televisual and key concepts of postmodern theory. A fuller exploration is another project altogether.[24]

Television itself is often considered by postmodern theorists to be the 'quintessence of postmodern culture' (Collins, 1992: 327). It is supposedly an arena where simulacra displace the 'real', where the (self) referentiality of intertextuality overtakes any overt references to reality. Television texts become part of an endless 'competition of signs' situated with a 'limitless televisual universe' (Collins, 1992: 331). Television's textual and technological presentness and liveness, and the apparently eternal and unstoppable flow of broadcasting, impact on our perception of television texts: we are aware of 'an endlessness of parallel worlds which go on whether switched on or not, whether we watch or not, a world which is a primary reference in daily conversation, which we may be equipped to enter or not' (Morse, 1990: 211–12).[25] In this way, a series of unreal worlds exists alongside the real world, blurring previously assumed distinctions between the two.

These ideas demand certain distinctions and provisos. As was suggested earlier, television's intertextuality does not necessarily constitute pastiche, and is not necessarily unreflective or anti-historicist (as will be shown in Part II). In addition, as television expands into the televisual context described above, its potential to connect with (and refer to) our daily lives and the 'real world' is increased. Television's representations, though 'parallel' and often imaginative, can thus have real-world referents, and can certainly have real-life affectiveness.

However, some of television's features are aptly described by concepts drawn from postmodern theories. Television's performativity imbues the television text with a playful, 'let's pretend' quality; added to this is television's playful use of intertextuality (Jameson, 1991: 12). Thus the idea of performance and the related notion of 'play' can illuminate our understanding of our enjoyment of television and the way in which its texts are structured.

Further, theorists have long conflated postmodern aesthetics with televisual aesthetics. Stephen Connor notes that 'rock video is ... the TV form favoured by ... theorists of the postmodern' (1989: 159), and Kaplan does indeed focus on MTV for her well-known study of television and postmodernism, wherein she argues that MTV, a particularly televisual form, 'marks its discourse as postmodernist' (1987: 144). Ellis asserts that 'The "spot" advertisement is in many ways in the quintessence of TV ... [Advertisements] are also the supremely televisual product: hence another part of their exhilaration, that of seeing a medium used for itself, and not weighed down by cultural presumptions that are not its own' (1992: 118).

These theorists select particular characteristics which they argue are 'typically' televisual, and which are also considered 'postmodern': both television and the postmodern are fast-paced, contemporary, fragmented, part of 'mass' culture ('not weighed down by cultural presumptions that are not its own').[26] The alliance of television with the postmodern means that negative feelings about either of these tend to affect theorists' attitudes to the other. Thus gloomy postmodern theorist Jameson is as downhearted about television as he is about the prospect of a wholly postmodern world, regarding the medium as failing to fulfil its potential and instead acting as comforter and analgesic for its viewers (1991: 70–1, 281, 355).

Jane Feuer asks, 'Should an aesthetics of television be historical and descriptive (based on received network practice) or speculative (based on an assumed essence of the medium)?' (1983: 12). It is an astute question. Although the characteristics of the televisual described in this chapter arise from the technical and ontological specificities of television, and are thus 'medium-specific', it is true that other characteristics could also have arisen (and will yet arise) from this very basis, and could equally be cited as 'televisual'. The features discussed here have been selected because they impact in particular on the genre of classic-novel adaptations, for certain recognisable features of the televisual appear to contradict particular generic features of classic-novel adaptations in a way that problematises previous theories about and interpretations of these programmes.

Classic-novel adaptations and the televisual

Many approaches to this genre focus on the programmes' rose-tinted representations of the past, and on the efficacy of these representations as part of a reactionary ideological project which builds nostalgia for the past. Yet these ideas are problematised by television's fundamental presentness. Beja writes:

> it is a commonplace to say that in reading a good story we 'lose ourselves' in the work, and often that is true; but even when we become so absorbed in the imaginary world we are reading about that we can say that it has happened, it has occurred because we have been willing to let it. And ultimately a part of us remains quite aware of what is going on. (1979: 12)

Just as this is true of literature, it is even truer of television. Television's temporality and performativity must be taken into account when postulating theories about the ideological influence of the television text. If a theory concerned with such an influence requires that the audience watch the text totally immersed in a state of imagining or (as some would have it) 'false belief' – if we must 'lose ourselves in the work' – then it fails to consider the undermining power of the audience's ability to read the text as 'present', intertextual performance.[27]

Further, how can a programme recreate the past (essential to its generic identity) if its overriding characteristic is its inability to move beyond the presentness of performance? The performance and viewing of these adaptations are firmly grounded (through transmission) within the present, and the textual television image is also perceived as present. Consequently, theories that are under-analytically preoccupied with these programmes' relationship with the *past* are less useful an explanation of the meaning, appeal and power of these programmes than one might hope. Classic-novel adaptations exist within the context of the continuous performance of television; this context, as well as the date of their production and broadcast, ensures their identity as contemporary television programmes. They thus display an extra-textual presentness: 'belonging to or found in the present time, contemporary' (*Chambers*, 1997).

In addition to precipitating this 'temporal clash', classic-novel adaptations, whilst existing within television, have traditionally rejected other features of the televisual. The key to understanding this apparent 'conflict of interest' is to recognise that the interplay that these programmes initiate between past and present is a vital feature of classic-novel adaptations. These programmes do not just show us a (fictive) past; they bring representations of a past into our present, through the medium of television. They actively construct meanings through the televisual synthesis of represented past and contextual present: this process creates and maintains the programmes' appeal to their audience, and constitutes a central part of the genre's wider cultural significance.

Two worlds collide

Perhaps then the most distinctive, yet abstruse, feature of classic-novel adaptations is their specific 'locus' within their televisual context. These programmes are marked out as different from other television programmes in several ways, and are often characterised as an escape, a refuge, both from run-of-the-mill television and from the present (our contemporary world). As adaptations clearly cannot 'escape' either their televisual or their contemporary context, especially because the televisual and the present are in some ways linked, they are instead seen to constitute an oasis amidst both television and the present, demarcating the world of the classic-novel adaptation on the inside (a generic microcosm) and the world of the televisual and the present on the outside. Thus the boundaries of the classic-novel adaptation microcosm are marked out, through textual characteristics and extra-textual 'announcements', in order to perpetuate a firm 'generic' identity that has historically been dependent upon the genre's attempted renunciation of both its present and its televisual contexts, paralleling the way in which 'classic novels' are said to exhibit a timelessness which allows them to 'rise above' the particularities of their socio-historical contexts.

If we are to take a non-comparative approach to this genre, using critical frameworks that are suggested by the programmes themselves, a whole range of potentially lucrative theoretical topics suggest themselves. This book takes up generic traits of content, style and mood in order to trace the genre's appeal, identity and recent development. Where others have focused upon the national(istic) or literary aspects of these pro-grammes, I am concerned with the genre's televisuality and its existence within television. This approach brings many benefits. To distinguish television adaptations from film ones recognises the differences between adaptations in these two forms; to focus on the televisual aspects of adaptations is often to find elements that challenge, contradict or undermine theories about 'literary adaptations' in general; to concentrate upon the programmes as a part of a television genre is to draw deserved attention to the fascinating generic development that television classic-novel adaptations are undergoing.[28]

There are potential clashes or contradictions between common-sense conceptualisations of literary adaptation and widely held perceptions of television. Common analyses of this genre represent it as bourgeois, elitist, reactionary, sedate to the point of being soporific, and nostalgically obsessed with our colonial past and national heritage. Meanwhile, the televisual medium is usually and increasingly characterised as fast-paced, postmodern, popular, consumerist and forever perpetuating the present moment. The apparent contradiction between these two 'worlds' seems to me to create extraordinary possibilities for interpretation. How do these worlds, so estranged from each other, collide? What happens when they do? To what extent do our perceptions of either one of them stand up to scrutiny? Classic-novel adaptations hold a unique place within televisual culture, straddling two apparently irreconcilable worlds. In a sense this curious locus can be considered as constituting the key dialectic of the programmes themselves. This dialectic generates a plethora of inventive and varying adaptations; similarly, exploring the programmes through a consideration of this dialectic promises to result in creative and respon-sive interpretations, greater critical and theoretical understanding of the programmes, and a fuller appreciation of the genre's socio-cultural signi-ficance. Part II explores these two divergent worlds and the adaptations that are the fascinating synthesis of elements of both.

Notes

1 Indeed, I would be willing to concede that the term 'sub-set' or 'cycle' might be more accurate and defensible here. It should be noted, however, that the broader arguments offered in this book are not dependent upon the reader's acceptance of the term 'genre' as a description of the group 'television classic-novel adaptations'. In addition, the 'traditional' classic-novel adaptation should not be regarded as set in stone, but as a particular combination of recognisable conventions with which contemporary television viewers are very familiar, and which 'mark out' these programmes to those viewers as classic-novel adaptations, and as different from other television 'genres'.

2 'Generic traits' are here taken to refer to necessary but not sufficient traits that are shared by almost all classic-novel adaptations and constitute a defining feature of them, even if the individual traits may also be found in other genres such as historical dramas or parodic sitcoms (e.g. French and Saunders' *Let Them Eat Cake* (BBC, 1999)).

3 Andrew Higson's influential work on the 'heritage film' is the best-known example of such an approach. See 'The Heritage Film and British Cinema' in *Dissolving Views* (1996), *Waving the Flag* (1995) and 'Re-presenting the National Past' (1993). Higson's work is discussed in Part II.

4 I realise that it is problematic to regard any 'era' of a genre as a 'consolidation' era, following Altman's critique of genre theory (*Film/Genre*, 1999) – I risk raising 'a subset of the genre to a representative position' (1999: 79). However, my analysis of *Pride and Prejudice* (1995) will reveal the archetypal nature of the programme, and will propose that it constituted the 'pinnacle' of a certain, traditional, mode of adaptation. In terms of viewers, critics and theorists of the late 1990s/early 2000s, this 'consolidation era' (1980s to mid-1990s) is still hugely influential in terms of both contemporary adaptations and theoretical analyses of them.

5 Please refer to my discussion of these writers' comments offered in Part I.

6 'Popular discourse' includes social conversation, newspaper reviews, television guides,

continuity announcements, programme marketing publications, etc., as opposed to scholarly books and journals, although there is not necessarily an absolute dividing line between the two areas.

7 Though it would be apt to describe the model of television proffered here as 'medium specific', it should be noted that it is not essentialist in the sense of being ahistorical or determinist. It is based specifically upon the televisual context in which the adaptations analysed were broadcast, i.e. British broadcast television from the 1970s through to the 2000s. Other forms of television may not fit this model, though they are likely to share some of the properties discussed.

8 Elsewhere, I put forward arguments regarding filmic tense, and argue that the film image is essentially tenseless, but that it is perceived as 'present' for various reasons. I also demonstrate how some films utilise sound and images to convey a shifting and indefinite sense of 'tense', referring in particular to the opening sequence of Adrian Lyne's *Lolita* (1998). See Cardwell (2000a).

9 Stephen Heath and Gillian Skirrow make similar points to Zettl's about the television image. See S. Heath and G. Skirrow (1977), 'Television: A World in Action'.

10 The perception that television bears a privileged relation to reality is enhanced by television's historical role as a primary communicator of news and current affairs.

11 Often writers discuss 'television' and yet imply several different definitions of the word. A useful unravelling of these myriad uses of the word is offered by Jostein Gripsrud in his chapter 'Television, Broadcasting, Flow: Key metaphors in TV Theory' in Christine Geraghty and David Lusted (eds) (1997), *The Television Studies Book*, 17–32. Deborah Malor also delineates various meanings of the word, and argues that 'television' implies all of them in 'commonsense usage'. See her chapter 'Touch TV: Finding Out What is at Hand in the Televisual Environment' in Tony Fry (ed.) (1993b) *RUA TV?*, 67–84.

12 An interesting discussion of television's ability not just to cross but to *re-negotiate* spatial boundaries is offered in Margaret Morse's chapter 'An Ontology of Everyday Distraction' in P. Mellencamp (ed.) (1990) *Logics of Television*, 193–221. Paul Adams extends similar ideas, relating them also to the 'presentness' of television, in his chapter 'In TV: On "Nearness", on Heidegger and on Television' in Tony Fry (ed.) (1993b) *RUA TV?*, 45–66).

13 Of course, other media share some features of television's time-space relations: the performance and viewing of a theatrical play is also simultaneous, but in the case of theatre spatial boundaries are not stretched; radio is 'live' to a far greater extent than television, but is not a visual medium.

14 Roger Silverstone's article 'Television, Ontological Security and the Transitional Object', *Media, Culture and Society* (1993), whence this quotation is drawn, offers a detailed consideration of the constant presence that television constitutes in our daily lives, and theorises its consequent psychological importance to us as viewers.

15 For example, a 'performative' utterance is one that can be understood as an action, not just as speech, a notion that derives from J. L. Austin (1971) *How To Do Things with Words*. Andrew Parker and Eve Kosofsky Sedgwick utilise this idea in relation to theatrical (and other) performances in *Performativity and Performance* (1995). 'Performativity' in the field of feminist theory refers to the notion that gender is separate from biological sex and is instead a mediated, socialised 'performance' – i.e. one may be female, but one must 'perform' femininity. See Judith Butler, *Gender Trouble* (1990). I suggest links between the Butler's notion of 'performativity' and my own (as outlined in this chapter) in my discussion of *Moll Flanders* (1996) in Part II.

16 In the early days of television, these two performances were united, as programmes were broadcast live. Television thus has a history of 'performance' in a way that cinema does not.

17 I use the word 'illusion' here because the idea that the audience either 'suspends disbelief', or engenders a 'false belief' in the filmic representation before them, is still prevalent in film theory. However, I would argue that such a theory of audience engagement cannot be maintained in view of the model of television viewing I am elaborating

here. The analysis offered in this book supports the notion of a more active engagement with television programmes; an 'imagining' process based on the visuals presented. This is not the place to develop a detailed account of audience engagement and imagining or to assess its advantages over a model based on the 'belief' paradigm. I would refer the interested reader to Noël Carroll, *Theorising the Moving Image* (1996), Gregory Currie, *Image and Mind* (1995) and Murray Smith, *Engaging Characters* (1995), in the first instance.

18 A note for the interested: the unknown actress was indeed Bonham-Carter, playing the pivotal role of 'lady at cricket match'.

19 If our mode of engagement is (mis)understood as one of 'belief' (of whatever kind: false, 'true' or temporary) in what we are seeing on the screen – belief in the representation of the past as it is seen there – then clearly these intrusive hiatuses, these moments when we are brought back to the present, reminded of the text's performative and contemporary nature, are of great concern. These breaks in the diegetic flow would disrupt our false beliefs, creating in us momentary irritation, even confusion; if we had to engender such beliefs in order to gain pleasure from a screen text, then clearly our regular television/film viewing would be fraught with displeasure.

20 The key exposition of this argument is offered in Jean Baudrillard, *Simulacres et simulation* (1981), reprinted as 'The Precession of Simulacra' and 'The Orders of Simulacra' in Paul Foss, Paul Patton and Philip Bleitchman (trans.), *Simulations* (1983).

21 This notion of postmodern playfulness, visible in the intertextual and performative elements of the television text, is something I shall return to specifically in my discussion of *Moll Flanders* (Granada/WGBH, 1996) in Part II.

22 It is rare for the marketing of a genre to be discussed within a broadly conceptual, theoretical and interpretative discussion such as this one. A notable exception is Rick Altman, *Film/Genre* (1999).

23 It is also important to note that the 'televisual', as elucidated here, becomes more and more a medium-specific conceptualisation, differentiating television from other media.

24 There is no definitive account of the relationship between television and postmodernism. However, for useful discussions of the subject see P. Brooker and W. Brooker (eds), *Postmodern After-images*, (1997); J. Collins, 'Postmodernism and Television' in R. C. Allen (ed.), *Channels of Discourse, Reassembled* (1992), 327–53; and S. Connor, *Postmodernist Culture* (1989), 158–72.

25 Though some (postmodernist) theorists might suggest otherwise, the 'parallel worlds' that television offers, which exist irrespective of whether we 'access' them or not, are not unique to television; literature is comparable in this sense.

26 Not all theorists agree on the quintessential television genre. In contrast, Charlotte Brunsdon asks us to 'accept that soap opera is in some ways the paradigmatic television genre (domestic, continuous, contemporary, episodic, repetitive, fragmented, and aural)' (1990b: 67).

27 Clearly the existence of a 'disengaged' type of watching is also better reconciled with a conception of audience engagement that hinges on 'imagining' and not 'believing', as I suggested earlier in my discussion of television and performance.

28 There are necessary exclusions, then, from this study. For example, although I refer to a range of 'postmodern' theories about nostalgia, intertextuality and performance, I exclude many other theories of the postmodern: I do not discuss notions of difference, plurality, fragmentation, and so on. Similarly, I have not addressed other areas that appear equally pertinent to classic-novel adaptations, such as debates regarding national identity. This study is primarily text-based, focusing upon textually related concerns, rather than, for example, issues to do with audience(s), production or institutions (although these issues are sometimes referred to).

The adaptations

Introduction to Part II

Through the close study of four examples, Part II illuminates the recent development of a genre: the television classic-novel adaptation. Writers and students persist in analysing these programmes in terms of blinkered, often outdated, conceptions of them. In fact the genre is rapidly developing and, whilst recent adaptations confirm some of its key conventions, they also alter, undermine, challenge, even disregard others. It is probably not surprising that, broadly speaking, the more recent the adaptation, the greater the likelihood that it will exhibit an awareness of its televisuality and a reflexivity regarding its place in the genre. In fact, the 'genre' of the classic-novel adaptation undermines Feuer's sceptical view of the evolution of television genres (1992: 157), following closely that which she regards as a teleological model of filmic generic development: 'a genre begins with a naïve version of its particular cultural mythology, then develops toward an increasingly self-conscious awareness of its own myths and conventions' (1992: 156).[1]

My particular choice of adaptations for close analysis was guided by each programme's wider generic significance. I have deliberately chosen four very different adaptations, for to do so is to emphasise the eclectic and sometimes contradictory nature of this genre, something that is frequently overlooked by theorists and critics. Chapters 5 and 6 are concerned with the establishment and consolidation of the genre during the 1980s and early 1990s, Chapters 7 and 8 with the later stages of generic development described above. Both *Brideshead Revisited* (ITV, 1981) and *Pride and Prejudice* (BBC, 1995) are in an important sense 'traditional', but the increasing influence of the televisual upon the genre is apparent through a comparison of the two. Whilst *Brideshead* attempts to deny its televisual context, rooting itself in the (literary) past, the later *Pride and Prejudice* partly surrenders itself to the extended televisual context. *The Fortunes and Misfortunes of Moll Flanders* (ITV, 1996) and *The Tenant of Wildfell Hall* (BBC, 1996) exhibit reflectiveness and reflexivity, revisiting and challenging generic traditions in very different ways. *Moll Flanders* wholeheartedly embraces its televisual identity, actively employing tele-visual features and appearing to reject traditional generic conventions. In contrast, *Wildfell Hall* seems at first glance to return to the recognisable generic microcosm of the classic-novel adaptation, but in fact thought-fully subverts and questions accepted features of the genre.

My discussion of the development of this genre is overtly based upon the alternative, non-comparative model of adaptation proposed in Part I, and assumes that there are many features of adaptations that refer not to a literary source but to previous adaptations or other films or pro-grammes. Ed S. Tan's delineation of sources of pleasure in film texts is employed as a rough framework for the study of this genre. Tan writes that 'there are two sources of primary satisfaction specific to the feature film: the first is the fictional world depicted by the film; the second derives from the technical-stylistic qualities of the medium' (1996: 32). I would argue that his comments apply equally to television programmes.[2] By exploring a genre in terms of its 'sources of satisfaction' one enables a focus on the generic traits which characterise the programmes them-selves, and which make them enjoyable. Thus to seek out 'sources of satisfaction' is to facilitate the generic analysis advocated in Part I.

In fact, though I refer (above) to these programmes as examples of a 'genre', it is perhaps more true to conceive of them as being part of a microcosm – a 'generic world', created and maintained by a continuity of shared content, style and structuring mood(s). This generic microcosm thus exhibits a certain solidity, a reassuring order, but it is necessarily affected by its place in the televisual context described in the previous chapter. The genre's locus has affected its development – at first through its conflict with its own televisuality, then (more recently) through its acceptance of this feature and an increasing interplay between the two 'worlds'; both the conflict and interplay can be seen within classic-novel adaptations themselves. The source of the genre's appeal and cultural significance is thus rooted in its identity and locus: it constitutes a distin-guishable generic microcosm within the televisual context.

Therefore, in turning to recent examples of the genre, I shall reveal these programmes as sites of interaction or interplay between the dis-courses of these two worlds, and consider the implications of each adapta-tion for contemporary cultural discourses about the past, the present, television and, reflexively, the genre itself. The resultant 'meanings' of the programmes are consequently diverse and ambiguous: there is no mono-lithic ideological bias inherent in the genre, nor can it be simplistically characterised as stuffy, institutionalised and elitist. The genre is growing, developing, flourishing. It is full of life.

Notes

1 It could be argued that to characterise the changes a genre undergoes in 'evolutionary' terms is problematic, as Altman (1999) argues. However, the reader can challenge the broadly evolutionary model implied here without invalidating my discussion of the development of this genre and my analyses of individual programmes.

2 Tan's comments are especially apt when applied to a genre such as classic-novel adaptations, which are almost always shot on film and exhibit cinematic traits, as I shall discuss shortly.

Brideshead Revisited (1981)

5

In 1981 the mournful notes of a plangent, romantic theme tune intro-
duced television audiences to the whispered messages of national loss and
decay that echo through Evelyn Waugh's threnody on the decline and fall
of the great house of Brideshead. This story of nostalgic sensuality, frustrated desires, corrupted principles and lost prospects was presented with
all the splendour that costume drama can provide. (Hewison, 1987: 51)[1]

Brideshead Revisited has served as a benchmark for television classic-novel
adaptations ever since its first broadcast. Additionally, *Brideshead*'s attempts at fidelity unintentionally provided an instigation of various traits of
content, style and mood which still define the genre today.[2] Yet in some
ways the serial is anomalous. Most notably, the novel *Brideshead Revisited*
by Evelyn Waugh (1945) is not one of those nineteenth-century classics
upon which this genre typically relies. As Giddings *et al.* have observed,
'of the many thousands of novels available to the programme- and filmmaker, the nineteenth century novel appears perennially attractive. Indeed,
[it] forms the core of the BBC Classic Serial output' (1990: 28). It is rather
curious, then, that the programme which, more than any other, established the generic identity of the traditional television classic-novel
adaptation was based upon a book written during the Second World War.
Similarly, E. M. Forster's books, which provided the inspiration for Merchant Ivory's four defining 'heritage films' of the 1980s, are published
alongside Waugh's as 'modern classics'.[3] The title 'classic' is indicative of
a widespread, relatively recent acceptance that Waugh's and (especially)
Forster's novels are 'good literature': novels are only regarded as modern
classics if they are still esteemed a reasonable number of years after initial
publication. Sandy Craig alludes to the reputation of Waugh's *Brideshead*
in the *Listener*, when she argues that what 'separates *Brideshead Revisited*
[the television serial] ... from the common herd' is that it is 'an adaptation
not just of any old novel but of a work of literature' (1983: 31). In addition,
Brideshead is a 'popular' classic: well known and well liked. Kingsley

Amis, who stated that it was 'the worst' of Waugh's *oeuvre*, nevertheless remarked that 'long before the Granada TV serial came along it was his most enduringly popular novel; the current Penguin imprint is the nineteenth in its line' (1981: 1352). It is possible that the adaptation of *Brideshead* itself helped to reinforce a popular perception that the source novel is a modern classic. The place of the serial within a now-established genre of 'classic-novel adaptations' retrospectively places *Brideshead* the source novel alongside novels whose adaptations are in the same genre: *Emma*, *Pride and Prejudice*, *Great Expectations*, and so on.[4]

The television serial *Brideshead* was highly successful. Contemporary commentators did not stint in their praise: 'An outstandingly strong production' (Saynor, 1982: 56); 'a production ... grand both in spectacle and performance' (Yakir, 1982: 58); 'It was, at worst, an illuminated reading to glorious pictures, at best some of the sharpest and most reson-ant drama seen on television this year, and at all times so far above the competition ... that one wondered where that competition had gone to' (Ratcliffe, 1982: 52). Excepting the familiar slight about the 'glorious pictures', most critics and scholars were full of praise (if occasionally grudging) for the serial.[5] Even the *Evelyn Waugh Newsletter* praised 'the splendid TV production of *Brideshead Revisited*' (Doyle, 1982: 1). Dan Yakir reported that

> Recently, when John Schlesinger watched a preview of *Brideshead Revisited*, he was heard to exclaim, 'This is where the British movie industry is!' Schlesinger – who started in television – may well be right. At a time when British cinema is barely beginning to recover from years of economic and artistic paralysis, British television is thriving. *Brideshead Revisited* gives the medium a respectability it has seldom enjoyed. (1982: 59)

Brideshead may have drawn upon film genres – the period film, the heri-tage film, the costume drama – but its success suggested that television could achieve parity of cultural status with film on its own terms.[6]

Within scholarly reviews of the programme, comparative criticism is apparent, although, surprisingly for the early 1980s, comparisons with the source novel do not dominate the articles. It seems reasonable that most writers noted the programme's fidelity to the book. As James Saynor wrote, 'a common and unrefuted remark about *Brideshead* is that it is "like watching the novel". Rarely has the television dramatist been so passive: practically nothing has been added and nothing taken away' (1982: 57). Nick Roddick concurs: 'John Mortimer's adaptation is so faithful and complete that at times it seems to be not so much adapting as transferring the whole text to television' (1982: 58), as does William Boyd: 'it is scrupu-lously faithful to the original' (1982b: 26). Mortimer admitted that fidelity was his intention: 'what I aimed at wasn't so much a drama as giving people the feeling that they're *reading* a long novel' (italics in original); the director, Charles Sturridge, stated that 'we used [Waugh's] dialogue almost verbatim. Ninety-six percent of the words you hear on the screen are his' (Yakir, 1982: 58). Given these facts, a comparative analysis of the programme is certainly justified, and, indeed, Boo Allen's unpublished Ed.D thesis offers an extended analysis within the comparative approach: 'A Study of Evelyn Waugh's *Brideshead Revisited* as Compared to the Telefilm Version'.[7] Less sustained comparisons are offered in contemporary scholarly reviews. In retrospect, however, these comparisons reveal that it was the programme-makers' aim of fidelity that inadvertently gave rise to now-established generic traits with which we are familiar. So, whilst critics understandably attributed the key features of *Brideshead Revisited* (1981) to fidelity to the source novel, from the vantage point of the twenty-first century it is clear that the nature of Waugh's novel and the ways in which the programme-makers attempted to achieve equivalences with it are in fact more notable in terms of establishing an important television genre.

Pace and style

According to most critics, the serial was faithful to Waugh's book in content, style (in particular, pace) and mood. As described above, the events and dialogue of the book are reproduced in the serial almost completely (although Charles Ryder's commentary, transferred to voice-over, had to be considerably reduced, it is generally conceded that the reduction was achieved with little loss of meaning). Though this was broadly commended, Saynor argued of the programme-makers' strict fidelity to the book that the 'cost in television terms … is the almost total lack of pace that results' and that *Brideshead* would therefore have 'a reputation for slowness' (1982: 57, 58); Boyd also argued that the adaptation's fidelity would mean that 'the charge of tedium is sure to be levelled' (1982b: 26). Indeed, *Brideshead* is 'slow paced': the two-hour first episode opens with Charles's recollections of his arrival at Oxford, and extends only to the end of his first term there; once the charismatic Sebastian leaves the story at the end of Episode Five (appearing only briefly in Episode Seven, in a Moroccan hospital), the final six episodes move even more slowly, with Episode Six consisting of an extended flashback of Julia's married life, and Episodes Eight to Ten almost exclusively charting the ultimately (and patently) futile relationship between Charles and Julia. Roddick summarises: 'the rhythms (and also the dead periods) of the novel become those of the television serial' (1982: 58).

It is not just the narrative development that is slow: this pace is echoed by the manipulation of the camera, which moves little within shots, and the editing, which is sparse. Though we are treated to montages – of Oxford, Venice and Brideshead – they are not rapid juxtapositions of images, but lingering series of decorative shots. At other times the slowness of the narrative, camerawork and editing combine to produce a scene so lacking in visual stimulation that it is reminiscent of the 1970s style of adaptation: Cordelia's lengthy explanation to Charles of Sebastian's exploits since he left Brideshead takes up twelve minutes of screen time and, unlike earlier scenes with Sebastian and Charles, though there are some scenic long-shots and a brief flashback, the scenery upon which we are focused is that of a fairly featureless wintry English landscape in hues of dull green and brown. Apart from an initial spectacular crane shot of the house, which pans, depresses and gradually zooms to find Cordelia and Sebastian walking through the nearby wood, the movement of the camera within shots is restricted to following the two characters as they walk – it does not create movement of its own, denying us Tan's 'second source of satisfaction' (as described in the Introduction to Part II). As Roddick noted, 'for all the adjectives heaped on it at the time of the first episode – sumptuous, magnificent, lavish and so on – [it] is not an extravagant production visually or stylistically: [with some exceptions] it is soberly shot, unobtrusively edited and visually coherent' (1982: 59).

In addition, in this scene Cordelia and Charles are dressed in colours that recede into those of the background and provide no visual appeal such as that offered by Sebastian himself. Visual interest is underplayed in order to focus attention on what Cordelia is saying. This 'wordiness' is echoed in 'Jeremy Irons' ponderous voice-over' (Saynor, 1982: 57) which frames the scene, and which carries us through the entire serial. Both dialogue and voice-over are used to reveal the characters' feelings, and are thus informative and emotionally significant, but the effect upon a television presentation of such 'literariness' combined with unadventurous filming is an inevitable lethargy.

The serial's trademark music also lends a certain gravitas to the proceedings, eliciting rare praise from Amis: 'I think the music is just right, grand, sad and rather brassy' (1981: 1352) (though he couldn't resist the implied criticism of the serial's supposed 'showiness' in his use of the adjective 'brassy'); Saynor also noted the 'liberal doses of Geoffrey Burgon's analgesic, if occasionally flagging music' (1982: 57). In fact, the music is vital to the mood of the piece, for it delimits the potential mood of the viewer, allowing for some responses, discouraging others. We are encouraged to experience subtle alterations in mood rather than sudden changes of emotion. As Roddick puts it, 'Geoffrey Burgon's music, minutely varying a major theme, shifts the mood from wistful nostalgia to uncomplicated happiness to gathering gloom' (1982: 59).

Whilst Saynor, Roddick and Boyd express a concern that *Brideshead*'s 'slowness' is a flaw on television, with Saynor specifically arguing that it is 'untelevisual', this feature in fact consolidated the unusual pace of classic-novel adaptations as a sign not of bad television, but of 'quality' television. This pace acts as a marker of distinction, in its dual sense of merit and differentiation (the serial's differentiation being enhanced by its 'wordiness' – an attempt at 'literariness'). At the time, Saynor, commenting on the use of voice-over, music and leisurely pace, noticed that 'the form bestowed on the dramatisation by this approach seems unique in the context of serial drama' (1982: 57). However, there was very little speculation on the potential for further development of this 'unique' presentation. Whilst Saynor and other writers should be commended for their recognition of the ways in which the text drew upon other television genres, they were perhaps too eager to attempt to reappropriate *Brideshead* into a recognisable television genre: costume drama (Hewison, 1987: 51, and Craig, 1983: 31: 'all the old familiar conventions of the genre remain intact') or soap opera (Saynor, 1982: 58: 'the soap opera model of television literary dramatisations'), or at least a film type (Roddick, 1982: 59: 'Hollywood').

The sedate pace of the narrative in *Brideshead*, though arising from fidelity to the source book, was subsequently adopted as a generic stylistic trait, along with other peculiarities of style such as its particular use of framing and editing. In its pace there is a textual resonance of its connection with literature, which is seen as a more leisurely, measured and thoughtful pursuit, for reading is carried out more slowly and quietly than watching television (or 'should be' – Thomson begs that we spare Jane Austen's novels 'the rape of speed reading' (1981: 74)). Robin Nelson praises the slow pace of *Middlemarch* (BBC, 1994) for exactly this reason: that it encourages a similar reading/viewing strategy in viewers to that which he believes the source book elicits in its readers; 'it is this aspect of the series which, with some success, attempts to retain the textures and moral seriousness of the novel' (1997: 147).

Brideshead's languorous pace makes good use of these associations. The slow, careful style indicates the amount of independent thought and imaginative activity that the audience is expected to contribute whilst watching: 'it demands an active and imaginative response from viewers' (Nelson, 1997: 147). At a time when we live our daily lives at a speed unimaginable to previous generations, a certain respect and admiration is reserved for those activities which demand that we take time to appreciate them slowly. Thus, whilst the filmic aspects of adaptations differentiate them from 'ordinary' television, their un-contemporary slowness acts to distance them from both fast-paced television and frenetic modern life – the present. In addition, their measured pace is defined negatively against youth culture and consumer culture, both of which value speed; classic-novel adaptations thus implicitly reject the new, the young, emphasising their connections with the durable, the old, the past.

Later adaptations are based less heavily on dialogue, rejecting more forcefully the 'literariness' of 1970s adaptations, but just as the cautious pace and the slow, admiring gaze of the camera employed in *Brideshead* have persisted within the genre, so too has the object of the camera's gaze: the 'heritage' so lovingly displayed in the first half of the serial. Again, *Brideshead* remained faithful to its source, but 'where the novelist can refer to those details in a description which are significant or relevant, the screen image is forced to introduce a whole array of background information' (Giddings *et al.*, 1990: 18). Waugh's descriptions became a wealth of objects for the camera's gaze – and to different effect than in the book. The objects (buildings, furniture, ornaments, etc.), when presented on film, are real or simulated relics which can perform the function David Lowenthal (1985) ascribes to them: providing valuable, possibly over-valued, links between past and present.

The past

> Aesthetes rather than historians are responsible for constituting our notions of period. (Samuel, 1994: 21)

> Inevitably, something happens on the way from the page to the screen that changes the meaning of the past as it is understood by those of us who work in words. (Rosenstone, 1988: 1173)

Whilst Raphael Samuel notes the importance of visual representations to our understanding of the past, Robert Rosenstone's statement about transferring written history into screen representations of the past unwittingly echoes the concerns of scholars who fear that adaptations alter the meanings of their source texts.[8] Their comments are a part of a relatively recent surge of interest in on-screen representation(s) of the past.[9] Many theorists have sought to explicate the popularity and power of classic-novel adaptations through precisely this feature: their representations of the past and the way in which these representations are filmed. This ongoing concern is a valid and constructive response to a prime aspect of this genre's aesthetic, dramatic and emotional appeal.

Brideshead exhibits a purposeful fidelity not just to its source text but also to the era in which the story is set. Kerr argues that

> in classic serials props are employed specifically as signifiers of the past and its faithful and meticulous reconstruction. Such ambitions of authenticity function to factify the fiction, literally to prop it up, performing a positivist role as the tangible trace of a lost era. There are different ways of achieving such aims but the commonest is simply that of painstaking historical accuracy. (1982: 13)

He thus highlights several salient elements: the way in which classic-novel adaptations are primarily concerned with representations of the past; the importance of their careful reconstructions of the past to their aura of 'quality'; and the fact that although the audience recognises the stories as fictitious, it accepts the validity of the programmes' representations of the past. Most significantly, Kerr implies the necessity of adaptations' reliance upon representations of the past, because they are based upon books written in past eras; due to the difference in period, where Jane Austen describes a drawing room, we see a reconstruction of a room from a past era, such as we usually see only in National Trust country homes.[10] Fredric Jameson, similarly, argues that a novel written in the past 'has necessarily become for us a historical one: for its present has become our past' (1991: 285). Thus the (faithful) adaptation of a novel written in the past ineluctably becomes a representation of a past world and is viewed in historical terms; there is an unavoidable distance between the time of our viewing and the era of the novel/adaptation.

However, the fact that a source text was written in (and is set in) a long-gone era does not necessarily mean that the screen adaptation of it will be. Consider the innumerable ways in which Shakespeare's plays have been adapted for stage and screen – often through radical updating.[11] Even relatively 'straightforward' adaptations of the plays, which leave the source text (words) fairly unaltered and claim fidelity to text and spirit, are often presented in a different era to that in which they were originally set.[12] Yet adapters of classic novels tend to be less creative with this aspect of their sources, preferring to present the story within its intended temporal setting. Close attention is paid by the makers of these adaptations to what is often called 'authenticity' (period accuracy): costumes, hairstyles, buildings, landscapes, furnishings, modes of travel, behaviour and speech are usually presented as being faithful not only (or not even) to the source text, but to the era with which the source text was concerned. The audience understands this to be a fundamental element of classic-novel adaptations – thus there are as many complaints, comments and criticisms made about inaccuracy in period detail as about inaccuracy in details taken from the source book. Indeed, the genre's obsession with such representations justifies the frequent inclusion of these programmes within the general group 'period drama'.

Some might claim that the existence of this widespread, apparently purposeful fidelity justifies an approach to adaptations that assumes the intention of fidelity and judges the adaptations on such terms; it might be argued that this is evidence that an adaptation tries to maintain strong links with the literary source. However, to take such an approach would be to conflate the apparent desire for historical accuracy (a desire to represent faithfully a particular era) with an assumed desire for fidelity to a source text. The two are not necessarily related; Cartmell even differentiates adaptations that move 'narrative from one textual site to another' from those that translate 'history and notions of the past into film' (1996: 2). After all, adapters are frequently accused of being deliberately 'unfaithful' to other, central elements of the source novels. Why, then, are adapters so concerned with *historical* fidelity, above other kinds? Why do adaptations tend to be set firmly in the past, apparently immune to the updating process? The extent of temporal fidelity within this genre suggests that it is more than a stylistic choice or convention, and that there is some other, more fundamental motive for the over-emphasis on the 'accurate' portrayal of (mostly) nineteenth-century England.

The answers to the above questions can surely be found in the seemingly widespread desire we have to connect with our (national) past[13] – something Robert Hewison calls 'a profound cultural need' (1987: 28).[14] The form this 'connection' takes has been typically conceptualised as nostalgia, though close analyses of the adaptations discussed in this book challenge this broad characterisation. However, one might reasonably concur with Wollen that within many films and programmes 'there would seem to be a set of ambivalent impulses driving the search for connections with the past', and that such texts offer 'distinctive routes to the past' (1991: 180, 187). It seems likely that the enduring popularity and influence of *Brideshead* can be explained partly in terms of its fulfilling a desire to forge imaginative links with the past.

It could be argued that the pictorial arts have always afforded us a degree of access to the past which non-pictorial arts cannot provide.[15] Paintings and photographs offer us additional visual clues about the people and places of the past.[16] Modern-day film and television can be seen as adding a further dimension to our understanding, for they allow us to engage in imagining what the past looked like, with the aid of the text being presented to us; this process is what Hayden White refers to as 'historiophoty' (the representation of the past through visual media), in comparison with historiography (written history) (1988: 1193). Being re-created, television programmes and films can bring together elements and facts known to be true, and re-present them to us, with the added dimension of realistic movement, as a 'slice' of the past, giving us an impression of what the past was like. They can 'recover all the past's liveliness' (Raack in Rosenstone, 1995: 26).[17]

Although the audience understands that these re-presentations are mediated and re-created, there is nevertheless a feeling that 'quality dramas' such as classic-novel adaptations achieve a certain level of accuracy – that there is a point at which their visual depictions of the past are fairly true to life. Whilst Barrie Bullen describes the audience's trust in terms of an '*illusion* of historicity' (1990: 52) (my emphasis), Hayden White seems more open-minded: 'Imaginistic (and especially photographic and cinematic) evidence provides a basis for a reproduction of the scenes and atmosphere of past events much more accurately than any derived from verbal texts alone' (1998: 1194).

The division of opinion here is due not to prejudices either against or in favour of the visual media, but to differing perceptions of the subject in hand: Bullen is concerned with history, whilst White is writing about the past. If history 'proper' is understood as the attempt to record, evaluate and narrativise details of the events, people and places of the past, no one can justifiably claim that screen fictions like classic-novel adaptations offer the audience access to history, for they are not based on real-life events but on fictive stories. Yet these programmes do depict the 'past' – a far more abstract concept than that of history – and one could even argue that just as these screen fictions attempt to represent the past, so too does written history;[18] the difference lies in the particular aspects of the past they attempt to represent, and the possibilities for representation open to them. As Wollen suggests, 'as dramatic narratives they are not the work of history-the-discipline, but the fictions allow millions access to knowledge about history through representation' (1991: 187). And Raphael Samuel argues, 'in the present day, television ought to have pride of place in any attempt to map the unofficial sources of historical knowledge' (1994: 13). However, by 'historical knowledge' he does not refer simply to the television audience's accumulation of 'facts' about history (through non-fiction programmes), but also to our development of perceptions of past times: our 'sense of the past, at any given point of time, is quite as much a matter of history as what happened in it' (Samuel, 1994: 15). In the generation and modification of this more vague abstraction (our 'sense of the past'), the generic microcosm of classic-novel adaptations – a visually accessible 'past world' – plays a vital role. As Rosenstone writes, 'in privileging visual and emotional data and simultaneously downplaying the analytic, the motion picture is subtly ... altering our very sense of the past' (1995: 32).

Thus Samuel and Rosenstone utilise expanded notions of 'history' to recognise the importance of images and the imagination to our sense of the past. It is with these aspects of audience engagement that so many theorists and critics are concerned, for they believe that it is because of our desire to connect with the past that, at the level of trust, of faith in the well-intentioned truthfulness of the recreation, we fall victim to the conscious ideological motives of the filmmaker or his/her unconscious ideological notions about history, the past, the present and society.[19] For, as Giddings *et al.* suggest, 'the media invite us to look back at our past through the refractions, flaws and distortions of our present' (1990: 35).

So what happens to the past when it is represented in the television adaptation of *Brideshead*? The type of relics presented gain greater significance when they are displayed to us visually, rather than described verbally: 'homes are middle-sized mansions with impressive staircases (for entrances and exits) and rooms stacked with furnishing ransacked from Sotheby's' (Craig, 1983: 31). The nature of the relics, the way in which they are filmed, and their presentation within a diegetic framework of nostalgia, reconfigures them not just as mementoes of the past but as examples of 'heritage'.

Displaying echoes of contemporary postmodern theory Hewison opined, 'Actual locations took on a hyper-reality: Oxford University became a Gothic jewel in a Renaissance setting, its honey-coloured stones (refaced in the 1960s) glowing in the warm sunshine of late adolescent memory. Venice rose out of the mists of soft-focus in a sparkle of tiny waves' (1987: 51). Thus *Brideshead* 'evoked a rich material past made all the more desirable by the knowledge that, except in memory, all this was lost' (Hewison, 1987: 51). The appeal of *Brideshead*'s distinctive look, arising from its fidelity to the source novel, consolidated generic conventions of style, pace and content that would be drawn upon by subsequent productions. What was innovative at the time is now accepted as conventional. But even more importantly, *Brideshead*'s fidelity to the *mood* of the novel guaranteed the nostalgic mood that was also to become generic.

Mood and nostalgia

Critics agreed that 'the tone of the novel has been preserved to a quite remarkable extent' (Roddick, 1982: 58), and the 'tone' of Waugh's book was undeniably nostalgic, as Waugh himself stated in his introduction to the 1960 edition: 'the book is infused with a kind of gluttony, for food and wine, for the splendours of the recent past, and for rhetorical and ornamental language' (1962: 7). The importance of nostalgia to Waugh's novel is clear: 'One of the themes of *Brideshead Revisited* was Waugh's sense that the aristocratic world of the Marchmain's [*sic*] was moribund'

(Saynor, 1982: 59); it was driven by 'nostalgia for a vanished era' (Boyd, 1982b: 25). Other commentators noted that, just as the Second World War explained Waugh's longing for a previous, simpler age, the particular context of 1981, when the adaptation was produced, was 'the ideal time to be recreating [the nostalgic fiction] *Brideshead*' (Saynor, 1982: 58).

The adapters' desire for fidelity, and the favourable context for nostalgia, guaranteed that the adaptation would be infused with a nostalgic mood that reflected the one in Waugh's book. However, the serial had to use televisual techniques, not literary ones, to achieve this, and these techniques have been appropriated, reused and developed in subsequent adaptations. Rather than conducting an extended search for equivalences between novel and adaptation, it is more constructive to accept the adapters' aim of creating a nostalgic mood on television, and explore how they have done so.

Continuities with the heritage film

One of the ways in which *Brideshead* attempts to recreate the mood of its source novel is to draw upon a contemporary film genre: the heritage film, as epitomised in the films of Ismail Merchant and James Ivory (Merchant Ivory Productions), sometimes derisively characterised as the 'Laura Ashley' school of filmmaking.[20] The influence of Merchant Ivory upon the genre of classic-novel adaptations is noted by Robert Emmet Long: 'the 1990s saw an upsurge of period movies, adaptations from classic novels by such writers as Jane Austen and E. M. Forster, which were sometimes said to be riding Merchant Ivory's coattails' (1997: 206). Long acknowledges the defining importance of the films' characteristic images and style beyond the films which they themselves made, quoting a critic who, at that time, complained that 'we live in an age of Merchant Ivory' (Long, 1997: 207).

Andrew Higson, observing the generic features of the heritage film, ascribes to the genre a deeper ideological function, and offers an analysis of the kind of relationship that it creates between the audience and the past. He utilises the notion of 'heritage' as being a limited collection of historical artefacts, which these films display, and argues that the display of heritage and the style in which this display is filmed work to create in the viewer a specific relation to the past depicted: namely, nostalgia.[21] Higson states that such programmes and films[22] display 'a museum aesthetic: the particular visual style of the films is designed to showcase these various heritage attractions, to display them in all their supposed authenticity', and thus concludes that 'one of the central pleasures of the heritage film is the artful and spectacular projection of an elite, conservative vision of the national past' (Higson, 1996: 233). Thus the style of filming is linked to a specific purposeful goal: to allow us to gaze at, admire, even fetishise the heritage settings before us. In contrast with Kerr's analysis of the ideological import of classic-novel adaptations, Higson's arguments are based upon solid and careful observations of the films themselves. Thus, he also offers the best characterisation yet of this genre in terms of its specific generic style – its aesthetic particularities.

Higson's work on 1980s and early 1990s film adaptations argues that the diegetically unnecessary (or at least excessive) lingering shots of various parts of English 'heritage' – landscapes, houses, furnishings, even ornaments – work not to further the narrative, build a discourse, etc., but to beautify and romanticise the objects portrayed thus, and infuse the audience with a sense of appreciation of and pleasure in these articles and a longing for the days for which they are referents; he characterises this emotional response as 'nostalgia' for a long-lost past. Higson does not deny the 'accuracy' of period detail – far from it: the details of set, costumes, props, and so on are carefully researched, and are combined to form fairly accurate (though very selective) reproductions of the era concerned. Rather, this level of accuracy is of some concern to him, for it is the combination of a faithful reproduction of period, and a heavily stylised and emotive filmic style, that endows these films with their ideologically reactionary force.[23]

The notion of 'heritage' is regarded by Higson as a bourgeois creation which valorises the cultural heritage of the middle and upper classes over that of the working classes; it is thus conceived as being closely allied to the creation and maintenance of a particular class identity. This point of view is not ubiquitous (see John Corner and Sylvia Harvey (1991) and Raphael Samuel (1994)[24]) but is widely held. This conceptualisation of heritage implies that classic-novel adaptations are not just working ideologically through the use of nostalgia, but also through the efforts to uphold a bourgeois cultural identity. Giddings, for example, links the depiction of 'heritage' with upper-middle-class identity when he argues that 'our class structure ... seriously distort[s] our perceptions of the past' (Giddings *et al.*, 1990: 35).[25]

In classic-novel adaptations the settings are a central, defining feature, and are frequently noted for their importance in building up the representations of 'heritage' deemed so reactionary by critics. Traditionally, classic-novel adaptations on film have relied upon both indoor and outdoor settings which can be roughly divided into three types: interior long shots of beautiful rooms full of heritage objects; exterior long shots of the central house or houses in the story in their (usually rural) locations;

and exterior long shots of untouched rural landscapes, characterised by rolling hills, hedges, farmland, some trees and an expanse of clear sky. Higson summarises these generic shots thus: 'large and small country houses, and the more select landscapes, interior designs and furnishings conserved by such bodies as English Heritage and the National Trust' (1996: 233). All three types of long shot are held for slightly longer than normal 'establishing' long shots generally are; this slowing of pace through extended shot length is characteristic. The shots are also, in general, beautifully framed: the interior shots appear well-balanced, if not near-symmetrical; the houses are central in the frames which include them; the landscape shots are framed as landscape paintings might be. The conventional style of filming is accurately described by Higson: 'the use of long takes and deep focus, and long and medium shots rather than close-ups, produces a restrained aesthetic of display' (1996: 234). Julianne Pidduck also asserts that 'such a staging of iconic "nostalgic" English countryside informs a 1990s costume drama aesthetic' (1998: 386).[26]

Generic heritage long-take long shots, originating in the film adaptations upon which Higson's work was based, lend themselves well to the filmic medium. The sense of expansiveness and tranquillity that these shots convey is well suited to the wide film screen, and each shot is held long enough for us to explore, or 'feast our eyes upon', the picture – to imagine the actuality of the scene before us. The use of wide-angle lenses and deep focus accentuate the detail of each extensive set. The rich colour of film highlights the somewhat ethereal quality of these shots, and adds to their general power and impressiveness. In view of these shots often being diegetically superfluous, it could be said that they favour impressiveness over expressiveness. As Hipsky writes,

> in these movies the setting is overpowering – is in fact *superfluous* to plot, history, and character portrayal. We are given an overdose of what I would call 'circumambience'; we do not need it to transport us realistically back into the period depicted. Instead, circumambience functions as escapist fantasy, spectacular *excess* of signification that is unironically meant to provide great sensual pleasure. (1994: 102) (italics in original)

The affective power of these images depends upon the viewer establishing a particular relationship with the text. Higson argues that 'the emphasis on spectacle rather than narrative draws attention to the surface of things, producing a typically postmodern loss of emotional affect: emotional engagement in a drama is sacrificed for loving recreations of the past' (1993: 118). In fact, our emotional engagement is with that 'second source of satisfaction', which 'derives from the technical-stylistic qualities of the medium' (Tan, 1996: 32), and our viewing pleasures are rooted in an appreciation of aesthetic beauty. As this implies, our 'gaze' upon these programmes is rather detached, somewhat distant. As Michael Roemer writes, 'a sequence of beautifully composed shots tends to leave the audience outside the frame – spectators who are continually aware of the director's fine eye for composition' (1971: 49); this relates to Higson's 'public gaze' (1993: 117), with which we regard the heritage displayed in the text. One might assume this to be exacerbated in the case of television, for our mode of engagement with television texts in general is understood to be distracted, in the sense that we 'glance' rather than 'gaze' at the screen. Our distracted engagement with television could be considered to accentuate the detached nature of our gaze upon the landscapes, buildings and interiors of classic-novel adaptations like Brideshead.[27]

A television genre: moving away from the heritage film

The heritage film was evidently part of the wider pool of sources upon which the makers of Brideshead drew, in addition to the novelistic source text. This serial, and many later television classic-novel adaptations, aware of the emotional and aesthetic appeal of the heritage film, relied to a certain extent upon its conventions. Television adaptations have also made heavy use of other 'period' scenes which have now become generic: ballroom, or at least 'dancing', sequences; scenes of refined conversations over afternoon tea; sequences where characters travel by carriage or horseback across rolling countryside (the latter usually being reserved primarily for male characters). The reason for this expansion of set-piece period scenes, Nelson suggests, is that 'in a medium where landscape is restricted, the sumptuous interior settings and costumes are in themselves a feature of popular spectacle on television' (1997: 149). As we shall see, all these shot sequences and scenes occur and recur within the adaptations discussed in Part II, confirming and perpetuating generic conventions.

The shots and shot sequences which originated in films such as Merchant Ivory's were not simply transferred to the small screen but were successfully adopted by the new medium. Watching television is not a 'filmic' experience, but audiences were prepared to accept such shots as signifiers of good television drama and not just attempts to recreate the cinematic experience (though their cinematic roots are still part of their appeal). Audiences' acceptance of these shots as part of a television genre was in great part due to their appearance in Brideshead. Nor was the traffic between heritage film and television classic-novel adaptation one-way: Brideshead also employed then unestablished, now generic, shots such as the one of Charles and Sebastian punting, and the medium-long and long shots of the Oxford colleges where they spend their first two years to-gether; these shots reappeared in Merchant Ivory's *Maurice*, six years later. Moreover, generic shots such as these, variations of which now appear regularly in classic-novel adaptations and other period dramas, are even more clearly televisual: not only were they conceived on television, they continue to thrive there in both adaptations and non-period dramas.

Note, for example, the popular 'quality' drama series *Inspector Morse* (ITV, 1987–92, 1995) and its idiosyncratic shots of Oxford University and the surrounding countryside – often long or medium-long shots, often long takes, and often superfluous in terms of their supposed function as establishing shots. Richard Sparks notes these features of *Morse*, and ascribes to them familiar connotations:

> [they announce] that this is quality television. ... *Morse* is at times quite cinematic in its pleasures, especially in its sheer visual and aural richness and the rather un-televisually relaxed pace of its narrative development ... Having been made with evident, patient and expensive care, *Inspector Morse* invites patient and involved viewing. (1993: 90)[28]

Certain features – the 'cinematic' style, slow pace and high production values – that mark *Morse* as being of 'un-televisually' high quality, are those which also characterise the quality classic-novel adaptation. The myth-making power of such images was noted by that great commentator on popular culture, Alan Partridge: 'no-one had heard of Oxford before *Inspector Morse*'. Though ironic, this communicates to some degree the way in which historical cities like Oxford maintain their mystique through the display of their 'heritage' on television.[29]

More broadly, Charlotte Brunsdon directly relates 'the England of *Morse*' to that of other 'heritage' television programmes, including classic-novel adaptations such as *Brideshead Revisited* (1981) and *Pride and Prejudice* (1995), as well as period dramas like *The House of Eliott* (BBC, 1991–4) and modern-day programmes like *Lovejoy* (BBC, 1986–94). She argues that their 'representational domain [is] a certain image of England' and their 'dominant structure of feeling [is] an elegiac nostalgia' (Brunsdon, 1998: 230). Brunsdon also concretises the notion that these programmes deny their televisuality and contemporaneity: 'just as *Morse* in some ways denies the 1980s, so the series also, in these moments of visual splendour often matched by an operatic soundtrack, denies that it is television' (1998: 231). Thus, these generic 'heritage landscape' long shots, which emerged in part from film conventions, in part within tele-vision, and which *Brideshead* consolidated, have become television con-ventions which we expect to see not only in classic-novel adaptations but also in other types of 'quality drama' programme, where they are assumed to carry similar meanings.[30] The characteristic style and mood of the genre is so influential that it has even begun to permeate into classic-novel adaptations usually kept distinct: a notable example is the use of the generic 'heritage' shots and sequences in *Oliver Twist* (ITV, 1999), in contrast with the ordinarily distinctive, dark and gloomy feel central to traditional Dickens adaptations.

Brideshead revisited

Brideshead established a coherent and evocative microcosm: a past world, distinct from both the present day and more 'ordinary' television, and marked by nostalgia. Yet a closer exploration of the way in which nostalgic relations are structured within the programme encourages moderation, and even revision of accepted theories about heritage films and pro-grammes. *Brideshead* is undoubtedly 'nostalgic', but its nostalgia is directed, structured and particular. The serial establishes a nostalgic mood which is then reinforced at moments of emotional intensity – moments Greg M. Smith has named 'emotion markers' (Smith, 1999: 116). The nostalgic mood is overtly rooted in the diegesis, and nostalgia is encouraged in the viewer through eliciting his or her sympathy for the characters, and through the use of the emotive music and reflective pace. Interestingly, the programme utilises a limited number of particular objects that act as focal points for our feelings of nostalgia. Perhaps understandably, these foci are more tangible, more specific than those in the book – Charles's nostalgia is less for his youth, and for 'pre-war English Roman Catholicism' (Saynor, 1982: 56), than for Sebastian, Oxford and Brideshead as symbols of his past. The adaptation shares with the book its nostalgia for the past aristocracy, but while in the novel the Marchmains' residence epitomises this, the specific visual treatment of the house in the adaptation draws attention to the aristocrats' abode and effects as targets of nostalgia in themselves, rather than as representatives of a 'disappearing' social class (figure 1). Additionally, there is a curious but powerful intra-textual nostalgia which develops through the latter half of the serial, as I shall reveal shortly.

Brideshead is for the most part a sustained flashback. It opens with Charles Ryder as an older man, employed as an army officer: his charac-teristically sober voice-over, which carries us through all eleven episodes, recounting his feelings of loss, ennui and resignation. His words emphasise the importance of his past over his present: when asked by a senior officer what job he had before the war, his reply 'I was a painter, sir' is underscored by the introduction of 'the mournful notes of a plangent, romantic theme tune' (Hewison, 1987: 51), with the result that particular emotional significance is attached to his past; in comparison, Charles's attitude to his present life is summed up in his words 'I'll live it out.' The mood of these opening 'army' scenes is unsettled as well as reflective – a mood enhanced by the feeling that we are awaiting something. Frequent references are made to the preparations of the soldiers for their removal to an unknown destination (of which both Charles and his colleague Hooper are ignorant), whilst the ominous score that accompanies the soldiers' journey from base to terminus increases our sense of disquiet and our desire for the soldiers to arrive at their journey's end.

Of course, while Charles and the soldiers are unaware of their destination most viewers, through their knowledge of the source book (or at least its story) or their exposure to trailers featuring Brideshead, are not. The weighting of Charles's past over his present; the disconcerting sense of expectancy; the knowledge that the story must move to Brideshead; the use of unspectacular shot sizes, ranging from close-ups to medium shots; and the dull, earthy brown/green colours of the army base, with its small, featureless, rather depressing settings all work as mood cues to establish in the audience a desire to return to Charles's past – to beautiful surroundings, happier moments, more charismatic characters and youthful freedom. From the beginning, then, we perceive Charles's nostalgia for his past; we also wish for our anticipated imaginative return to this past. Through alignment with Charles and a careful use of colour, music and limited shot variation, the programme attempts to ensure our desire to 'return' to Brideshead and our consequent emotional and aesthetic appreciation of it.

When Charles is finally told that the place at which the squadron is encamped is Brideshead, the emotional focus of his nostalgia is specified: it is not his youth in general but his youth at Brideshead – the house becomes a concrete emblem of his loss.[31] The name of the house and its significance in Charles's past life are not just emphasised through his speech: 'I've been here before' and his thoughts (in voice-over): 'he had spoken a name that was so familiar to me'; 'I had been there before – I knew all about it'; again the serial's melancholy theme tune resounds at the mention of Brideshead, linking the house with the theme, and reinforcing the theme as an emotion cue. Charles's long-awaited gaze upon the house – shown through the now-familiar long-take long shot customarily used to display such impressive properties, and accompanied by the theme music – allows us to experience our own rush of satisfaction; the first generic shot of the serial acts entirely as one might expect: it provides that sudden burst of emotion necessary to maintain the wistful mood that we are beginning to identify as nostalgia. Roddick notes that the serial 'hold[s] back on purely visual sumptuousness until moments ... when some magical quality is needed' (1982: 59), considering this a stylistic technique; in fact, the 'moments' he accurately pinpoints act as emotion markers.

However, this shot, in its context as described above, deviates in one very important way from conventional descriptions of the genre. Higson argues that such shots are usually

> offered direct to the spectator, unmediated by any shots of characters within the diegesis looking at the view. Such shots in fact, *follow* the views, rather than preceding and thus motivating them ... In this way, the heritage culture becomes the object of a public gaze while the private gaze of the dramatis personae is reserved for romance: they almost never admire the quality of their surroundings. (1993: 117) (italics in original)

Yet in *Brideshead* the nostalgic gaze is diegetically motivated and personalised. Charles feels nostalgia for his past, and his mood (combined with his perceptual view) provides the justification for the lingering long shot that acts as an emotion marker for the audience. Any nostalgia we experience cannot be divorced from the text and its diegesis, for it is the mood that has been established in previous scenes that ensures that the audience desires and revels in the gaze themselves. As Anne-Marie Cook (1998) contends, in her critique of Higson's work, 'narrative regulates and directs our interpretation of mise-en-scène'. Thus there are significant particularities in the way in which the text addresses us and expresses and frames its nostalgia.

As the scenes of Charles's youth and his relationship with Sebastian Flyte are played out, two other key foci of emotion (ultimately, nostalgia) besides Brideshead are established: Oxford (University) and, even more significantly for the serial, Sebastian himself. The first focal point is perhaps more straightforward than the second. The narrative transfers us to Oxford via several long-take long shots, moving from cityscape to spires to college to quadrangle. Both these shots and subsequent scenes set in Oxford are softly lit, pictorially framed and accompanied by the haunting theme music. Ratcliffe compared the representation of Oxford in Waugh's source novel with that in the adaptation: 'The spell of delayed, eternal childhood at the University of Oxford, on the other hand, has rarely been so bewitchingly cast as in Waugh's novel, and by its absolute fidelity to the original ... the spell was cast again in the opening episodes to stunning, mesmerising effect' (1982: 53).

Again, although the makers' intention was fidelity, this stylised depiction of Oxford was so appealing that repetition has now confirmed it as generic (as discussed above). The serial's images of the Italian landscape have been appropriated in a similar way: the picturesque views of Sebastian's and Charles's trip to Italy (Venice) are echoed in Merchant Ivory's later *A Room with a View* (1985) and in the film *Where Angels Fear to Tread* (1991), directed by Sturridge. *Brideshead*'s epigrammatic portrayals of particular locales – the English country house, Oxbridge, the English and Italian countryside – were in great part responsible for the constitution of a clear generic microcosm to which later adaptations were faithful.[32]

At Oxford, crucially, amidst these soft-toned, golden images of the University, we are offered a glimpse of Sebastian, though his identity is not immediately revealed to us. He stands in the sunlight, framed symmetrically by an archway, so that the arch and foreground are dark whilst his bright blond hair, pale clothes and faithful teddy-bear Aloysius are bathed in a gentle golden light, lending him an angelic, almost ethereal air. (Anthony Andrews's 'angelic' light-blond hair was a deliberate addition to the on-screen Sebastian – in the novel Sebastian has dark brown hair, like Julia's.[33]) This is Sebastian as we shall always remember him. Our glimpse of him is significant, for his striking appearance, enhanced considerably by the way in which the shot is arranged, and by its place within shots of buildings and black-robed students, emphasises his importance, yet his difference from that which surrounds him; he seems 'someone too pure to live in the world, too ethereal and delicate to cope with harsh reality' (Toynton, 1998: 135). In fact, Sebastian 'symbolises' the world of the early part of the serial – the youthful, enchanting world in which he plays a central role.

The relationship that is formed between Sebastian and Charles dominates the first five episodes of the serial, which are rooted firmly within what we now understand to be the classic-novel adaptation's generic microcosm. The couple enjoy youthful frolics at Oxford, in the surrounding countryside and at Brideshead, and these episodes are regularly punctuated by romantic scenes such as Sebastian and Charles punting on the Isis, and having a picnic in a meadow (figure 2). Sebastian in particular is depicted in a loving way – lying on the ground, gazing up at the sky, with his hands clasped behind his distinctive shock of blond hair; pictured in medium shot with that sad, winsome smile whose poignant plea for understanding and consolation is seen only by Charles. In fact, Sebastian is regarded through Charles's perceptual and emotional point of view; he is the object of Charles's gaze and his fascination, whilst Charles's role in these five episodes is really only that of onlooker.[34] As the voice-over and the narrative have aligned us from the start with Charles, and continue to do so, we see Sebastian similarly: we may have sympathy with the latter, but we are aligned with the former.

When Sebastian rejects Charles, at Brideshead, concluding that he is 'no help', Charles ruminates:

As I drove away, I felt that I was leaving part of myself behind, and that wherever I went afterwards I should feel the lack of it, and search for it fruitlessly ... A door had shut, the low door in the wall I had sought and found in Oxford; open it now and I should find no enchanted garden. ... I have left behind illusion, I said to myself. Henceforth I live in a world of three dimensions – with the aid of my five senses.

Thus he reminisces about Oxford, his youth, Brideshead and Sebastian. His words consign the 'world' we enjoyed in the previous episodes to the past, and to a romanticised image of the past – an 'illusion' – but, as Charles discovers that the present and future that follow are no more real than this illusion, and empty and cold in comparison, our nostalgia for the ideal world we inhabited with him is assured. Charles's nostalgia for his 'ideal' past is echoed in the paintings he produces. Whilst his earlier paintings were tender studies of England, his later ones are detached observations of 'foreign lands', accentuating his nostalgia for a previous, ideal homeland. Repetition and contrast are used similarly in the case of the Marchmains' house. In the adaptation each subsequent view of Brideshead brings more immediately to mind the times we saw it previously, and reveals the disparity between past and present. Nowhere is this more patent than when Charles explores the house at the end of the serial, as an army officer, and sees the vandalised paintings that we watched him create and the abandoned, dusty rooms we remember as being full of beautiful furniture – the stage for so many of the emotional scenes of his youth. While Waugh conveys the poignancy of this return, our relation to the house in the adaptation is more immediate, and our responses to the alterations in it arise directly from the house itself, rather than from an emotive description of it.

In the novel Charles attempts to specify what it is he has abandoned: 'I had left behind me – what? Youth? Adolescence? Romance?' (Waugh, 1962: 163); in the serial, though all these things are implied, it is Sebastian whom Charles has just deserted, and Brideshead that we see him leave. His wider, more unspecified losses are symbolised in Sebastian and the world of Oxford and Brideshead that the two of them inhabited. Any attempt by Charles to repeat with another man the kind of relationship he had had with Sebastian could never match its precursor: he would 'find no enchanted garden'. But the text is not just simplistically nostalgic for Sebastian as a lost love, or as a symbol of Charles's youthful past; Sebastian has a greater significance within the text and is a focus of nostalgia for more than Charles's personal feelings. Again, the serial attempts to follow its source, in which Sebastian was 'the central presence ... of the first half of *Brideshead*, whose absence haunts the remainder of the book' (Toynton, 1998: 135). When Sebastian left the novel 'we were stuck with Charles and Julia for the rest of the course. Charles without Sebastian is a man without a mirror to reflect in' (Ratcliffe, 1982: 52). We viewers know the ending already – we have seen Charles in the army – and we watched the first half of the serial with a wistful pleasure, knowing that the world Charles inhabits there cannot last; we view the second half of the serial longing for the past as he does. But we are longing for a *textual* past – a past we have seen, that exists within the text, and this past is signified by Sebastian, its loss precipitated by his departure. The first half of Waugh's novel exhibits a different mood from the second half, due to the presence of Sebastian. Thus in this faithful television serial, nostalgia is internal to the text in the same way: we are 'nostalgic' for the first section of the serial when we watch the second section. The mention of Sebastian's name in both book and adaptation acts as an emotion marker, bringing with it nostalgic associations, but in the serial, every mention of Sebastian inspires in us an additional, particular longing for a visual sight of him.

The mood of the latter half of the serial is altogether more melancholy and bleak. Sturridge described the serial thus: 'it starts in high summer, where everything is bathed in bright colours and sunshine, and then changes into Christmas and Easter, with gray skies and more night scenes' (Yakir, 1982: 58). But in fact the time span in *Brideshead* is much longer than this, and Sturridge's comments are therefore as much metaphorical as plainly descriptive of the narrative. The transformation of 'bright colours and sunshine' into dull weather and darkness is obvious in the serial as a whole, for the second section is characterised by gloomy interior shots and dull countryside (rather than ornamental gardens and pictori-ally framed landscapes) and Julia, 'one of the most lifeless heroines in modern fiction', in place of Sebastian, 'an excellent leading character' (Boyd, 1982b: 25). Though the serial is slow-paced throughout, 'rather like the book itself, I suspect that it was the first half that got us watching the second. The departure of Sebastian, leaving centre stage to Charles Ryder, consigned most of the final episodes to a level of infuriating dullness' (Boyd, 1982a: 23).

While in the book 'it is ultimately the friendship between Sebastian and Charles that lingers after the final page' (Yakir, 1982: 58), in the television serial it is the 'world' the two characters inhabit that lingers through the second half of the serial, and beyond – a world accessible to us only through fictional representations and those tangible traces that relics (such as Brideshead/Castle Howard) provide, and that forge con-nections between a fictional past and the real past, and both these pasts and our present.

1 'Brideshead'. *Brideshead Revisited* (1981)

2 'Charles and Sebastian picnicking'. *Brideshead Revisited* (1981)

3 'Pemberley'. *Pride and Prejudice* (1995)

4 'Elizabeth and Darcy flirt'. *Pride and Prejudice* (1995)

5a and b 'Elizabeth breaks into spontaneous skipping'. *Pride and Prejudice* (1995)

6 'Moll accuses us'. *The Fortunes and Misfortunes of Moll Flanders* (1996)

7 'Moll makes her move'. *The Fortunes and Misfortunes of Moll Flanders* (1996)

8 'Moll and Jemmy conclude their adventure'. *The Fortunes and Misfortunes of Moll Flanders* (1996)

9 'Moll indicates her intentions'. *The Fortunes and Misfortunes of Moll Flanders* (1996)

10 'Echoes of *The Shining*'. *The Tenant of Wildfell Hall* (1996)

11 'Framing repetition'. *The Tenant of Wildfell Hall* (1996)

12 'Helen on the moors'. *The Tenant of Wildfell Hall* (1996)

13 'The edge of the world'. *The Tenant of Wildfell Hall* (1996)

14 'Leaving the past behind'. *The Tenant of Wildfell Hall* (1996)

Brideshead's contribution to the genre

Fidelity to the source book is ultimately less important to the serial *Brideshead* than the unintended consequences of this fidelity in generic terms. The depiction of Brideshead and its contents on screen, and the nostalgic mood of the scenes based there and at Oxford, were so successful not necessarily because viewers were pleased with their fidelity to the book, but because they were impressive in themselves and because such images struck a chord with the audience. Further, Pearce names nostalgia as 'the novel's abiding specularity' (1982: 60); specularity becomes even more salient when we are discussing a television programme. While the lens of nostalgia through which the novel's events are seen is a metaphorical one, the serial utilises a set of stylistic features – shot sizes, shot lengths, framings, editing pace – that construct a more literal nostalgic specularity and a distinctive style which are perpetuated within the genre. Contemporary commentators noticed these traits but (understandably) did not comprehend their significance for the 'genre' or predict that their appeal would mean their extensive repetition. It is vital that the importance of *Brideshead* in defining the generic style, content and mood of British television classic-novel adaptations is now recognised: this serial constructed a generic world (microcosm) – its fidelity resulted in genre.

> [*Brideshead Revisited*] carries with it, not merely an aura of epic, but a sense of total commitment to the cultural values of the project which tends to place it, by its own standards and quite possibly by any standards, close to the peak of British television achievement, a visual masterpiece of awesome proportions. (Roddick, 1982: 58)

Roddick's heartfelt response to *Brideshead* expresses not just an appreciation of its aesthetic merits but also the powerful cultural and emotional significance the serial holds for so many viewers; these are the reasons that the serial maintains a special place in popular culture. Indeed, it could be suggested that the strong, uncompensated sense of loss and sense of unsatisfied nostalgia created by the structure of the serial induced later programme-makers to compensate and satisfy us through their own adaptations. Certainly the 1995 *Pride and Prejudice*, an archetype of the genre, provides the pleasant, warm feeling of nostalgia that *Brideshead* first elicits, then eschews.

Notes

1 Hewison actually cites the date of *Brideshead* as 1976, not 1981. Assuming this to be a typographical error, I have amended the date in this quotation.

2 Some of the genre's seeds had been sown in *The Forsyte Saga* (BBC, 1967), where one can see elements of style and mood that are apparent in *Brideshead*. However, I would argue for *Brideshead* as the exemplar of the genre as we know it, because of its complexity, coherence and influence.

3 Penguin Modern Classics, previously known as Penguin Twentieth-Century Classics. The catalogue includes Virginia Woolf, Vladimir Nabakov, James Baldwin, etc.

4 This could also be argued to be the case with 'The Raj Quartet' by Paul Scott (1966–75). The quartet undoubtedly gained wider acclaim due to its serialisation in 1984 (ITV) under the title of its first novel: *The Jewel in the Crown*.

5 Though there were two notable exceptions: Australian reviewer Edward Pearce described the serial as a 'desolating experience' due to its 'snobbery' (1982: 59); Kingsley Amis launched a witty but scathing attack on both the book and the serial in the *Times Literary Supplement* (20 November 1981: 1352), though his later volte-face in a more populist publication undermines his position somewhat (*TV Guide*, 16 January 1982: 33–4) (for details see Doyle, 1982: 2).

6 Though highly successful in terms of critical acclaim, initial audience figures for *Brideshead* did not scale similar heights. It is perhaps even more impressive, then, that the serial has had such a powerful influence in shaping the genre of classic-novel adaptations.

7 Allen, B. (1990), unpublished Ed.D thesis, East Texas State University.

8 Meanwhile, Robert Brent Toplin, another historian, offers a similarly familiar argument in defence of 'the past on screen': if successful, screen texts will raise awareness of the past and encourage the audience 'to ask questions and seek further information through reading' (1988: 1213). That is to say that the best screen adaptations of the past will send viewers back to books (if not a single esteemed 'original').

9 This interest in the 'heritage' aspects of films and programmes, and their influence upon our perceptions of past times, burgeoned at the beginning of the 1990s, with Andrew Higson's contributions (1996, 1995, 1993 – see Bibliography for full details) being the most prolific. His work is discussed in detail in this chapter.

10 The connection between the National Trust, English Heritage and classic-novel adaptations is echoed throughout Part II.

11 Clearly, the huge variety of ways in which Shakespeare's work has been adapted is due partly to the sheer number of times his plays have been performed, and due also to the rather different attitude audiences have towards the performance of dramatic texts from that which they have towards the 'performance' of literary texts. They appear to be generally far more accepting and open-minded towards the reinterpretation and updating of the former.

12 Branagh's recent *Hamlet* (1996) is a prime example. See my discussion in Part I of *Hamlet*'s 'fidelity' in relation to source and ur-text/work (pp. 26–7).

13 Most writers in film studies understand these films/programmes to be part of our search for a contemporary British national identity. I do not have the space to discuss in greater detail the 'national' (nationalistic?) aspects of the past depicted; I shall instead assume that the past depicted is pre-theoretically understood by the audience of classic-novel adaptations and heritage films as being British (or, more specifically, English). Jeffrey Richards offers a good discussion of this issue (see Richards, 1997); also of interest, in the face of a standard belief in the Western (or even British) basis of this process, is Richard Kearney's argument contesting the 'commonplace view that Western culture is more committed to such historical retrospection than its Eastern counterpart' (1998: 85).

14 Unfortunately, there is not space here for a digression into a discussion regarding whether this desire is innate, culturally formed, dependent upon individual personality or

social identity, or a societal tendency at particular moments in history. Fred Davis, in his book *Yearning for Yesterday: A Sociology of Nostalgia* (1979), offers a wide-ranging exploration of many of these issues.

15 This is a crude delineation. I include in the pictorial arts photography, painting, film and theatre; in the non-pictorial literature. This differentiation, though problematic, is adequate for my purposes here.

16 The use of such visual source material is common by adaptations' designers who are researching a particular period that they hope to 'recreate'. The BBC website provides an extensive overview of just this kind of primary-source research, as carried out by the designers of *Our Mutual Friend* (BBC, 1998) (*bbc.co.uk.dickens* (August 1998)).

17 In this sense, classic-novel adaptations can be considered part of a wider movement towards the 'simulation' of history also seen in museums, heritage centres and theme parks, in their presentation or 'performance' of 'the past', and their emphasis on the viewer's/participant's imaginative and playful engagement. Indeed, Higson notes that 'the heritage film and its reconstruction of the past thus represents just one aspect of the heritage industry as a whole' (1993: 112).

18 Rosenstone has also suggested this similarity (1995: 34-7).

19 Understandably, other disciplines have different concerns arising from the audience's faith in the historical 'accuracy' of these programmes. There is an ongoing debate amongst historians about the historically educative usefulness of such texts. An entire *AHR Forum* – 'History in Images/Images in History' – was dedicated to debate about the representation of history in both fictional and non-fictional films (*American Historical Review*, 94: 5).

20 This cutting, but amusing and pertinent, description is attributed to Alan Parker.

21 The term and concept 'nostalgia' are discussed in greater detail later in this chapter, and throughout Part II. Here I shall only note that the extended meaning which Higson ascribes to the term is becoming more and more widespread; as Patrick White notes, 'we have come to apply nostalgia to worlds separated from us by time rather than by space' (1982: 5). The original meaning of the term was 'homesickness'.

22 Higson bases his arguments only upon *film* classic-novel adaptations, not upon television programmes; I am, perhaps, taking liberties here. However, other theorists have begun to extrapolate elements of his work and relate them to television.

23 In addition, there is in Higson's work an implicit Marxist critique of commodity fetishism – the valuing of objects retrospectively endowed with meaning (commodities) over people, through the 'fetishization of period details' (1993: 113). The use of many characters as 'clothes-horses' and the abundance of extras (servants, etc.) in adaptations, mean that people are often regarded as no more than mere objects. This combination of an excessive fetishisation of detail and 'the creation of heritage space, rather than narrative space' (1993: 117) determines commodities, not people, as emotional foci, and thus as meaningful and valuable.

24 Corner and Harvey, in *Enterprise and Heritage: Crosscurrents of National Culture* (1991) offer a convincing argument to the effect that ' "heritage", that which is inherited from the past, can be inflected in a variety of different political directions' (1991: 14), and Samuel, in *Theatres of Memory: Volume I* (1994) offers a careful analysis of heritage that leads us to the same conclusion. For an excellent, wide-ranging and historical discussion of 'heritage' see 'Semantics' in Section III of Samuel (1994) *Theatres of Memory: Volume I*. Indeed, if one utilises a wider notion of 'heritage', the monolithic view of it as reactionary and elitist is not sustainable. However, I do not have the space here to develop this debate, and refer the reader to these two texts, which offer extremely good counter-arguments to the dominant view of heritage.

25 Many critics ascribe to these programmes and films a high cultural status, branding them either elitist and exclusory or firmly bourgeois. These claims can be supported to some extent by details of the generic style of classic-novel adaptations. The slow, steady pace of

both narrative and editing here can be regarding not just as aiding the display of heritage, but also as validating the 'slower' arts of art-film and literature traditionally conceived as bourgeois.

26 Pidduck's inverted commas around the term 'nostalgic' admit the problems in affixing such a term to a landscape. In my discussion of *Pride and Prejudice* (BBC, 1995), I explore the relationship between the landscapes of these serials and their perceived 'nostalgic' nature.

27 It should be noted, however, that viewers probably watch these serials in a different way, as they repay closer attention in both aesthetic and emotional terms.

28 Charlotte Brunsdon (1998) argues that *Inspector Morse* can be included within a category of 'heritage television'. The link was also suggested by Amy Sargeant in a paper given at the 'Cinema, Identity, History' conference held at the University of East Anglia (10–12 July 1998), and previously by Simon Barker (1994) in his article '"Period" Detective Drama and the Limits of Contemporary Nostalgia: *Inspector Morse* and the Strange Case of a Lost England', *Critical Survey (Oxford)* 6: 2, 234–42.

29 Alan Partridge made the observation about Oxford and *Inspector Morse* during the episode 'A Room with Alan', in which he pitched ideas for various new television series to the commissioning editor at the BBC. One of Alan's ideas was for a detective series, *Swallow*, based in Norwich, which he claimed would 'put Norwich on the map', just as *Inspector Morse* did for Oxford. Yet again we glimpse the connection here between the 'heritage industry', accounting for much of England's tourist trade, and depictions of 'heritage' in films and television programmes such as classic-novel adaptations and modern 'heritage television' programmes like *Inspector Morse*.

30 In view of Altman's work (*Film/Genre*, 1999), a note on genre is necessary here. The fact of such cross-genre intertextuality places limitations upon the notion of a completely differentiated, self-contained genre, which is perhaps to be expected in our (post)modern times, but it is still true that we can expect to see certain generic shots and scenes when we watch a classic-novel adaptation, whether they occur elsewhere or not. It is its particular combination of generic tropes that defines this genre.

31 In addition, the serial both concretises and expands the significance of Brideshead, conflating the fictional Brideshead with the real Castle Howard, and thus forging extra-textual links between fiction and the 'real world'.

32 It is also true that these particular locales have ideological values associated with them that cannot help but influence the programmes and films that utilise them (as Higson *et al.* suggest). However, I am concerned at this point primarily with the programmes' aesthetic and emotional salience.

33 It is possible that the filmmakers also intended a visual reference to Sebastian's 'holiness' here (implied in the source novel).

34 I have chosen to omit an exploration of the representation of Sebastian and Charles's relationship in terms of its implied homosexual nature. Their relationship as depicted in the serial can be read in two ways – either as an attempt to sanitise and deny its homo-erotic/homosexual nature, or as an attempt to offer an understated and romantic por-trayal of homosexuality (and to align the audience with the couple, implicating them in these values). I avoid this debate primarily for reasons of limited space, but also because the very ambiguity of the presentation allows various readings, and rejects firm, stereo-typical representations of homosexuality and heterosexuality, instead blurring the distinc-tion between the two (in a manner which could, in itself, be considered progressive).

Pride and Prejudice (1995)

6

Brideshead initiated specific generic conventions that have become more firmly established in television adaptations since it was first broadcast: conventions of content (the display of 'heritage' as representative of 'the past'), style (a languorous pace and 'filmic' use of the camera) and mood (nostalgia). *Pride and Prejudice*, first broadcast fourteen years later, holds an equally important position as a generic archetype, drawing upon and developing the same conventions as *Brideshead*. However, as a television programme produced in the 1990s, *Pride and Prejudice* did not establish such firm boundaries separating itself from the televisual context, in the way in which *Brideshead* did. Instead, *Pride and Prejudice* recognised its place within the televisual context, whilst strongly asserting its generic identity and continuity with classic-novel adaptations like *Brideshead*.

Austen and adaptation

Pride and Prejudice (1995) was produced at the height of the consolidation of generic tropes of content, style and mood. Crucial, then, to a generic analysis of this programme is an awareness of the adaptation's intertextual links with other classic-novel adaptations made in the 1980s and 1990s.[1] As Imelda Whelehan notes, a classic-novel adaptation is 'a recognizable film genre which is, in turn, an adaptation of other films, with intertextual links with its contemporary filmic counterparts' (1999: 4) – the same applies to television adaptations.

It is equally important that the 1995 *Pride and Prejudice* be regarded specifically in the context of other 1980s/1990s Austen adaptations. This is not because adaptations should be categorised according to (the author of) the books from which they are adapted. Rather, 'Jane Austen adaptations' bear textual similarities to each other not necessarily due to the authorial connection which links the various source books, but because of the way in which Austen and her work have come to be regarded, and because of the impact of Austen adaptations upon the wider genre of classic-novel adaptations. In the first place, Austen adaptations tend to share particular traits which differ to a certain degree from those found in adaptations of works by some other authors, such as Dickens. These traits have arisen from common perceptions of Austen's work. Theorists have picked up on this commonality: the edited book *Jane Austen in Hollywood* (Troost and Greenfield, 1998) postulates an entire genre of films and television programmes constituted by adaptations of Austen's novels. In the second place, and even more significantly, Austen adaptations had by the 1990s become representative of the genre of classic-novel adaptations as a whole. Ruminating upon Austen's possible responses to adaptations of her work, Rachel M. Brownstein concludes that

> she would have been distressed by dramatized episodes of *Pride and Prejudice* and *The Golden Bowl* and *Brideshead Revisited* that look and feel like chapters of a single interminable Classic Serial. A genre was being developed in the literal-minded literary films made for television in the 1970s and 1980s: the particulars and peculiarities of individual novels and novelists were absorbed in its over-eager embrace. (1998: 16)

What Brownstein fails to consider is that Austen adaptations have not simply been assimilated into wider, monolithic generic constraints, but have rather played a vital role in consolidating the traits which adaptations share (and which make them all 'look the same'). To some extent, in the 1990s Austen adaptations became synonymous with 'classic-novel adaptations', and the 1995 *Pride and Prejudice* was of particular significance because of its outstanding success. Therefore *Pride and Prejudice* serves as a consolidation of the genre less because of its place in the chronology of television classic-novel adaptations (the 'consolidation era'), and more because of its importance as an Austen adaptation in confirming the archetypal image of the genre.

Thus in 1995, the choice of a book by Austen as a source text for a screen adaptation implied a conscious decision to work within the traditional bounds of the classic-novel adaptation genre, which had itself been consolidated through previous (Austen) adaptations. The fervour for adapting Austen's gentle tales of insular middle-class families has worked to consolidate a slow-paced style and 'heritage' content. In terms of mood, Austen's novels are not overtly nostalgic like *Brideshead*; Austen was rarely given to nostalgia. However, her work is not inimical to nostalgic re-presentation, because it is commonly regarded as being broadly uncritical of the present about which Austen wrote (our past). Cartmell, though doubtful as to the real extent of Austen's uncritical nature, notes the impact of Austen's image as a 'conservative literary icon': 'The first candidate must be Jane Austen, alongside Shakespeare, as a conservative literary icon. Both are identified by the word 'heritage', and screen adaptations of their work tend to perpetuate their assumed conservative ideology in spite of critical readings which suggest otherwise' (1999: 24).

As Cartmell suggests, Austen critics have noted various kinds of radicalism in her work, reconfiguring it as feminist, postcolonial and so forth. Devoney Looser defends Austen's ideological credentials, criticising the fact that a 'glaring difference in the ways Austen adaptations have been written about, compared to those of E. M. Forster, Henry James, Edith Wharton or even Shakespeare, is the tendency to label the Austen revival as part and parcel of a conservative cultural turn' (1998: 160) However, the evidence offered by the adaptations of Austen's work offers convincing reasons for this apparent 'bias'. Even the programme-makers' 'conservative' desire for fidelity to Austen's work has played a role in maintaining her image: 'the fact that the discourse generated by Austen adaptations has so insistently been one of conservation, reverting to a notional, pre-existing standard of the original and the authentic, has worked in itself to reinforce Austen's position within the conservative hierarchy' (North, 1999: 39). Therefore, the popular view of Austen as 'a conservative icon' (North, 1999: 38) can be understood with reference to adaptations of her work.

It could be argued that source texts which can be fairly easily recruited into a nostalgic portrayal of the past were sought out due to the cultural desire for further (nostalgic) connections with the past of the type that guaranteed *Brideshead*'s appeal and success. Thus, though it is certainly admissible that 'those [authors] at the top of the canon (Austen, for one) must be treated respectfully and faithfully in adaptations due to their position high up within a "hierarchy of texts"' (Cartmell, 1999: 27), it is also likely that these adaptations continue to be 'faithful' because that is the best way to achieve their own goals – including the emotive, nostalgic representation of a stylised past – not that fidelity is their goal per se. Besides, fidelity is a less sufficient explanation for the generic content, style and mood of these texts than it was for *Brideshead*.

Landscapes, long shots and stately homes

Pride and Prejudice (BBC, 1995) is a particularly good example of the classic BBC literary adaptation, and is historically important. It is generally perceived as being 'faithful' to its source book, and also as conforming to our expectations of high-quality, 'good' British costume drama. It is not wooden, nor does it appear 'un-televisual', unlike many earlier television adaptations. The move around this time towards more energetic, engaging film adaptations is noted by Brownstein: in comparing the BBC's 1985 *Sense and Sensibility* with the 1995 film *Sense and Sensibility*, she says one is 'astonished by its slowness and dullness' and its use of 'shadows and muted colours' (1998: 16). A similar comparison could be made between the 1980 BBC *Pride and Prejudice* and the 1995 version. The latter makes for interesting and entertaining viewing, as the audience figures bear out.

The programme follows closely in the footsteps of its televisual and filmic forebears, rarely straying from the path, apparently aiming for respectful fidelity to the source novel as did *Brideshead*. Indeed, *Pride and Prejudice* is doubly conventional for it is also faithful to the genre now established, and appears to resist the powerful influence of the televisual and generic experimentation apparent in other classic-novel adaptations of the 1990s.[2] Its striking fidelity to the traditional conventions of the genre is clear in its use of so many typical generic shots and shot sequences that can be traced back to classic-novel film adaptations and heritage films from the 1980s, television adaptations from *Brideshead* onwards, and previous 1980s/1990s Austen adaptations. In *Pride and Prejudice* (1995) one can see the confidence of a genre clearly established (and at a peak of popularity) and able to build on its relations with other classic-novel adaptations. The programme fits broadly into Altman's definition of a paradigmatic genre film (programme), as it was 'produced after general identification and consecration of a genre when shared textual material and structures lead audiences to interpret films not as separate entities but according to generic expectations and against generic norms' (1999: 53).

Long shots of rolling countryside open the 1995 *Pride and Prejudice*, and are repeated throughout the serial. They are also ubiquitous in other contemporary (1980s/1990s) television and film adaptations such as the 1980 *Pride and Prejudice*, the two 1996 *Emmas* (television programme and film), *Sense and Sensibility* (1995), and non-Austen adaptations such as *Middlemarch* (1994), *Howards End* (1992) and *A Room With a View* (1986). It is significant that these shots are termed 'landscape' shots, and are not just images of countryside, for 'landscape' typically implies both a particular formal composition and a specific form of specularity. H. Elisabeth Ellington explores the use of landscape in the 1995 *Pride and Prejudice*, especially in one of its key scenes: Elizabeth Bennet's visit to Darcy's estate, Pemberley. Ellington combines a detailed analysis of the programme with a comparison of the source book and its screen counterpart, arguing that the novel is 'easily the most visual of Austen's six completed novels ... lending itself to cinematic adaptation more readily than her other novels through its extensive use of visual imagery and language' (1998: 91). Both the novel and the adaptation, Ellington argues, encourage us to 'become, in effect, consumers of landscape' (1998: 91), a landscape that was first determined (by agricultural changes, etc.) and first appreciated (toured, written about, visually represented) at the time Austen wrote the source novel. Ellington thus forges new links between novel and adaptation that are concerned less with textual/literal fidelity and more with the specific historical and cultural contexts of each text. For example, she explains that in the late eighteenth century

> influenced by theories of the Picturesque and the rise of landscape painting, landowners went to great pains to conceal their houses along the approach until a 'considerable eminence' was reached which would afford a commanding view of the property, transforming the land and house into a picture. (Ellington, 1998: 99)

The sequence in the adaptation when Elizabeth and the Gardiners arrive at Pemberley corresponds exactly to this description (figure 3).

It appears, therefore, that the adaptation is not only historically accurate, it also displays directly the pleasures of eighteenth-century tourism to which the modern-day lay reader of Austen's *Pride and Prejudice* would not be privy. Yet to evaluate this scene, and others like it, only in terms of either textual or historical fidelity would be to repeat the mistake that comparative critics of *Brideshead* made: such shot sequences are significant beyond this context, in both cultural and generic terms. Ellington wisely acknowledges the cultural import of the programme within a framework of other 'tributes to the English countryside and nostalgia for a bygone lifestyle' (1998: 92), figuring these landscape images as targets of a 'visual consumption' that, she argues, is a 'decidedly middle-class phenomenon' (1998: 98). Historically, the viewing of landscape 'allowed the middle classes imaginatively to own land ... through looking at land, they could make it, in a sense, their own' (Ellington, 1998: 98); adaptations like *Pride and Prejudice*, it is implied, serve a similar function.[3]

It is interesting that in Ellington's analysis, the gaze over land is historically situated and has precedents. Although limited to a specific group of people, there is a suggested continuity between past and present, through the activities of touring and of looking. Equally, this historically grounded gaze is focused upon referents that have solidity in 'real life'.[4] Indeed, much of our emotional response is reliant upon a certain stability or continuity in the object of our gaze: the countryside and buildings that constitute these landscapes are solid and enduring – they act as Lowenthal suggests, constituting a continuous link between past and present. Raphael Samuel explicitly notes the importance of these particular 'memory places':

> Finally, and perhaps as a result of the collapse of ideas of national destiny, there is the growing importance of 'memory places' in ideas of the historical past. Landscape, and in particular those vast tracts of it which now come under the administration of the National Trust, is now called upon to do the memory work which in earlier times might have been performed by territorial belonging ... Old houses, formerly left to decay, are now prized as living links to the past, a kind of visual equivalent to what used to be known as 'a stake in the country'. (1994: 39)

It is vital, therefore, to move beyond an evaluation of these characteristic shots that offers only a criticism of their aesthetic appeal. Nor should the shot sequences be automatically assimilated into a framework of unquestioning nostalgia. Ellington's work reveals the history of our gaze upon these landscapes, a gaze which was not initially nostalgic – thus we cannnot assume that nostalgia is the only possible response to the gaze as re-presented in classic-novel adaptations, just as 'heritage' is not intrinsically reactionary.

It is true that the specificities of our cultural and historical context affect the mood in which we view landscapes. Adam Nicolson, in his introduction to a coffee-table picture book, *Panoramas of England*, explores with impressive acuity the nature of our relationships to the kinds of landscapes (panoramas) the book contains. He does not underestimate the complexity of our feelings about the pastoral landscape, noting that 'we know as we look at them they are not true to the real state of the country, that they are the most obvious of selective fictions' (Nicolson, 1992: 14), yet that 'everything the English continue to think about England is poured into these pictures like milk into a bucket. They seem to be overbrimming with the English national consciousness, which is not consciousness of a flag, or a language or even really a race, but of a landscape' (1992: 28).

Whilst Nicolson recognises, therefore, the ideological nature of our engagement with pictorial presentations of landscape, he refuses to dismiss or denigrate the presentations themselves simply on this basis, acknowledging that our emotions are far more nuanced than that. He instead concludes that 'the landscape of England is sacred only in the sense that almost anyone can recognise who has been moved by a place ... the ineffable sensation of something there beyond material facts' (Nicolson, 1992: 27).

So far we have been concerned with these images in terms of their (and our) relationship with the past, and in terms of the pleasures of viewing. However, we should not lose sight of the importance of these generic sequences to the genre itself: they are vital to the generic microcosm, and to the microcosm's place within television. Whilst Ellington does attempt to explore *Pride and Prejudice*'s cultural importance, she limits her comments on the matter of its generic significance to a brief note that technological developments mean that 'landscape imagery is thus much more developed in the 1995 version' (1998: 91). It is worth emphasising that in almost every case, these archetypal shot sequences are not derived from the source books to which they claim to be faithful; they are supplementary. Though Ellington's attempt to place the shots within a historical framework of 'viewing' is useful, one cannot extract any one adaptation from its place within a network of generic, specifically televisual practice. It must be recognised that these shots also appear to work as establishing shots, such as those we are accustomed to see in quotidian television dramas, whilst their subject matter (grand residences or charming country cottages) is drawn directly from the Merchant Ivory school of film adaptations, and from film adaptations of Austen such as *Sense and Sensibility* (1995) and *Emma* (1996). These shots are therefore semi-televisual, semi-filmic, and historically related to the visual arts and the real-life appreciation of landscape but (comparative theorists might like to note) barely grounded in literature.

What strikes the viewer of *Pride and Prejudice* is that although that programme follows generic convention in including these shot sequences, it seems to take them further: the houses are grander, the composition of the shots more precisely orchestrated, the length of the shots extended. Confidently refusing to 'scale down' for television, these long-shot sequences appear 'filmic' and impressive, aided by improved sound reproduction and the use of climactic music to highlight moments of awe. Ellington's reference to technological development is no doubt correct, but her 'thus' conceals the fact that what we see in *Pride and Prejudice* is not just the result of technological development, but also the result of generic development: these two things are not one and the same. Generic development draws upon technical advances, but also upon previous textual conventions – both televisual and filmic – and cultural changes. These shot sequences reveal *Pride and Prejudice* to be an archetype of a television genre at its height, a complex configuration of the above factors.

Ellington's analysis of the historical origins of the 'views' in the serial does not illuminate the opening sequence of the adaptation, which employs common generic conventions. *Pride and Prejudice* begins with a traditional opening shot sequence: two characters, Darcy and Bingley, ride on horseback up a gently sloping hill, pausing at the apex to look down upon the large country house that is Netherfield. This is an arche-typal shot sequence that occurs within many classic-novel adaptations: we are first shown a shot of one or more characters traversing the country-side to a flattering vantage point, then a long shot of (one of) the central houses of the adaptation. The sequence is often repeated on the intro-duction and exhibition of each new building. In *Pride and Prejudice* it occurs just so: we see Rosings in long shot through the eyes of Elizabeth and her friends as they walk up the extended drive towards it; Pemberley (the most spectacular residence of all) is revealed in long shot from the other side of its lake, again from Elizabeth's point of view, as her carriage halts to allow a clear view between the trees upon a stunning aspect of the house. A similar shot sequence opens the 1995 adaptation of Austen's *Persuasion* (BBC and WGBH), as Mrs Clay and Mr Elliott return by carriage to the Elliotts' country house, and the 1994 adaptation of Eliot's *Middlemarch*, as Tertius Lydgate arrives in the town. The 1980 adaptation of *Pride and Prejudice* begins with a long shot of the Bennets' house: a country home rather larger than one might have expected. In these other adaptations, though, the initial long shots of the main residences of the programmes are not obviously point-of-view shots, our gaze upon the houses being impersonal, and not through the eyes of an on-screen character – a significant difference.

As nostalgia and heritage theorists have noted, despite Andrew Davies's protestations,[5] these shot sequences are not just establishing shots. First, they follow and confirm established generic convention. Second, and more importantly, they are a significant source of the programme's affective power. A routine establishing shot of a location does not require a preceding 'point-of-view' shot as a diegetic motivation for the long shot. In fact, both establishing shots and conventional 'heritage' shots are ordinarily impersonal: 'it is a characteristic of the heritage film that its gaze is often not identified with character point-of-view but with an anonymous public gaze' (Hill, 1999: 104). But in *Pride and Prejudice*, the character's gaze upon the building works to guide our mood – our response to the building. Bingley looks favourably upon Netherfield; Elizabeth looks with awe upon Rosings and with wonder-ment, longing and wistful regret upon Pemberley. The point-of-view shot encourages us to view the buildings as the characters do. The fact that these buildings are usually 'new' to the onlooking character also means that the preceding 'looking' shot offers a diegetic excuse for the sub-sequent long take which is characteristic. The more splendid the building, the longer the take – the shot of Pemberley is held long enough for us to fully appreciate its sheer magnificence.

All this is not to suggest that these shots are diegetically *unnecessary*, though they are perhaps superfluous. The generic long shot works to establish a setting, and the combination of this shot with a preceding point-of-view shot also introduces a character and implies his or her relationship, or potential relationship, to that setting. In a similar way, the recurrent paradigm of *movement* works to link a character even more strongly with the building towards which he or she is travelling. As stated above, this shot sequence, including the travelling paradigm, appears again and again: in *Brideshead*; in the 1995 *Persuasion*, at the beginning; at the start and throughout the 1994 *Middlemarch*; and in other adaptations of the time. The ubiquity of these shots renders them somewhat over-determined, leaving diegetic explanations unconvincing. In fact, these shot sequences bear far greater significance than that of narrative aids. The 'travelling' paradigm allows us to 'come upon' these buildings, to discover them nestled in the rolling English countryside. Their presence within the countryside as representative of rural and historic England is naturalised not only by surrounding sheep – in *Persuasion* (1995) and *Middlemarch* (1994) – but also because we 'burst in' upon them as they sleep in their natural environment; they are concealed by trees or hills, and we encroach upon them; they are permanent, eternal, our presence is ephemeral, even intrusive.

These landscape shots therefore follow the historical precedent set by 'tourists' of the eighteenth century, but to explain their presence in those terms would be to overlook the specific features of an on-screen representation of a real-life precursor. The type of camera movement involved in these sequences works to elicit a contemplative, appreciative gaze, giving us time both to look and to experience emotion. In combination with the typical pace of classic-novel adaptations, the use of mobile framing within a long-take long shot means that 'as the camera lingers on a fairly "full" visual field, the spectator has more opportunity to scan the shot for particular points of interest' (Bordwell and Thompson, 1993: 236), as well as to experience the rush of emotion these images elicit. The use of music is also pertinent: it 'builds up' to a climax. Music which peaks at the full display of certain objects suggests that they should be regarded as emotional foci. Clearly this choice of foci is ideologically significant, but of equal concern is the objects' aesthetic and emotional importance.

The mood encouraged here can be described as appreciation and pleasure in aesthetic beauty, mixed with other diegetically motivated feelings such as regret and awe. It is salient that all these responses are 'wistful' and thus rather more vague than, say, anger, fear or sadness; it is also important that 'nostalgia' is not listed. There is no evidence here that the programme either contains or directly elicits anything that can be called 'nostalgia'. However, as it shall be argued later, the wistful, vague mood that the programme *does* create can be reconfigured as nostalgia in the space between text and audience.

Nostalgia in the making: taking a closer look

It is clear by this point that nostalgia is extremely important to this genre, both textually and extra-textually. The affective power of these images depends upon the viewer establishing a particular relationship with the text, namely a nostalgic one, to the extent that the genre is routinely labelled nostalgic. Torben Grodal elucidates the link between the naming of genres and their peculiar emotional address/affects, pointing out that many 'genres … have strong and characteristic emotional effects' (1997: 161), and that 'emotion-evocation' can be used as 'a principle of generic construction', alongside 'iconology or certain themes' (1997: 162). 'One prominent way (among several others) of categorizing visual fiction in relation to consumer information is by emotion evoked: horror, comedy, melodrama, or thriller' (Grodal, 1997: 3).

Thus claims concerning 'nostalgia films/programmes' recognise the importance of the texts' affective specificities; as indicated by Noël Carroll, it is not 'only the case that a great deal of our experience of films is saturated with emotion; it is also that our emotional engagement constitutes, in many instances, the most intense, vivid, and sought-after qualities available in the film experience' (1999: 23–4).

The locus of nostalgia

The apparently simple question that arises, then, is 'Where is the nostalgia?' If we are to argue convincingly that *Pride and Prejudice* and the genre it epistomises are nostalgic, a close analysis of the text can precipitate serious problems. In the case of *Brideshead*, the nostalgia felt by the viewers is inspired by a diegesis that actually contains nostalgia: the text aligns them with Charles Ryder, who is nostalgic for the old days at Brideshead with Sebastian. But in *Pride and Prejudice*, the shots and scenes that we instinctively single out as eliciting nostalgia from the audience do not 'contain' it. Elizabeth Bennet, for example, does not feel nostalgia when she gazes upon Rosings or Pemberley in the sequences mentioned earlier. So, where is the 'nostalgia' located?

Other theorists have neither asked nor answered this question about the locus of the nostalgia they so frequently cite. Even where textual details have been proffered as evidence of the texts' nostalgic tendencies, those details tend to be unspecific. Therefore the relationship and differences between textual style and mood (i.e. the style and mood that can be 'found' within the text) and extra-textual 'nostalgia' (broadly, the audience's feelings or emotional response) remain unexplored. Grodal notes the complexity of this issue:

> There is a traditional objection to dealing extensively with the emotions of an artwork by describing its impact on an addressee: if the emotions are closely related to other structural features or the visual fiction, why describe the emotional impact on the viewer, instead of just describing the emotional structure of the artwork? The emotions, it might be said, should be implied in the structures and meanings of the artwork itself. (1997: 3)

Grodal disagrees with the view that an explanation of an artwork's emotional affects can be sought solely within the emotional structures that the artwork 'contains', arguing instead that a 'simple argument against this position is that feelings and emotions are states and processes in humans, not in texts' (Grodal, 1997: 3). In contrast, Fred Davis argues that

> so frequently and uniformly does nostalgic sentiment seem to infuse our aesthetic experience that we can rightly begin to suspect that nostalgia is not only a feeling or mood that is somehow magically evoked by the art object but also a distinctive aesthetic modality in its own right, a kind of code or patterning of symbolic elements, which by some obscure mimetic isomorphism comes, much as in language itself, to serve as a substitute for the feeling or mood it aims to arouse. (1979: 73)

Referring more specifically to the way in which the artist achieves a 'distinctive aesthetic modality', Davis continues:

> he or she 'knows' by training, intuition, and prior exercise what configuration of lines, pigments, sounds, movements, or words will touch nostalgic 'chords' in the audience. The audience, too, without necessarily having any immediate or 'real' reason for feeling nostalgic, will upon seeing or hearing the material respond nostalgically since it, too, has through long associative exposure assimilated the aesthetic code that evokes the emotion. (1979: 82)

The existence of particular much-used (one could say 'generic') traits within traditional classic-novel adaptations, which are so often repeated that we can identify one of these programmes by the presence of those very traits, suggests that there is some set of textual features that bear some sort of connection with nostalgia. Grodal concludes:

> My hypothesis is, then, that there is a systematic relation between the embodied mental processes and configurations activated in a given type of

visual fiction and the emotional 'tone' and 'modal qualities' of the experienced affects, emotions, and feelings in the viewer. Prototypical genres of visual fiction will evoke typical tones and modalities. (Grodal, 1997: 3)

It is perhaps most useful, then, to understand that there are differences between textual style and mood and extra-textual moods and emotions (affects) but also to accept that there is a relationship between the two.

Nostalgia – feeling, emotion or mood?

Carroll, Grodal, Carl Plantinga and Greg M. Smith all distinguish feelings from emotions similarly. First, 'feelings are often non-object-directed (I feel sad, happy, and so on), whereas emotions often have an object-directed quality' (Grodal, 1997: 4). Second, and relatedly, emotions tend to incorporate cognitive elements, whereas feelings do not: 'it was once commonly thought that emotions were coextensive with feelings ... [but] not only does thinking accompany and in many cases determine emotion, but emotions can themselves be rational or irrational' (Plantinga, 1997: 378); 'emotions consist of (at least) physiological changes, feelings and thinking' (Plantinga and Smith, 1999: 6). In summary, whilst a feeling is neither object-directed nor 'cognitive', an emotion has a 'thinking part ... with thinking consisting of the emoter's evaluation or judgement about the object of the emotion' (Plantinga and Smith, 1999: 6). Carroll offers a broader notion of '*affect* where everyday speech might talk of the emotions, reserving the term emotion to name a narrower subclass of affect, namely, what might be even more accurately called cognitive emotions (i.e., affects that include cognitive elements)' (1999: 21). It is difficult to determine from such explanations whether nostalgia is better understood as a feeling or an emotion. One can certainly experience nostalgia in an object-directed and cognitive fashion – if one seeks out photographs of a lost relative or friend and indulges in nostalgic memories of that person, for example. In comparison, an aroma, or a type of weather, or a sound, can induce a generalised feeling of nostalgia for which one may then seek a 'focus'. Nostalgia appears altogether more difficult to pin down than the categories of 'feeling' and 'emotion' may allow. There are two further possibilities that can be suggested as avenues for exploration: Fred Davis's work on nostalgia as a 'form of consciousness' and Greg M. Smith's work on film and mood(s).

Davis asks us 'to treat nostalgia as a distinctive *form of consciousness*' (1979: 74) (italics in original). Drawing on the work of Alfred Schutz,[6] he attempts to define the experience of nostalgia:

nostalgia as a form of consciousness can be characterized in Schutzian terms as: a heightened focus on things past (time perspective) along with an enhanced credence in them (epoché), accompanied by considerable musing (form of spontaneity), mild detachment from the affairs of everyday life (tension of consciousness), an essentially appreciative stance toward the self (form of experiencing the self) and attenuation of that sense of we-ness (form of sociality) which in everyday life frames and constrains our conduct. (Davis, 1979: 81)

Davis's detailed description of the nostalgic state is pertinent to our understanding of nostalgic films and programmes, as there appears to be a close correspondence between his description and our viewing of such texts. Respectively, the texts' detailed and meticulous display of a past world encourages a 'heightened focus on things past' and 'an enhanced credence in them'; the imaginative process involved in watching such films and programmes, enhanced especially by the slow pace of the presentation, allows for 'considerable musing'; finally, our engagement with the fiction constitutes a 'mild detachment from the affairs of everyday life' and a relative withdrawal from 'sociality'. Though Davis's description of 'an essentially appreciative stance toward the self' is perhaps not straightforwardly applicable in this case, these films and programmes certainly induce such a stance towards 'our' past, our country, our national identity, so that we feel tenderly about ourselves as members of something greater – a wider 'imagined community'.[7]

Whilst Davis's account of the nostalgic experience applies aptly to the viewer of nostalgic fictions, it applies only analogously or loosely to the fictions themselves. In order to understand more fully the possibility of a text like *Pride and Prejudice* being 'nostalgic', we must look elsewhere – to Smith's coherent account of filmic mood(s). Smith argues that 'the primary emotive effect of film is to create mood. Because it is difficult to generate brief, intense emotions, film structures attempt to create a predisposition toward experiencing emotion' (1999: 115). Elucidating 'mood' (as distinct from emotions or feelings) more fully, he continues:

> the primary set of orienting emotion states is mood. A mood is a preparatory state in which one is seeking an opportunity to express a particular emotion or emotion set. Moods are expectancies that we are about to have a particular emotion, that we will encounter cues that will elicit particular emotions. (Smith, 1999: 113)

Smith notes that it is very often film style that is used to establish the desired mood. Extrapolating from his theory, to label *Pride and Prejudice* 'nostalgic' is to describe the mood created and maintained within the text by its aesthetic particularities of style. This understanding of nostalgia as a 'mood', rather than an emotion, feeling, or even 'form of consciousness' is more useful, as a mood can be shared by text and viewer. This brings us a little closer to supplying an answer to my initial question about the locus of the nostalgia.

Smith contends that films use 'mood cues' or 'emotion cues' to establish in the viewer the above-described predisposition to feel certain emotions. He also notes that mood cues 'can fairly reliably create an emotive predisposition (a mood); once that mood is created it has a tendency to sustain itself. A mood is not entirely self-perpetuating, however. It requires occasional moments of strong emotion [emotion markers] to maintain the mood' (Smith, 1999: 116). By applying Smith's ideas to this genre, several problematic areas are clarified. The generic, romanticised representations of the past and, more specifically, the way in which they are filmed are, as Higson and others have argued, of fundamental importance. But these generic shot sequences, said to elicit nostalgia (thus characterised as an emotion), occur far less frequently than close-up shots of characters, traditional point-of-view shots and scenes of conversations which utilise classic shot/reverse shot edits. If we take traditional analyses literally, we would have to accept that the audience only feels nostalgia on a few brief occasions during a classic-novel adaptation; this would leave our film theorists' analyses looking unbalanced, as they are concerned with only one aspect of the genre. But if we accept Smith's arguments, and combine them with traditional analyses like Higson's, we can see that these generic scenes act to reinforce an overall *mood* of nostalgia – they are the 'occasional moments of strong emotion', the emotion markers, required to maintain the mood of the programme or film.

Smith argues, 'A primary task for a film's early sequences ... is to establish a [*sic*] emotional orientation that will guide the audience through the film, encouraging them to evaluate cues in mood-congruent ways' (Smith, 1999: 120). On almost every occasion, and markedly in the case of *Pride and Prejudice*, classic-novel adaptations begin with generic long-take long shots of generic content (carriages, large houses, countryside) accompanied by elegant classical music. These shot sequences establish a mood that is then reinforced, developed and heightened through the use of other generic shots and scenes throughout the adaptation.

In generic terms these opening shot sequences are also fundamental in serving to establish the microcosm of the classic-novel adaptation, and in many cases to delineate this microcosm clearly from the televisual one within which it is situated. In the 1994 adaptation of *Middlemarch* this delineation is foregrounded: we 'arrive' at the beginning, as described above, and then 'leave' at the end, as we watch a carriage leave Middlemarch, and the sheep we saw at the beginning spill onto the road behind the carriage, emphasising the carriage's – and our – departure from the generic world which they mark.

So Smith's work reveals that our mood (and subsequent emotions) are established through cues in a film's style, and that mood is also integral to the text in the sense that it is created through (stylistic) features inherent in the text itself – the text itself can be said to have a mood. If generic shots and shot sequences are seen not as distinct, separate moments but as emotion markers that reinforce the framing nostalgic mood, a definition of the genre as 'nostalgic' is more fully supported.

Ballrooms and backdrops

A close analysis of the use of generic interior 'heritage' shots in the 1995 *Pride and Prejudice* supports the view that the methods by which the serial establishes its 'nostalgic' mood and generic credentials are far more intricate than most theorists allow. From even the 1971 *Persuasion*, through the 1980 *Pride and Prejudice* and the 1995 *Persuasion*, to this 1995 *Pride and Prejudice*, interiors have been presented as elegantly furnished, and the use of frequent medium to long shots allows us to gaze at the furnishings as well as the characters.

In particular, *Pride and Prejudice* includes generic 'ball sequences' we have come to expect, one of which is the well-known scene in which Darcy and Elizabeth undertake a tense but amusing sparring flirtation (figure 4). Aesthetically, this is a standard generic sequence, recognisable to regular viewers of classic-novel adaptations. Through the manipulation of various elements of mise-en-scène, and the integration of movement and dialogue, it shows the social conventions of the time to be admirable. The shape of the dance mirrors the careful verbal volley of conversational shots being bounced between the two, suggesting a congruence between social conventions and the instinctive, natural behaviour of a young courting couple. The characters' interactions, vital to the narrative's progression, are not hindered by the rather formal and restrained movements of the dances, but are instead aided by the same. Though Pidduck views such sequences as providing 'a dynamic, complex, and largely non-verbal forum for Austen's trademark plays of gesture and glance' (1998: 398), these scenes are equally significant (more significant, for the viewer who has not read the source novel) for their contribution to the overall mood of the serial. As Alain J.-J. Cohen suggests, dance 'is a richly polysemic and common occurrence' in films and television programmes, and 'every dance scene presents specific image and narrative integration' (1999: 130). In *Pride and Prejudice*, Darcy and Elizabeth find apparent freedom of personal expression within the mores of the time, and their desires appear literally in step with their expected behaviour and roles. This imbues their interaction with a certain ease, grace and simplicity, which inspires pleasure in the viewer; the mood is relaxed, 'upbeat', contemplative, romantic.

The mood of this sequence is not specifically nostalgic. However, because the affects elicited are not strong emotions but subtle moods, they can be co-opted into, or reconfigured as, nostalgia. As the scene is marked as 'past' through a plethora of period details, many viewers may feel wistful admiration, as they compare Elizabeth's and Darcy's 'naïve' flirtation with the complexities of sexual politics and interaction in the 2000s. The use of mise-en-scène and movement, then, works to deny the restrictive nature of contemporary social conventions, whilst the narrative enforces the viewer's sense that the real barriers to any relationship are the pride or the prejudices of those involved in it. Thus the serial combines an apparent realism, justifying a cognitive response that assumes veracity, with a romanticisation and simplification of the past, casting a favourable light over these symbols of days gone by. It offers a reactionary, uncritical representation of the past, achieved through the careful manipulation of details within an appealing aesthetic on screen.

These ball scenes are representative of the serial as a whole; the characters live very happily within the constraints to which they would have been subject. Elizabeth seems so contented and appears to feel so free within her traditional feminine role that younger, less knowledgeable viewers might envy her her situation, unaware of the restrictions that the expectations of 'ladylike' behaviour and a 'lady's' role in life would have placed upon them. The long gowns never hinder Elizabeth's spontaneous 'skips' across the countryside (figures 5a and b); the lack of anything worthwhile to do is disguised by the narrative thrust, so that it is only rarely that one becomes aware that dialogue is the central activity; some of the source novel's lines are surreptitiously cut (such as Mr Bennet's advice to Elizabeth that she find a dominant husband if she wants to be happy); and even the entailment away from the five daughters of the Bennets' house is taken as read – only Mrs Bennet objects – and is not used to highlight the realities of the era's social context. Thus, the congruence between heritage locations and mores, and the characters' desires and feelings, casts a favourable light over these symbols of days gone by. The generic sequences are not merely 'heritage backdrops'; they work with the diegesis to establish a mood (a mood which is not nostalgia).

In the archetypal case of *Pride and Prejudice*, nostalgia does not exist on the screen, nor is it overtly elicited. In essence, to say that this programme is 'nostalgic' is correct; in another sense, such a statement is generalised, vague and inaccurate, for it is more complex than that. The serial works to 'prepare' us for nostalgia and break down any barriers to it. Using mood cues in style, working together with the narrative, it elicits a non-specific mood that is appreciative and open to the pleasures of viewing, and that is often wistful. It aims to conceal awkward historical realities and present the past favourably through the subtle manipulation of mise-en-scène and camera movement, to emphasise its ease, grace and simplicity. The type of landscape chosen for the programme may have been determined by generic conventions, cultural proclivities and the programme's literary source, but Sue Birtwistle, producer, emphasised that in their choice of locations they actively tried to exclude unpleasant images. Birtwistle discusses the depiction of Meryton, stating that the town is only there to 'look nice', and that we see it through the girls' eyes, so the focus is on 'soldiers and hat shops'. On the issue of historical realism, she explicitly states: 'We're not going to be interested in beggars; we're not going to be interested in any poverty, because that's not what's required by the script' (in interview, 1996).[8] This undermines the audience's critical distance and reflection that could hinder their nostalgia for the past. Simultaneously, *Pride and Prejudice* increases the potential for a nostalgic response because it puts the past within reach, by emphasising the apparently eternal nature of human relationships and the permanence of relics and extant artefacts such as the houses. Therefore we feel that the 'ease, grace and simplicity' of the past is potentially attainable today.

A close analysis of the serial reveals the fundamental importance of generic, social and cultural contexts. *Pride and Prejudice*, unlike *Brideshead*, is not nostalgic itself. The 'nostalgia' of so-called nostalgic fictions is frequently a 'secondary' emotion – it is often nigh impossible to point to any textual feature and say 'there is nostalgia' or 'this is nostalgic', unless nostalgia is directly inherent within the narrative. Nostalgia is instead often a synthesis of various elements; it exists in the space between text and viewer. The perception of *Pride and Prejudice* as 'nostalgic' is dependent upon the individual viewer, his or her knowledge of the genre, and the vital cultural context of viewing.

The existence of recognisable generic tropes is extremely important to creating a 'shortcut' to desired affects, for 'the main genre-formulas and modes of fictive entertainment are often constructed to produce certain emotions' (Grodal, 1997: 161). *Pride and Prejudice* utilises 'genre-formulas' in order to suggest that a nostalgic response is an appropriate one to the fiction presented, and in order to provide the cognitive and emotional space for such a response. As this genre's eponymous nostalgia is dependent upon viewers' responses, the importance of the audience's generic knowledge should not be underestimated, for 'the generic expectations of dominant emotional impact ... play an important role in the viewers' reconstruction of a given film' (Grodal, 1997: 163).

Just as we learn the rules of genre – when and how to respond to generic tropes – we are also 'socialized to know what the experience of [a particular emotion] is like and when we should inhabit this "role"' (Plantinga and Smith, 1999: 9). It is vital that we consider

> the social nature of the emotions. Social constructivists assert that cultural forces are not merely overlaid onto more essential biological foundations of the emotions ... Instead, they argue that emotions cannot be understood outside of culture and the shaping forces of society. (Plantinga and Smith, 1999: 9)

Whether we fully accept the constructivists' views or not, most theorists agree that the 'shaping forces' of cultural and social contexts are both powerful and historically specific. In order to understand a programme's 'emotional ambiguities and novel emotional timbres' (Carroll, 1999: 34) it is necessary to appreciate the vital role of context. *Pride and Prejudice* encourages a nostalgic response, and although this response can be resisted (for example, by theorists like Higson and Fredric Jameson), the contemporary cultural climate guides the receptive viewer towards nostalgia.

Nostalgia and postmodernity

So, whilst the source of *Brideshead*'s nostalgia could be found in the text, *Pride and Prejudice*'s nostalgia is far less tangible and harder to locate, being understood as present in a wider cultural and social sphere. In a sense, *Pride and Prejudice* can be regarded as a manifestation or symptom rather than a cause of nostalgia. Describing this rather more vague 'nostalgia' is a difficult task. Eric Larsen offers a definition of nostalgia which echoes commonly held perceptions: an immersion in a falsified, glorified past, where 'the past serves effectively as an escape from the present', this escape occurring as a result of

> the relationship between the past and the future in our time. For a number of reasons, the age we live in has lost its ability to draw people toward the future with a sense of vitality, security or hope. One result of this fact is that what comes to seem most desirable, and most meaningful also, is not the promise or release of a cleansed future, but the security and comfort of a known past. (1983: 464)[9]

Theorists who are primarily concerned with the ideological function of nostalgia understand it thus: a yearning for the past which does not recognise the shortcomings of previous eras – restrictive, oppressive class structures, unquestioned nationalism and colonisation, and expected and enforced modes of gendered behaviour. This yearning, created by the representation of past as 'heritage', is judged not just idealistic and unrealistic but also reactionary, for the audience not only fails to recognise the social problems of the past, but also succeeds in forgetting the social problems of the present.

This idea that 'heritage' films and programmes offer us an escape from the present into the past is widely held. Bullen writes of the appeal of a 'retreat from the present' (1990: 52), whilst Simon Harcourt-Smith pleads: 'by all means let us escape on the wings of the movies to less troubled epochs than the present' (in Cook, 1996: 56). The past is characterised as an escape, and thus too is the genre, which 'falsifies, turning the past into a safe, familiar place' (Friedburg, 1993: 118). The way in which we escape the present through nostalgia is echoed in the classic-novel adaptation's escape from its televisual present. Both the past and this genre are 'safe, familiar place[s]'. Hipsky, writing about *Howards End* (1992), describes the house Howards End as 'the refuge-within-the-refuge, the purest inner sanctum of the beauty-enhanced historical space we have come to the movie to escape into' (1994: 102).

As Larsen implies, our tendency to feel nostalgia and our desire to 'escape' to/through it is rooted in our everyday cultural and social context. Nostalgia (again, understood as a mood not an emotion) exists within our culture outside the realms of art, and is an effect of our (post)modern condition. Larsen and Friedburg suggest that the appeal of nostalgia can be traced to our feelings of uncertainty and despondency about our present times; Fred Davis writes that nostalgia arises due to 'present fears, discontents, anxieties and uncertainties' (1979: 34); and Hewison opines, 'nostalgia is felt most strongly at a time of discontent, anxiety or disappointment ... [our present] is a time going nowhere, a time that leaves nothing for our imaginations to do except plunge into the past' (1987: 45–6).

These are familiar claims. Friedburg, with other theorists of the postmodern, argues that it is postmodernity[10] that precipitates our search for roots in the past (and yet determines that this search is unsuccessful). Fredric Jameson, in his famous essay on postmodernism and nostalgia, describes our relationship with 'nostalgia' films (within which classic-novel adaptations can be included) in a conventional way: 'we peer across our historical gap and try to focus the landscape of the past through nostalgia-tinted spectacles' (1991: 290). The lack of historicism and 'objectivity' in the gaze we cast over the 'landscape of the past' is, in his opinion, less a result of our relationship with the past than a consequence of our relationship with our present. As Friedburg neatly puts it,

'Jameson diagnosed the "nostalgia" film as a sign of postmodern cultural malaise' (1993: 188).

 Pride and Prejudice, as an archetype of the genre, is regarded as a symptom of postmodernity.[11] It elicits nostalgia as its defining generic mood; as an example of the genre at its peak, it utilises generic tropes of style and content in an overt, even exaggerated fashion. This does not mean, however, that the programme's identity can be explained simply within the terms of 'nostalgia'. Despite its reliance upon this traditional mode of address, this serial was highly successful because of its simultaneous embrace of the popular and televisual. A close look at the cultural event that it constituted, and the popular discourses in which it was placed (how it was marketed, discussed and evaluated) makes this clear.

Televisuality

Especially since the early 1990s, classic-novel adaptations have been as heavily marketed as any other 'quality' or expensive television programme. There are a significant number of internally produced marketing aids: trailers, *Radio Times* features, merchandise and so on, which relate not only to the original broadcast, but also to the adaptation's release on videotape and the customary republication of the source book as a television tie-in. Those writers who, following Kerr, have written about classic-novel adaptations as examples of 'bourgeois' television, claiming a certain cultural status through their links with 'great literature' and 'art film', often misunderstand the true nature of adaptations' identity as constituted within the bounds of the televisual. It is true that there is an overt emphasis upon the adaptation's literary origins and high production qualities, but if one looks closely at real examples of 'contemporary popular discourse', one sees that it recognises and supports generic development and experimentation. In fact, there is a discernible response within recent popular reviews to the adaptation as a site of contradictory discourses (between the generic microcosm of the classic-novel adaptation and the world of the televisual); viewers and critics seem increasingly aware of the potential clash or renegotiation between these two 'worlds'. In contrast with the critical and evaluative response offered to *Brideshead*, viewers and critics of *Pride and Prejudice*, whose writings themselves constitute part of the wider televisual context, engage with the text as a site of competing discourses within the 'playground' of the televisual.

 Austen's iconic status within this genre is evident from the emphasis laid upon the use of her name, which is often closely associated not just with the source book but also with the adaptation itself: thus we are presented with '*Pride and Prejudice* by Jane Austen' (1990), '*Persuasion* by Jane Austen' (1995), 'Jane Austen's *Pride and Prejudice*' (1995), and so forth. Of course adaptations are ordinarily 'announced' through references to their source novels, and adaptations of classic novels especially foreground their references to their source books and the respective source authors. Yet this is not necessarily evidence of an attempt to deny or escape the televisual context for a more highly esteemed 'literary' one. For one thing, these references are important because they sell. For many viewers, knowing that *Clueless* (1995) was based on *Emma* was enough to make them go and see the film, something that they may not otherwise have considered.[12] Such an influence does not only apply in this country: the BBC relies on this 'recognition effect' to boost its international sales in a time when they are under increasing pressure to compete, as a profitable company, with the commercial television stations.[13] Similarly, as we have seen, 'Austen adaptations' are the archetypes of the classic-novel adaptation genre, so to emphasise an adaptation as being one of 'Austen' is to advertise the expected characteristic features of the programme (its generic style, content and mood), as much as to highlight its source text. It could be argued that many more viewers know and recognise an 'Austen adaptation' than have read the books upon which they are 'based'.

No doubt the BBC considered very carefully the marketing of the videotape release of *Pride and Prejudice*, to achieve the staggering sales they did: 50,000 videotapes in the first week of sales, 200,000 in the first year (Troost and Greenfield, 1998: 1). On studying the presentation box for the videotape release of this serial, we find these words:

> *(on front)* BBC *Pride and Prejudice* by Jane Austen
> Stunning BBC TV dramatisation of a classic romance.
> *(on back)* The romance, drama and humour of Jane Austen's greatest novel, perfectly captured by an all-star cast in this 1995 adaptation by award-winning writer Andrew Davies.
> 'It is a truth universally acknowledged, that a single man in possession of a good fortune must be in want of a wife.'
> Amid a host of delightful characters and against a background of grand, stately homes and beautiful countryside, this famous romance runs its rocky course.
> Director: Simon Langton
> *(followed by list of cast and crew)*

This certainly seems convincing evidence for the traditional view of classic-novel adaptations, with the deliberate ambiguity over the 'author-ship' of the BBC serial, and use of the novel's famous opening lines. However, it is important to bear in mind that this 'advertisement' was written not to sell the original broadcast (to attract viewers) but instead to induce buyers who had probably already watched the serial to buy it on video. The writing attempts to convince us of the quality of the serial and its status as a classic piece of television – as a programme that will take its place amongst the glowing successes of (BBC) television history. Potential buyers are thus convinced to buy the video, not just to watch the programme again, but also because to do so is to preserve a moment of broadcasting history of which, as viewers of the original broadcast, they were a part. In other words, we are referred to the programme's significance within its televisual context, not its 'literary' one. The programme is also described in terms of its fidelity to generic iconography ('grand, stately homes and beautiful countryside'), as well as in terms of its fidelity to the source novel.

Most importantly, when one looks at examples of the marketing of the original broadcasts of *Pride and Prejudice*, one finds that references to the cultural status and literary origins of the programme are employed to a much lesser extent than one might expect. The above references to the source novel, used to sell a post-broadcast videotape, are not typical. There are other emphases which predominate in the publicity that aimed to attract first-time viewers.

The position of even 'traditional' classic-novel adaptations within a contemporary televisual context is made clear in a 1997 *Radio Times* feature, 'My goodness, how they've changed' (Graham, 1997). The *Pride and Prejudice* serial was due to be re-shown on BBC1, and the purpose of this article, therefore, was to publicise it.[14] Yet the article, though printed next to a three-quarter page photograph of Jennifer Ehle and Colin Firth dressed in costume as Elizabeth Bennet and Fitzwilliam Darcy, barely mentions the serial, being based, in the main, on an interview with Firth, and the writer's assessment of his sexual attractiveness and analysis of his personal life. The title of this piece ('My goodness, how they've changed') places the two actors concerned firmly within the present time of the article, and the original run of *Pride and Prejudice* within the time scale of two contemporary actors' careers. This stresses not the 'classic', lasting nature of the adaptation (in the way, perhaps, that a screening of Olivier's *Henry V* (1944) might be advertised), but the *performative* aspect of the adaptation – the performance of two roles by two now well-known actors, two years previously. In place of an emphasis on the literary origins of the serial and its 'classic' nature, we have an emphasis on a characteristic associated purely with the televisual nature of the serial – its identity as a performance.

This wider performative (televisual) aspect of the adaptation is also stressed through a distinction made at several junctures by the feature-writer, Alison Graham. On the topic of Firth's purported sex-appeal, she writes:

> as Mr Darcy in the BBC adaptation of *Pride and Prejudice* he was lusted after by millions of otherwise sensible women. All it took was for him to smoulder on a staircase or rise, dripping and fully clothed, from an impromptu dip in a lake, and women across the country – and later the world – melted like toasted brie.
>
> And there's the rub. It was Mr Darcy they were swooning over, not necessarily Colin Firth ... Firth would be the first to admit that he doesn't turn heads when he walks into the pub. And even at the height of Darcymania, he was rarely stopped on the streets. (Graham, 1997a: 23)

Graham's unflattering comparison of the rather average-looking Firth with his attractive, brooding alter-ego Mr Darcy verges on the offensive; to add insult to injury, the piece finishes with the note 'turn to page 126 for the second and final token for your Darcy poster'. Obviously there cannot be the clear separation intimated by Graham between the dull Mr Firth and the sexy Mr Darcy, for they are inextricably physically linked in the unique way that actors are with the roles they play. The effect of this 'double identity' (actor/role) is to heighten our perception of the adaptation as contemporary, rather than 'past', to increase our sense of the adaptation-as-programme.

In addition, the 'Darcy phenomenon', noted by popular writers like Graham and explored by academics like Lisa Hopkins (Hopkins, 1998), extrapolated Darcy/Firth from his place within a(n) (Austen) text, and placed him as a 'free-floating signifier' within the televisual context. Darcy 'enters a moment of autonomy, of a relatively free-floating existence, as over against its former objects' (Jameson, 1991: 96). This 'postmodern' aspect of the *Pride and Prejudice* experience qualifies Jonathan Miller's assertion that 'The fact that someone is in a novel ... does not mean that they are *in* the novel in the same way that someone else might be *in* Birmingham or *in* a cubicle. They cannot be taken out of the novel and put in a film of it' (1986: 238–9) (italics in original). The unique nature of performance and the extended televisual context allowed Darcy to escape both novel and adaptation, to become a popular character who, like Superman/Christopher Reeves, exists in the form of actor Firth, but is simultaneously greater than him.[15]

The *Radio Times* article in question concludes, 'like it or not, Firth and Ehle have moved on. *Pride and Prejudice* was another country', which interestingly invokes the well-known phrase 'the past is another country', and thus knowingly gestures towards *Pride and Prejudice* as an archetype of the classic-novel generic microcosm. Of course, this 'other country' can be revisited if one purchases the video. Our nostalgia is thus directed not just towards the fictional world *Pride and Prejudice* represents, but also towards the serial itself. An advertisement for the video release on 1 August 1997, run in national newspapers, boasts, 'The best in Classic Drama, available on video'; this sentence stands below a flattering photograph of Elizabeth Bennet and Mr Darcy, with a much larger heading: 'Remember the first time ... *Pride and Prejudice*'. Even the purported claim to 'classic', elite, literary drama is undercut, as we are referred to our memories of the televisual event – the performance itself, and not our memories of its literary source. 'The first time' does not refer to one's reading of the book by Jane Austen but one's viewing of the first screening of the BBC's adaptation of it. There is also, of course, the deliberate (and postmodern) play on words: the 'playful and allusive' (Brooker and Brooker, 1997: 1) reference to another memorable 'performance' – isn't everyone supposed to remember their 'first time'?

Finally, a review in the *Radio Times*, printed just after the 1997 re-run, again written by Graham, makes perfectly clear that the performance of *Pride and Prejudice* was a truly televisual, contemporary and popular event, and not a restrained retelling of a worthy literary classic. Graham writes about the fate of those who miss a 'TV event' first time around. Employing the only overt reference to Austen's book in the whole article, she says, 'It is a truth universally acknowledged that if you miss a big television event, you feel a bit daft. Not only that, those who watched the first time round will never give you a chance to join their little club, particularly if this great event is repeated' (Graham, 1997b: 122). Her later comment, 'The thing about big television events is that they are national unifiers, the kind of things people talk about in the newsagent's next morning', places the re-run of *Pride and Prejudice* firmly in the context of the reception (and appropriation) of a popular television text, and thus within the wider, contemporary context of the televisual. Her sense of being outside the television-created 'community' of *Pride and Prejudice* viewers, who are connected with each other through the televisual event, echoes the model of the 'televisual' elaborated in Part I: the televisual has become a context, expanding its affective sphere beyond its programmes. Graham's comments also reveal a nostalgia for the 'television event', both in specific terms (for *Pride and Prejudice*), and in more general terms (for times when a television text could constitute a shared national event – something now much rarer in a multichannel, twenty-four-hour television culture). Her words betray a feeling that in trying to 'relive' the *Pride and Prejudice* experience, she is also attempting to recapture the significance of early television events like *Brideshead*. In this sense, then, *Pride and Prejudice* attempts to satisfy a nostalgic yearning for the televisual past.

Pride and Prejudice's place in the wider televisual context also determines its place in popular culture, distancing the programme from traditional notions of elite, literary culture. The programme was shown first in 1995, then re-shown in July 1997. The two intervening years, however, seemed to allow no respite from rampant 'Austenmania'. The *Radio Times* feature whence this term derives, written in July 1996, notes for its evidence *Pride and Prejudice, Persuasion* (BBC/WGBH, 1995), *Sense and Sensibility* (Mirage/Columbia, 1995) and the 'forthcoming' ITV *Emma* (Meridian/A&E, 1996) (which, unmentioned in the report, followed hot on the heels of the film *Emma* (Miramax, 1996)).

This *Radio Times* report is obviously concerned to highlight critical and commercial BBC successes, the *Radio Times* being historically and loosely linked to the BBC, which faces increasing financial pressures. Yet this emphasis on market forces undermines the notion that BBC productions are marketed primarily in terms of their status as 'bourgeois' television based on classic novels. And instead of presenting the programmes and films as examples of an elite, literary culture, the texts are presented as part of an extended popular culture. The feature notes trends in popular culture which have arisen from Austen adaptations: 'thanks to Colin Firth's smouldering Darcy, sideburns have undergone a revival, while bra manufacturers have been cashing in on the Bennet girls' "rounded and uplifted" look. Elizabeth's romantic wedding dress has also been much copied by brides' (Lock, 1996a: 66–7). In addition 'the UK Jane Austen Society has ... seen membership climb sharply, with more than 260 joining since *Pride and Prejudice* was screened last year, bringing its total to more than 2,000'. There are references to web-pages devoted to Jane Austen, such as that containing the strange 'picture of her ... lounging by a pool, complete with bonnet, mobile and laptop'. In comparison with Austen adaptations themselves, these are examples of participatory activities organised by members of the public for their own pleasure – the programmes acting as catalysts for these reactions.

This is not to suggest that such activities, being 'popular', are for that reason radical or subversive (*contra* Fiske).[16] Wearing a wonderbra and getting married hardly constitute a rejection of patriarchal values. However, these examples of the 'ripple effect' from one televisual event certainly render traditional analyses of the genre no longer unproblematically applicable. They also corroborate the conceptualisation of the extended televisual context elucidated in Part I. As Whelehan notes, classic-novel adaptations set up 'a chain of references, local and immanent to the new adopted form, [which] are generated and infinitely dispersed' (1999: 8). Indeed these references are 'generated' and 'dispersed' beyond the bounds of television, beyond even the bounds of the televisual, as they extend into new media like the internet. And perhaps it is significant that the main Austen website is 'The Republic of Pemberley' – 'republic' bearing connotations of equality and freedom in a monarchist country, even for those who might not want to inhabit a 'real' republic.

Moments of change

Brideshead Revisited and *Pride and Prejudice* established and consolidated tropes of content, style and mood that together constitute the traditional generic microcosm of the television classic-novel adaptation. Both programmes are characterised by their mood (nostalgic, and wistful and pro-nostalgic, respectively), and the consequent mode of our connection is nostalgic, although close analysis reveals the complex and sometimes ambiguous nature (and locus) of this 'nostalgia'. Interestingly, though, *Pride and Prejudice*, despite being a 'traditional' and highly esteemed classic-novel adaptation, does not attempt to escape the bounds of contemporary televisuality, in favour of maintaining links with a 'past' literary culture; the programme is instead happily located within the televisual context.

Continuities in generic tropes perpetuate the distinctiveness of a genre that is still identifiable, but there is also evidence of broad developments within the genre. In particular, one should be aware of the increasing importance of the televisual to the genre's stylistic features and affectiveness. Later examples of the genre reveal simultaneously significant continuities and dramatic alterations in content, style and mood. Specifically, later examples have tended to exhibit more 'postmodern' features, a greater recognition of their loci in the televisual context, and a reflexivity not apparent in the 'traditional' mode of classic-novel adaptations.

Notes

1 This is in keeping with the alternative model of adaptation proffered in Part I.
2 See, for example, the following two chapters on *Moll Flanders* (1996) and *The Tenant of Wildfell Hall* (1996).
3 Additional implications regarding the 'framing of landscape' have been suggested. Julianne Pidduck, for example, notes how 'capitalist and patriarchal relations of ownership inform the British landscape painting tradition' (1998: 388), thus revealing how the constructs of nationhood, class and gender have impacted upon the ways in which we have traditionally displayed and viewed landscape. See Pidduck, 'Of Windows and Country Walks', *Screen* 39: 4 (Winter), 381–400.
4 The solidity and historical veracity of these links with the past challenges dominant (postmodern) notions of history, the past and nostalgia, upon which many film theorists like Higson rely. See later in this chapter for a discussion of these postmodernist theories.

5 Andrew Davies was interviewed in *Pride and Prejudice: From Page to Screen* (BBC, 1995).

6 Alfred Schutz (1962) 'On Multiple Realities'. Davis notes that 'Schutz speaks of realities. For present purposes I have chosen the alternative term *form of consciousness*, in part because it better conveys the notion of a more or less distinctive organization of inner experience and in part because it avoids the ambiguity of Schutz's use of the term "reality"' (Davis, 1979: 78) (italics in original).

7 The term 'imagined community' is taken from Benedict Anderson's oft-cited work *Imagined Communities: Reflections on the Origin and Spread of Nationalism* (1993).

8 Sue Birtwistle is interviewed in *Pride and Prejudice: From Page to Screen* (BBC, 1995).

9 See also Robert Hewison (1987: 43–7), for a similar analysis to that of Larsen.

10 As I stated in Chapter 4, there is not the space here for a lengthy discussion of the postmodern. I am therefore being necessarily selective in my choice of features of 'postmodernism' and brief in my references to 'postmodernity'. As Peter Brooker and Will Brooker emphasise (1997: 3), a distinction must be made between these two terms. Friedburg and Jameson refer here to the latter, something Barry Smart defines as our 'contemporary social, cultural and political condition' (1993: 12). 'Postmodernism', by contrast, implies a particular aesthetic style, which the Brookers call 'self-ironic eclecticism' (1997: 3). Within film and television studies, postmodernism has attracted considerable interest; Smart offers an excellent overview of postmodernity for the interested reader (Smart, 1993).

11 I shall investigate the claims of postmodernist writers at greater length later, specifically in Chapter 8.

12 This point was made by Jean Wilson in her paper 'Adapting Jane Austen? The Battle for Jane Austen', given at the 'Classic Fiction and Modern Adaptations' conference, Centre for Extra-Mural Studies, Birkbeck College, University of London (April 1997).

13 It is also important to remember that the emphasis placed on fidelity in the publicity, promotion and marketing of an adaptation does not always reflect the nature of the actual screen text; the commercial and institutional context of these particular programmes explains, to a great degree, the emphasis seemingly placed on fidelity.

14 The serial was broadcast twice: first in 1995, and again in 1997.

15 Darcy's transformation from character to extra-textual icon is discussed in 'Darcy's Escape: An Icon in the Making' (Cardwell, 2000b).

16 As John Fiske defines it, popular culture is produced by the people, for the people, and is often inspired by mass culture provided for them. He also argues for popular culture as potentially radical (1989a; 1989b). His definition of 'popular culture' is useful here, but I withhold judgement regarding popular culture's radical potential.

The Fortunes and Misfortunes of *Moll Flanders* (1996)

7

A conceptualisation of the classic-novel adaptation genre, and related notions of nostalgia, were more useful in constructing an interpretative framework for *Brideshead* and *Pride and Prejudice* than was an understanding of the televisual. Despite the increasing influence of the televisual context on the positioning and identity of the later *Pride and Prejudice*, the influence of the televisual was limited in terms of its textual repercussions. Few intra-textual aspects in either adaptation suggested the salience of televisual features such as contemporaneity, presentness or performativity. Only intertextuality proved to be of considerable importance, as generic traits borrowed from other classic-novel adaptations were vital in marking out the programmes' generic identity.

However, other recent television classic-novel adaptations demand a new way of illuminating them. In a sense, the 1995 production of *Pride and Prejudice* marked a peak in the production of archetypal, nostalgic classic-novel adaptations. The adaptations discussed in this chapter and Chapter 8 appear somewhat more self-conscious, more sophisticated, than their forebears. *Moll Flanders* (ITV, 1996) and *The Tenant of Wildfell Hall* (BBC, 1996) reflect a wider generic shift in classic-novel adaptations. It is clear that even on an immediate level, contemporary adaptations frequently differ in setting, content and mood from earlier examples of the genre. While the adaptations are still set in the past and are still careful to pay attention to details of period accuracy, the period details themselves, and their manipulation within the texts, are different. It is immediately apparent that many recent adaptations do not romanticise the past in the same way as the films upon which 'nostalgia' theorists have focused. Settings are often employed in a different way: they are no longer 'excessive'; they often serve definite narrative purposes; they are not always beautiful; and there is considerably more variation in their use, across the genre. Contra John Hill's assertion that of the 'three main emphases within heritage culture – the aristocratic, the rustic, and the industrial – it is clearly the aristocratic, or upper-middle-class, emphasis which the heritage film prefers' (1999: 77), adaptations since the late 1990s challenge this characterisation.[1]

Observe the images of eighteenth-century squalor, degradation and darkness in *Moll Flanders*: there are no shots of rosy-cheeked street urchins here (such as those first presented in Lionel Bart's stage show *Oliver!*).[2] Instead, the disgusting prison and the grubby flats, streets and inns that form Moll's habitat hardly romanticise an era when the only option open to a woman like her was the alternative imprisonment of marriage. Comparably, *Far From the Madding Crowd* (ITV, 1998) was acclaimed for capturing 'Hardy's Wessex', and was filmed on location in Dorset, with each actor carefully coached in the regional accent. Yet *Madding Crowd* reveals the best and worst of the English countryside: the fertile, expansive beauty of the land alongside the miserable rural dwelling of Gabriel Oak and the reliance of the rural people on good fortune and hard labour.

The 1996 film *Jude* (from *Jude the Obscure*) included a now infamous computer-generated long shot of Christminster, taking the most picturesque aspects of Oxford's spires and electronically mixing these with shots of Berkshire and Edinburgh. This outraged many Hardy fans, yet the manipulated image looks suitably specious and romantic, and is juxtaposed with the miserable, dark and dirty streets Jude encounters upon his arrival in Christminster – thus exposing the difference between his distanced, idealised gaze upon the town and the grim actualities of class-bound, city society.

This varied use of setting reveals a move towards greater narrative depth, achieving a higher level of both symbolic and (socially) realistic representation. This use also contributes to the creation of a specific atmosphere, as opposed to a general, generic mood, that reflects the tone of the particular adaptation's narrative (which sometimes, though not always, echoes that of the source book). It is also significant that programme makers began, in the mid to late 1990s, to select different authors (of source novels), leaving Austen behind and choosing others whose work was more accessible to this new style of adaptation. Dickens has always been popular with adapters, and adaptations of his work tend to stand out from the genre for their darkness of humour and tone, but there was a sudden glut of adaptations of his books: *Martin Chuzzlewit* (BBC/WGBH, 1994), *Our Mutual Friend* (BBC, 1998), *Great Expectations* (BBC, 1999), *Oliver Twist* (ITV, 1999) and *David Copperfield* (BBC, 1999). Hardy has for some reason never been looked upon quite as favourably as Dickens, but in the 1990s we were offered *The Mayor of Casterbridge* (BBC, 1991), *Far From the Madding Crowd* (ITV, 1998) and *Tess of the*

D'Urbervilles (ITV, 1998). The Brontës' dark, sometimes menacing, work also gained attention, and adaptations of *Jane Eyre* (ITV, 1997) and *Wuthering Heights* (ITV, 1999) joined *Wildfell Hall*. It can surely be no coincidence that all these authors offer a relatively darker view of society than Austen does, and focus on characters who, if not working-class, are at least 'workers'; in addition, Hardy's and the Brontës' novels ordinarily focus on the 'rustic', and Dickens's frequently on the industrial, undermining Hill's argument that these aspects of 'heritage culture' are ignored in screen representations.

The cynic could level a familiar charge here: the increased 'realism' and change in mood could be explained through customary motives – the aim to be faithful to the mood of the source novel and at the same time 'fool' the audience into thinking that this was what the past was really like. It is, after all, because of their grimness that these adaptations seem less fanciful, magical and romantic, more real, honest and truthful about the times they depict. As McArthur argues, 'historical drama ... is the area where we are most off our guard' (1978: 45).

There is some mileage in this accusation. Certainly, the emotional, imaginative and educative links that these programmes forge between the audience and past times are still centrally important to the genre's cultural salience, appeal and endurance: 'Although the screen cannot possibly show everything "as it really was", the popularity of these dramas lies, apart from their narratives and characterizations, in their claims to historical authenticity, and to the pleasures gleaned from their discovery of times lost from view' (Wollen, 1991: 187). In that sense, these are still 'heritage' programmes, for as Raphael Samuel noted, 'heritage' is not inherently reactionary or elitist, but can refer to the process of tracing the impact of our past upon our present.[3]

Yet my response to the cynic is a tentative rebuttal. Recent television adaptations must be understood as creating, affirming and renegotiating our relationship with the past, but as doing this in terms of a constant affirmation of the present moment. They set up and foreground a complex interplay between the pastness and the presentness of the adaptation text. The two adaptations discussed in this chapter and the next create such an interplay in very different ways. *Moll Flanders*, rather than attempting a traditional rejection of the contemporary televisual context, constantly affirms it, even textually; our relation to the past is filtered through this present 'lens', offering us a critical distance from it. Notions of televisuality and, in particular, performance, as discussed in Part I, are absolutely central to a coherent analysis of *Moll Flanders*, and provide key foci for my discussion. *The Tenant of Wildfell Hall*, in comparison, offers a reflexive play on generic conventions which questions and subverts our traditional nostalgic relationship with the past; indeed, it offers a postmodern commentary upon the genre itself.

Stand aside, Jane Austen ...

Daniel Defoe's *The Fortunes and Misfortunes of the Famous Moll Flanders*, written in 1722, has undoubtedly been read by fewer of the general public than either *Brideshead Revisited* or *Pride and Prejudice*. This relative lack of personal knowledge of the book, probably due in part to its less accessible form and eighteenth-century use of language, seems to have been a positive boon to the adapter Andrew Davies, whose adaptation of it is far more adventurous and revisionist than his previous *Pride and Prejudice*. Few critics noticed or cared about the omissions and amendments made by Davies – indeed the adaptation received plaudits from almost all corners. Public perception of Defoe as a writer of more adventurous tales than Austen would have arisen from the more widely read *Robinson Crusoe* (1719), whilst general knowledge of *Moll Flanders* is likely to have been limited to a vague notion that the central character was a tough, immoral, even lewd (in contemporary terms, exciting) woman who bore no resemblance to the Elizabeth Bennets and Anne Elliots of Austen's novels. Greater public awareness of the character 'Moll Flanders', rather than knowledge of the novel *Moll Flanders*, aids Moll's transformation into a 'free-floating signifier' – thus the curious 1996 cinema-release film *Moll Flanders* was 'based on the character in the novel by Daniel Defoe', not on the novel itself, and indeed substituted an almost entirely different narrative for that of Defoe's novel. Added to the audience's supposed knowledge only of Moll's character, and not of Defoe's novel, is the 'categorical instability' (Blewett, 1989: 23) of Defoe's source novel, which also permits greater freedom of interpretation even for adapters aiming for fidelity.

Moll Flanders was marketed mostly on the strength of its bawdy, even subversive (carnivalesque) qualities. Employing a direct comparison with the more traditional style used for Austen adaptations, a pre-publicity article in the *Radio Times* begins, 'Stand aside, Jane Austen: polite society is about to be shocked as Daniel Defoe's bawdy Moll Flanders comes to TV', and continues, '*Moll Flanders* is no *Pride and Prejudice*: Daniel Defoe's 18th-century tale of a woman who uses her sexuality to advance her fortunes has been turned into a full-blooded, full-frontal series, starring Alex Kingston' (Lock, 1996b: 41). A preview in the same edition, under 'Today's Choices', repeats the same comparison: 'Andrew Davies presents his latest adaptation of an English literary classic. Say goodbye to the uptight, upright characters of Jane Austen, though: in *Moll Flanders* we're plunged headlong into the bosom-heaving world of Daniel Defoe' (Anon., 1996: 86).

Such comments accurately signal the stylistic differences between *Moll Flanders* and *Pride and Prejudice*, and it is noteworthy that the writers are not so much comparing Austen with Defoe as Austen adaptations with this Defoe adaptation. Taking into account the probable lack of public knowledge of Defoe's source novel, the article mentions the two authors only in order to compare two distinct televisual styles; the reviewers keep the programmes firmly within their televisual context. The notion of Austen adaptations as 'typical' of the classic-novel adaptation genre, and of *Pride and Prejudice* as the archetype of these, is used as a benchmark against which other adaptations can be categorised.

The bawdiness of *Moll Flanders* is its key selling point. The *Radio Times* stated that 'the producer David Lascelles *promises* a lot of sex and nudity, and perhaps stronger language than people may be used to in the classics' (Anon., 1996: 86) (my emphasis). Later, the cover of the videotape release of the serial boasts an 18 certificate due to the inclusion of 'sequences exclusive to video'. Though the potential for a licentious serial by Davies arises from the content of the source novel, the actual presentation is heavily dependent upon the use of television conventions and references to features of the televisual. Reviewers and critics seemed aware of this, and worked with it to place the programme firmly within its televisual context. While it is true that Defoe's source novel is considerably more risqué, action-packed, scandalous and socially aware than any of Austen's oeuvre, the way in which this crudity is 'sold' to us does not rely upon references to the source book, but rather on similarities between the 'shocking' aspects of the *Moll Flanders* adaptation and those of other television programmes and films: 'incest, prostitution, bigamy and theft: if this sounds like a *Brookside* story line, you might be surprised to learn it all happens in TV's latest period drama' (Lock, 1996b: 41); and, under a picture of a cavorting Moll and Daniel Dawkins: 'Carry On up the classics: Alex Kingston and Christopher Fulford get down to some serious romping in *Moll Flanders*' (Anon., 1996: 86).

The overt use of intertextual references, along with the repetition of each actor's 'form' after his or her name – 'Alex Kingston (*The Knock*)' and 'Daniel Craig (Geordie in *Our Friends in the North*)' – not only emphasise the performative, contemporary nature of the adaptation, but also its identity as a programme amongst others. In comparison with *Pride and Prejudice*, *Moll Flanders* is identified even more obviously as a televisual text. References to Defoe's text are not given; his name only appears occasionally. *Moll Flanders* is marketed as a television programme, born, bred and living in the televisual context.[4]

The programme *Moll Flanders* itself acknowledges its televisual context. *Pride and Prejudice* depicted that curious, traditional generic microcosm, constituted within the televisual, which asserts its identity by rejecting televisual conventions and the contemporary world. *Moll Flanders* constitutes a radical challenge to generic norms: the programme still works to faithfully recreate the past, and there are several 'set generic pieces', but these are employed to very different effect than in previous adaptations. Most importantly, the programme asserts its televisuality through its intertextuality, presentness and, most of all, its performativity, which works to highlight the constructed and 'performed' nature of the text and (simultaneously) the illusory nature of adaptations' generic representations of the past and our insecure relationship with that 'past'.[5]

Temporality

As *Moll Flanders* was broadcast on ITV, there were advertisements before, during and after each episode. However, rather than being broken up into disparate fragments, the adaptation was integrated into a wider televisual flow that included advertisements and programmes. Before each episode began, the sponsor of the programme, Midland Bank, ran a short promotion. However, this promotion did not openly advertise the bank or its services. Instead, we saw 'live' the man who was at that moment reading the continuity announcement to which we were listening. That is, we saw him sitting at a microphone, reading the words 'Good evening. Tonight you're going to see the ITV drama premiere. The programme starts in just a few moments ...' (cut to pseudo-live footage of a row of largish suburban houses. As the camera tracks along in front of the row, we see the 'residents' gathering up gardening equipment, closing garage doors, entering houses and drawing curtains. The voice-over continues):

> So, if you hurry, you've just got time to finish that phone call, put the dishes away, say goodnight to the toddlers, close the upstairs window, push the cat aside, and settle down on the sofa. If the tea isn't brewed yet, bring the teapot in with you. You can finish that crossword later, because it's time for tonight's ITV premiere, in association with Midland Bank.

At each advertisement break, we saw a brief clip of the same houses, now in a darker street (later in the evening), with downstairs windows lit as (we assume) their residents enjoyed the same drama premiere as we were; after the programme finished, we saw a resident come to the front door to put empty milk bottles out, as the voice-over thanked us for watching.

This overt address to the television audience served three functions, only one of which was to advertise the sponsor, Midland Bank. The trailer also worked to grab the audience's attention by utilising television's presentness, its potential liveness. Because the viewers were likely to be taking part in exactly the kind of activity described by the voice-over, they would feel more directly, even personally addressed; as Allen argues, television's 'texts are not only presented for us but directed out at us' (1992: 120). To be directly addressed in a way that corresponds to one's actual situation is incredibly appealing. This directed address asserts the existence of a community of television viewers; though separated by 'mobile privatisation' (Williams, 1975), we are brought together, to form an audience, through television. The third function of this trailer was to create a television event, highlighting the performative nature of the adaptation. Like the event that was *Pride and Prejudice*, *Moll Flanders* was being announced as a performance. We are asked to settle down, abandon whatever we are doing, and set aside time to concentrate on the programme; at the end of the broadcast, we are thanked for our attention (attendance). It is all rather formal, rather polite, for television – it is almost like attending a theatrical or cinematic performance. Robin Nelson observes that with 'the profusion of channels and the incessant flow of television ... any specific TV drama – whatever its form or content – is diminished in impact' (1997: 23). In order to overcome this problem, *Moll Flanders* is marked as special, not because it is an adaptation, nor because it is based on a classic novel, but because it is a unique performance offered 'live' within the eternal performance of television. Tony Wilson also implies that television continuity announcements themselves can highlight the programmes' performativity, undermining any notion we may have of television as a 'window on the world': 'continuity announcements ... may be read as denying permission to treat the text as veridical, as giving an unproblematic access to reality' (1993: 114). It is unlikely that any viewer would be 'fooled' into confusing *Moll Flanders* with reality, but Wilson's observation that continuity announcements are influential in positioning programmes as presentations, as performances, is a perceptive one. And as we shall see, performance is vital to *Moll Flanders* in more ways than this one.

Direct address

Alex Kingston, as Moll, provides a running commentary throughout the serial, mostly in the form of a voice-over. This feature of the serial can be regarded as traditional in two senses: first, the voice-over appears to be a result of fidelity to the source novel, which is written in diary form;

second, the technique of first-person narration has historically been used in classic-novel adaptations. *Brideshead*, as previously discussed, utilised this convention in order to attempt to maintain the novel's personalised point of view on the diegesis, but there were other precursors, such as David Lean's famous *Great Expectations* (1946). First-person narration, achieved through voice-over, is typically used to allow us direct access to the narrating character's thoughts and feelings. However, it is in the form and effect of this filmic/televisual feature that *Moll Flanders* breaks with convention.

In its formal variation from the norm, this programme mixes voice-over with direct address. At the beginning of the serial, the camera follows a jailer of Newgate prison to Moll's cell, where the jailer encourages his on-screen followers (visitors) and us to look at 'Moll Flanders, wickedest woman in the world'. The use of a hand-held camera in this sequence is the first surprise of this adaptation: rather than the slow, controlled, filmic movements of a camera as it surveys a scene, we are offered a confused, jolting trajectory through the hideous jail, as the equally grotesque inmates jostle the visitors and the camera itself. Most unusually, though, our gaze upon Moll is followed not by the expected shot from Moll's point of view, but by a jump-cut shot of Moll taken from a completely different angle. Suddenly we view her as if from inside the cell, and she turns to the camera and beckons: 'Come on, come closer. Come ... You want to know how I came to be in this place of horrors, how I fell from pride and pomp ... You see, for me the wheel of fortune came full circle – I was born here ...'. Her direct address continues as she begins to tell us the details of her early childhood, mutating into a voice-over narration as the scenes she describes are shown on screen.

Though unusual, this opening does not completely undermine the audience's expectations of generic conventions. The use of direct address is surprising, but its mutation into voice-over narration – a familiar convention of the genre – identifies Moll's initial address to us as a 'beginning'. Like the earliest film adaptations that began by showing the first page of the source novel on screen, followed by the turning of the novel's pages by a sudden gust of wind (again, see *Great Expectations*, 1946), the use of direct address can be assimilated into our traditional conceptions of the genre. Moll introduces us to her world, appearing to bracket the world of *Moll Flanders* off from the wider televisual context. If a little taken aback by the jump cut and direct address, the audience can now assume that they are safely inside the presented diegetic world; we do not expect to see the technique of direct address used again (except perhaps at the end, to 'seal off' the story).

However, direct address *is* used again, and is used throughout the serial as a powerful diegetic tool. Most often, Moll addresses the camera directly to ask 'What would *you* do?', forcing us to consider whether we would act as she is doing. The technique employed here is almost Brechtian, forcing us to historicise the action in front of us, and it is vital to the relationship with the past this programme engenders.[6] The moments of direct address create hiatuses within the diegesis, as Moll almost 'steps out' of her role, while her role within the diegesis remains one grounded in apparent historical realism. In addition to bearing resonances of a Brechtian nature, the direct address in this programme echoes a much wider use of direct address within television (as compared with theatre or film). We are accustomed to this 'particularly televisual' (Wilson, 1993: 132) mode of address through its use in primarily non-fictional television programmes, and its use here highlights the specificities of televisual address. In a novel, one cannot easily distinguish direct address from voice-over narration: a clear distinction between these two is only possible on screen.

The structure of the relationship formed between viewer and viewed alters with the diegesis, as direct address becomes not a simple tool for direct communication, but an additional source of Moll's discomfort, as we are positioned as her conscience or her judge. Just after Moll has left her fifth and sixth children (by Mr Bland) with two strangers, she walks towards us and, with guilty defensiveness, says, 'They're my husband's relatives. They're good people. Well, what else could I do?' Her relationship with the viewer here seems strangely antagonistic. Similarly, after Moll comes close to murdering a young, rich child whom she robbed, she turns to the camera which is trailing her, ranting about how the girl's parents should have taken better care, until she attacks the viewer with her culminating remark: 'Why do you stare at me?' (figure 6). Aggressively spoken, this moment of challenge, where our very viewing of Moll is foregrounded, and implied to be intrusive, engenders in the viewer a sense of awkwardness and a desire to look away. It reminds us of both our role as viewers and our involvement in the narrative, as the emotional and ethical implications of that very involvement are thrown into question. Moll subsequently puts her hand over the camera lens, in the customary style of celebrities pursued by the press. Direct address is utilised again as a challenge to our intrusive viewing when Moll fails to help Lucy, her partner; as the latter is arrested for pick-pocketing, Moll orders us to 'Leave me alone'.[7] The notion of the classic-novel adaptation audience as unwelcome or irritating pursuers is quite unique, but the notion of an intrusive camera revealing the shadier aspects of someone's life is familiar to television viewers who enjoy investigative journalism, from *Channel Four News* to *The Cook Report*. The use of this predominantly televisual convention (far rarer in film) grounds the programme within a strictly televisual mode of address.

This highly unusual use of direct address has several implications. Direct address repeatedly emphasises our status as viewers, and 'appears to reject the possibility of a more distanced, voyeuristic relationship with the text' (Wilson, 1993: 35), to 'prevent us ... from achieving that customary magical identification with the vicarious world unfolding on the screen' (Battestin, 1967: 40–1). Thus its use here denies us one of the central pleasures of the traditional classic-novel adaptation: engaging in admiring contemplation. Whilst most 1980s and early 1990s adaptations allowed us to gaze, often impersonally, at landscapes, rich interiors or beautifully clothed people, this programme questions the nature of that gaze, and indeed the object of it, as we shall see. Direct address is used here to question us regarding whether or not we would have acted as Moll did, and this forces us to think and feel, rather than simply to feel. In terms of our relationship with the past depicted, the detailed historical realism of the text is such that we can allow our imaginations to fully engage with the era it depicts. However, Moll's constant pleas that we consider her actions pulls us back to the present moment (which we are also aware we never left), so that our responses to her questions are not based on whether we would act as she does in our own lives, nor whether she should have acted as she did, but whether we would have acted thus if we were she, and if we were living in her time. Tony Wilson points out that the way in which we watch television (in relaxed, 'untheatrical' surroundings) appears, unlike film, 'to allow a particular space for awareness of self and the world to be retained during viewing' (1993: 47). This viewing situation, combined with the serial's believable settings and the encouragement Moll offers us to actively involve ourselves in the narrative on an imaginative level, allows a specifically televisual mode of engagement with the text, and the potential development of an alternative relationship with the past depicted.

The programme encourages us to condone, rationalise or at least understand Moll's decisions, in terms of the difficult social conditions within which she lived. It achieves this by aligning us with her in a way that is interestingly different from Defoe's strategy. Whilst Defoe asks the reader to excuse Moll's sexual relationship with Roland (from which she descends further and further into 'sinfulness'[8]) on the basis of Moll's naivety and impressionable nature, while admitting also her rather high sex drive, the adaptation entreats its viewers not just to excuse Moll's indiscretions but to positively support her in them. Moll as depicted by Alex Kingston is indeed initially naïve, but she is also extremely desirous, and the first scene in which Moll and Roland clinch is so appealingly filmed, so steamy, that, when the two lovers are interrupted, modern viewers are frustrated and desire fulfilment (so to speak). When a breathless, dishevelled Moll turns to us and asks 'What would you do?', the viewer is clearly expected to respond 'Go for it!' We therefore condone the decisions which will eventually lead Moll into ruin – we imagine responsibility for them, though safe in the knowledge that this is only a performance, only play.[9]

Moll Flanders convincingly depicts the problems of survival for an impoverished woman in the early eighteenth century. Thus the audience is encouraged to engage on a historical level, but also to utilise imagination to aid cognition, rather than revelling in the imaginative process just for its own pleasurable ends. Though viewers may gain little knowledge of 'history' beyond details of lifestyle, it is possible that they will gain greater emotional awareness of social history and greater rational understanding of how people responded to their social problems. Whilst Austen's women sought, like Moll, to make 'sensible' marriages that combined both love and financial security, the visual splendour of Austen adaptations such as *Pride and Prejudice* – from clothes to landscapes, from the grandiose Pemberley to the less impressive but equally appealing and spacious Longbourne – undermines viewers' understanding of the importance of 'marrying well'. If the consequence of not marrying money is to live in a house as pleasant as Longbourne, the viewer may find it hard to conceive exactly what all the fuss is about. In *Moll Flanders*, where the houses are dark, damp and unfurnished, where Moll has to go without food for days on end, and where there are no relatives upon whose kindness she can rely, the urgency of finding money in order simply to survive is far more tangible, and the appeal of marriage more understandable.

Vital to this process of engagement and evaluation is the fact that we are fully aware of the performative nature of *Moll Flanders*. Direct address, used as a way for Moll to 'step out' of the diegesis, highlights Alex Kingston's role as Moll as a performance: it reveals an overt recognition that she is performing. The theatricality of her performance is emphasised during her marriage to Jemmy[10] (James Seagrave), when she directly addresses us through a faux-theatrical aside, asking us whether or not we would go through with the marriage, knowing we had two husbands still alive. This is the only time in the programme where direct address is utilised in front of other characters – they 'ignore' her aside, and the action is suspended until she turns back to the on-screen priest and says 'Go ahead, Father'. This use of direct address in an aside is a well-known device on the stage, and serves to emphasise the theatricality – the performativity – of the adaptation.[11]

The illusion of genre

The audience of *Moll Flanders* is treated to few of the generic pleasures ordinarily derived from impressive landscapes or interiors. The majority of interiors are herein deployed merely as 'settings', and are not a key source of pleasure; indeed, the settings are generally fairly miserable. Moll's living conditions vary considerably throughout the serial; she does not permanently reside in the kind of upper- or upper-middle-class houses and estates that constitute the traditional generic world of adaptations. Her frequent changes in habitat also mean that the audience barely has time to become accustomed to (settled in) one place before Moll and they are uprooted to begin again in another place. The pace of the adaptation is thus accelerated, and the audience's attention is drawn away from the mise-en-scène as the object of its gaze, and towards the action occurring within the settings.

Of Moll's home in London, we are shown only her bedroom and the living room she shares with the other tenants. Both are dull and dirty, and lack any finery – they contain barely any furniture at all. Neither is filmed in long shot. Newgate prison is foul: dark, overcrowded, rat-infested, damp, and the scenes there are generally shot in close-up or with a hand-held camera, emphasising the cramped and claustrophobic nature of the space. Rather than grand society balls, *Moll Flanders* offers rowdy, riotous evenings in dark, crowded inns and public houses. These scenes clearly reflect the wider shift towards more socially realistic depictions of the past, showing more truthfully the brutish aspects of existence for those without money or relations. However, even more interesting is the use made of the rare generic shot sequences and scenes that this serial contains; most importantly, they are positioned within a discourse of 'performance' which problematises classic-novel adaptations' conventional representations. In this way, *Moll Flanders* utilises performance to highlight the performative and illusory nature of the genre's representations of the past and our relationship with it.

Two locations are filmed lovingly in *Moll Flanders* in the way that Brideshead and Pemberley are: the castle where Jemmy resides, and Moll's large house in Virginia. The long shots of the castle are relatively brief, but long enough to impress upon us the magnificence of the location and to establish Jemmy's apparent wealth. Yet we discover later in the serial that this castle, nestled in the countryside, is a 'front'; Jemmy does not own it – he has procured it for the specific purpose of attracting a rich wife. Thus both his and our connection with it is shown to be pretended, false. We, like Moll, are taken in by an impressive view, only to discover that we have no claim on it (in her case, literally).

Virginia is presented as a promised land. Endless green fields are displayed for us in long-take long shots: a rural idyll virtually uninhabited, dotted with only a few houses and pretty little country churches. The contrast with London as we saw it earlier could not be greater. Where England is urban and overpopulated, Virginia is bucolic and spacious, providing *Moll Flanders'* only archetypal generic landscapes. When Moll arrives at her new home there with her American husband, Lemuel (Lemmy), her approach and first sight of it are filmed in concordance with the traditional generic sequence I isolated in *Pride and Prejudice*: we see her carriage approaching, filmed in long shot across the countryside, and are then offered a point-of-view long-take long shot of the house, symmetrically framed and surrounded by trees. The house itself is impressive – large, symmetrical, pastel-coloured and lit by sunlight. For the first time, non-diegetic music is audible on the soundtrack, creating intertextual echoes of the moments when Elizabeth Bennet sees Pemberley and Charles Ryder sees Brideshead. Unlike these two characters, though, Moll does not stroll through the house in a restrained and dignified fashion, offering appreciative comments, but instead tears up the stairs and runs from room to room like an excited child (not a very 'English' reaction). Her appreciation discloses that such grand dwellings were as rare for most people then as they are today.

In effect, *Moll Flanders* does not glorify 'old England', but escapes it, instead emphasising the potential of the new-found land of America. When Moll returns to England, she unpatriotically dreams only of returning to Virginia, and eventually does so with Jemmy. And it is not only an escape from England's depressing urban settings and poverty that Virginia offers – it also offers an escape from the rigid class system within which Moll is trapped. Those transported to Virginia can work to establish their own small plots of land and build up their own savings. Whilst the source novel notes this fact literally, the adaptation utilises recognisable generic shots to make this point even more forcefully. As Lemmy's mother, Mrs Golightly, explains to Moll that many of the most respected citizens there began as transported convicts, an upright, middle-aged man rides past in his carriage, doffing his hat to the two women, and calling 'Good morning' in a recognisably upper-middle-class accent. Lemmy's mother nods in his direction, and reveals in hushed tones that Major Bastock is one such example. Therefore, whilst Major Bastock is the type of incidental character one might come across in an Austen adaptation, where his class and status remain unques-tioned, here these aspects of his character are thrown into relief, and class and status are shown not to be based in nature or heritage but to be established by money and maintained through signifiers such as material goods, fine clothes and the right accent (indeed, through 'performance').

Though the promised land of Virginia is, of course, in America, the land depicted is not that which we commonly associate with America, for the images we are offered of that country are often urban, jet-setting and (post)modern. Indeed, I would suggest that in this context it is not America that Moll and Jemmy aspire to, but a new England. The use of generic landscape shots for these scenes alone encourages the audience to associate Virginia with (the real) England: rural, unspoilt, fertile and beautiful, for it is usually England that is presented in this way. Perhaps in this sense these shots can be read as nostalgic not just for old England, but also for the times when we valued the landscape of that England as Moll and Jemmy clearly do: not as a 'view', but as a land of promise.

There are two types of generic set scenes in *Moll Flanders*: two dining scenes, at the Richardsons' house in Colchester where Moll is brought up, and the ballroom scene at Jemmy's castle. The Richardsons take Moll in, and raise her as 'almost' one of the family, although, as Moll points out, 'I never could forget that "almost"'. As one of the family, Moll eats with them in their modest but attractive dining room, but as an 'outsider' of lower status, she is also required to take on the role and duties of servant girl.[12] As Moll says, 'I never knew quite what I was in that house: one of them, or a servant, or something in between the two.' This in-between status is utilised to offer an alternative view of the servant/ employer divide in the dining scenes at Colchester. In most other adaptations, our attention is drawn to those characters who are enjoying the food in generic lavish dining scenes, whilst the servants who create and present the meal exist only as background, part of the 'heritage backdrop'. Admittedly, some adaptations have underscored the servants' role in supporting the society depicted on screen. In *Persuasion* (BBC, 1995) the numerous servants are ever-present, and when the Elliot family are forced to leave their country home for Bath, the servants' work is foregrounded, and the uncertainty of their own future employment emphasised through a lingering shot of their faces as the family departs. In *Emma* (ITV, 1996) a generic scene of the central characters taking a picnic amidst glorious English countryside is curiously inflected by the camera's pointed emphasis on the servants who must carry and lay out the feast. Similarly, in *Wildfell Hall*, there is a generic dining scene in which the presence of servants is a vital diegetic component, as will be revealed in Chapter 8.

However, in all these examples, the servants act primarily as signifiers – they 'represent' the servant (working) class in order to emphasise the class 'labouring to make the genteel dream come true' (Craig, 1996: 92). In *Moll Flanders*, Moll's unique position as half servant, half 'served' allows a focus on the servant as a complex, central character in her own right. Instead of noticing the servant presenting the food only to the extent that she represents a wider section of society, we focus our attention upon Moll to a greater degree than upon the seated family. We are already aligned with Moll's character, and through the use of a mobile camera we enter the room with Moll and the other servants, and leave it in the same way. The silence and servility demanded from someone in a servant's role are underlined as we watch Moll undertake her tasks; knowing her to be a more interesting, attractive and robust character than the petty and jealous daughters, patronising and lascivious sons and hypocritical father (a deeply 'pious' man who is having an affair with another woman) whom she serves, the iniquities of a system which deems them superior to her are emphasised. When the family has visitors over for dinner, Moll is not allowed to eat with them, though Mrs Richardson ensures that she boasts that when no 'company' is present, Moll is permitted to eat with them 'and we think nothing of it'. As the guests and family discuss Moll in the third person, while she waits on them, Moll is often placed centrally in the frame between two diners, standing silently as they talk. To deny the person who is placed centrally (re)action or speech is a powerful way to highlight the injustice and 'unnaturalness' of the situation. These scenes also have some historical generic roots: they are visually reminiscent of equivalent scenes in Merchant Ivory's *The Remains of the Day* (1993), where Mr Stevens, the butler, is placed in a similar situation.[13]

The ball sequence at Jemmy's castle does not undermine established generic conventions in the same way as these dining sequences do. Moll's position in this scene is one of an equal to the other guests, for she is pretending to be a rich widow, Lady Flanders, and the other guests treat her with respect. The iniquities of a rigid class system are not a focus here; the servants melt into the background as they do in similar conventional ball scenes. Yet this sequence is emblematic of the serial as a whole in one key feature: whilst purporting to be a traditional, generic ball – glamorous, colourful and appealing to the viewer – it is also fake. Later, when Moll and Jemmy are married, we discover that it was all a performance put on by Jemmy and his ex-lover/whore, in order to capture for him a rich wife. As with many other salient moments, performance is central here, and it is *Moll Flanders'* use of performance that sites the programme firmly within the televisual.

Performativity

One of the foremost narrative themes is Moll's own performances; even the name we know her by is not her real name, of which we are ignorant. On one level, Moll's performance is the same in source novel and adaptation: it is mere pretence. Moll 'lives a life of pretence' (Blewett, 1989: 19), purporting to be a rich widow, in order to be admitted to the right circles where she can ensnare a rich husband. Defoe himself had personal experience of pretence – David Blewett notes that 'he delighted in role-playing and disguise, a skill he used to great effect as a secret agent, and in his writing he often adopted a pseudonym or another personality for rhetorical impact' (1989: 5). On another level, though, the visual nature of adaptation and the construction of this particular one add a further layer to Moll's performance, at the level of gender.

Judith Butler (1990) proposes that 'femininity' (and indeed 'masculinity') are not characteristics of behaviour and attitude determined by the biological categories female and male, respectively; they are not expressive of an underlying essence. Rather, femininity and masculinity are 'performative': they are acts we choose to perform (though we may be pressured to perform appropriately by society), and are not determined by our biological sex. Butler thus utilises the feminist distinction between sex (biological sex) and gender (constituted by socially constructed notions of how a woman or man ought to behave). Moll's performance is illuminated with reference to Butler's notions of gender performance.

A notable scene in this context is the one in which Moll sets out to gain a marriage proposal from Lemmy, her American sailor suitor. She does not just pretend to be a rich widow, she also offers him a performance of the kind of traditionally feminine woman she knows he desires. By this point in the adaptation, Moll has been married twice and abandoned two children, and has sought to survive on her wits and dissembling from early childhood, yet for Lemmy she acts in a winsome, helpless and flirtatious fashion (as she later does for Mr Bland, her fifth husband) (figure 7). As she steps onto his ship, she pretends to falter and, as he lifts her on board, declaims admiringly, 'You're so strong!' Despite her ribald past, when Lemmy makes a mildly flirtatious comment, Moll chides him with the words 'Please Sir, I beg you, you will make me the common talk of the town', feigning an innocence and propriety far removed from the truth. Once inside his cabin, Moll's covert seduction of Lemmy through her faux-naïf punning remarks about his bed – 'It's not very big, is it?', though big enough for two 'with a squeeze' – drive Lemmy to make the first physical move and thus to assert his masculinity. During the sex scene that follows, Moll's voice-over emphasises the calculated, strategic nature of her love-making: 'This was not love, not on my side, though far from unpleasant. This was a business venture, and in that venture I determined to risk all, to lay out everything I had to draw him in, to give him, in short, a taste of paradise – that paradise that women can offer men, when they've a mind to it.' Moll's face, turned to the camera, reveals neither displeasure nor passion, just calm deliberation. Finally, to ensure his proposal, Moll 'cries', revealing to him that she is not rich, and sobbing that she is sure he will not want to marry her now. Knowing him to be soft-hearted, and having simpered her way into his affections by making him feel 'manly' in comparison, she secures her prize with no further effort. The nature of a televisual presentation (as opposed to a literary one) means that Moll's performance is highlighted as exactly that: we understand Alex Kingston to be performing Moll; we also comprehend Moll to be performing a different 'Moll'.

'As in other ritual social dramas, the action of gender requires a performance that is *repeated*' (Butler, 1990: 140) (italics in original). Moll repeats this performance throughout the serial. Thus a similar incident of this kind of gendered performance occurs when Moll tries to rebuff the advances of the dorkish Robin, Roland's brother, in Colchester. He accosts her in the garden and declares his love – Moll at first looks genuinely troubled, and begs him not to get her into trouble, for she could be thrown out on the street. When Robin magnanimously declares that he would always take care of her, her play for sympathy ends and she loses her patience with him, telling him angrily to go away and leave her alone. At first we, the audience, believe her earnest words of concern for her position, and her stance of feminine virtue, especially because we are accustomed to the traditional depiction of women in classic-novel adaptations; we are shocked when her expected behaviour is shown to be only performance. However, by the time we reach Moll's seduction of Lemmy (above), we are far more knowing, and can enjoy her performance for what it is.

Our enjoyment is grounded in our recognition, through Moll, that 'there is no gender identity behind the expressions of gender; that identity is performatively constituted by the very "expressions" that are said to be its results' (Butler, 1990: 25); unlike us, Lemmy, Mr Bland, and most other men within the serial believe in a solid, essential, gendered identity that underlies Moll's performance: they believe that the way she acts is an expression, not a performative constitution, of identity. As Butler argues, 'the distinction between expression and performativeness is crucial' (Butler, 1990: 141); while diegetic characters (with the exception of Jemmy) fail to grasp this distinction, the audience has no choice but to do so. Herein lies a significant portion of the radical potential of *Moll Flanders*

– it forces an audience who may not have had the opportunity to engage with Butler's arguments directly to consider the possibility of gender as performance, rejecting biologically essentialist ideals. Moll cannot be characterised in gendered terms, for although she certainly reveals an underlying identity, which shows itself in those rare occasions when her performance breaks down, this identity is not portrayed as gender-determined. In breaking away from the extremely rigid and traditional presentations of gender offered in other adaptations like *Pride and Prejudice*, *Moll Flanders* holds an original and transgressive appeal for its audience; the source of that appeal is performance, and its effectiveness is dependent upon our understanding of this feature of the programme.

The performative nature of Moll Flanders also works 'to overthrow both the category of sex and the system of compulsory heterosexuality that is its origin' (Butler, 1990: 115). It is argued by some feminist theorists that heterosexual relations are vital to the maintenance of differentiated gender roles. In the serial, not only does Moll directly challenge hetero-sexual norms through her relationship with Lucy Diver, she also subtly undermines expectations of female sexual enjoyment. Her response to every sexual encounter she has (and there are many) is different from the last: she categorises sex with different partners across a wide range of 'types': boring but bearable, passionate, nice but dull, terrible, dangerous and exciting, routine but loving, disinterested, and so forth. This challenges the audience's conventional expectations of women's sexual and emotional needs and engagements.

Without comprehending the programme's performative nature, we cannot fully understand its appeal. Yet, despite our growing awareness of the extent of Moll's performance, we are often shocked to find that we too, like the on-screen characters, can still be taken in. Most significantly, the tone at the end of the adaptation is dramatically different from that in the source novel. In the novel, Moll's dissembling nature is broken by her desperation in Newgate prison as she faces execution. Eventually, she repents of all her former wickedness:

> I joyn'd heartily in the [priest's] Petition, and must needs say I had deeper Impressions upon my Mind all that night, of the Mercy of God in sparing my Life; and a greater Detestation of my past Sins, from a Sense of the goodness which I had tasted in this case, than I had in all my Sorrow before. (Defoe, 1722: 368)

As a result of this repentance, and Moll's conformity to the values of Christian redemption, the priest pleads for her death sentence to be commuted to transportation to Virginia, whither she leaves with Jemmy. Defoe emphasises the moral values of his novel, as Moll asserts that her repentance 'is really the best part of my Life, the most Advantageous to myself, and the most instructive to others' (Defoe, 1722: 368–9). The adaptation appears to be faithful to the source novel's sequence of events: towards the end of the serial, we see Moll in her cell, desolate and desperate, and, voice breaking, she mutters, 'So now I am come full circle to the place where I was born. And now I am here I find the horrors of the place are not so unbearable as I had thought. For has not my life been like unto a prison these long years – a prison of wickedness, and despair?' Then, unexpectedly, Moll smiles, turns to the camera, and says, 'You see, I'm rehearsing my repentance'. Thus even her final moment of truth, self-recognition and self-knowledge in the novel becomes yet another aspect of her eternal performance in the adaptation. We never see Moll repent, and it is not a priest who saves her, but Jemmy, who appears as she is about to be hung, waving a pardon. (The pardon has been obtained, it is important to note, not by her 'hero' Jemmy, but through Moll's own wit and cunning: Sir Richard Gregory, who paid Moll as a prostitute, arranges the pardon in return for Moll's silence on his impropriety.) The moral nature of Defoe's cautionary tale is subverted, allowing Moll control of her own destiny, and condoning her ceaseless dissembling, rather than condemning it.

In fact, Moll's performance is so continual, and so central to the programme, that it is those moments in which Moll does *not* perform that are most visceral and striking. When Moll overtly threatens the child whose jewellery she has stolen, her performance as a friendly stranger having failed, her sheer brutality shocks us. As Moll first prostitutes herself, with Sir Richard Gregory, we watch the cold contempt and tired resignation on her face as she first undoes her corset, then lifts her skirts to sit on her client's lap. She makes no effort whatsoever to 'perform' either with her face or body: her face reveals only her true feelings, and she is completely passive during the encounter, merely offering her body to Sir Gregory, for him to do as he pleases. In all other intimate scenes like this, Moll offers some kind of performance, even if only with her body – the lack of it here renders the scene abnormal, brutal, shocking. In contrast, the pivotal moment when Moll and Jemmy discover they have tricked each other into marriage is a moment of self-recognition: Jemmy too is a master of disguise, a man of many names, a pretender. It is the fundamental shared element of 'performance' that reveal Moll and Jemmy to be destined for one another.

Moll's failure to perform also works to further emphasise the performative nature of her gendered identity, for in those moments she fails to act in a 'feminine way', rejecting accepted female characteristics as performance, as unnatural to her. Her failure to feign enjoyment in some sexual encounters; her failure to be sympathetic and protective towards the child she almost murders; her failure to experience heart-felt regret at abandoning all her children – these failures undermine traditional, essentialist notions of female emotions. As Butler writes, 'the possibilities of gender transformation are to be found precisely in the arbitrary relation between such acts, in the possibility of a failure to repeat, a de-formity, or a parodic repetition' (1990: 141). Moll offers both parodic repetition (in her entrapment of husbands through her 'helpless', feminine acts) and a disconcerting 'failure to repeat' – to maintain a consistent performance of gender. Moll's individual performance, which is separated from any determining biological imperative, is further bound up with the postmodern in its adherence to 'postmodernism's anti-universalism and anti-essentialism' (Brooker and Brooker, 1997: 3).[14]

There are overt moments of performance to the camera which appear non-diegetic, and seem to jar within the story. For example, there is a curious sequence of tableaux of Lemmy, Moll and family in Virginia. The family is gathered as if for a family photograph, and they stare directly into the camera, fidgeting and giggling as if waiting for the camera's flash. Obviously entirely invented, even to those who have not read the source novel, this strange sequence foregrounds the actors' roles as performers, bringing to mind a 'post-shoot' photograph session, and drawing attention to the image as televisual. Similarly, the serial concludes with a close-up of Moll and Jemmy, who walk directly towards the camera and stare, smiling and relaxed, straight into the lens (figure 8). The shot seems to indicate that their performances are over, that they can now relax 'out of character'. These instances emphasise the performative and contemporary nature of the programme itself – and therefore its televisuality.

An alternative mood: playfulness

Overwhelmingly, the mood associated with *Moll Flanders* is not nostalgia, but playfulness. The performative nature of the serial animates 'the critical effect of play with narrative conventions, character and cultural stereotypes' (Brooker and Brooker, 1997: 7), playing with our expectations of generic narrative and visual conventions, and with character traits that are commonly configured, both generically and socially, in gendered terms. The serial's emphasis on its performativity is in keeping with the 'playful and allusive' character of postmodern texts (Brooker and Brooker, 1997: 1). It is true that the sense of playfulness inherent in this adaptation, and lacking in so many other earnest classic-novel adaptations, derives in part from the source novel, such as in the use of characters' names to suggest personality traits: Mr Bland, and Moll Flanders herself. However, much of the playfulness of the programme is rooted in the televisual medium: there is a wealth of visual humour here, a sense of postmodern playful irony that pervades the serial. The comments of one critic earlier in this chapter that *Moll Flanders* is in some way comparable to a *Carry On* film were most apt, for not only is this playful humour primarily (tele)visual (hard to embody in literary form), it is also highly sexualised. *Moll Flanders* trades on an English tradition of humour epitomised in the *Carry On* films, seaside postcards and farce. So, Englishness *is* important to this adaptation, after all.[15]

I have already described Moll's punning seduction scene with Lemmy, which revolves around a discussion of the size of his 'bed'. Indeed, this scene is prefigured as Moll walks towards the cabin entrance, on deck. As she 'innocently' comments that she would like to see his cabin very much, her hand reaches out to gently caress the rounded end of the tiller, openly revealing to us (though to no one on screen) her intentions (figure 9). Her playful performance here is offered only to us, as viewers. A similar moment occurs between Moll and her prospective fifth husband, Mr Bland. Mr Bland has gallantly agreed to sit in Moll's bedroom at an inn, to guard her from villains: we are offered a shot/reverse shot sequence, showing Moll sitting in bed, and her view of the back of Mr Bland's chair, where he sits facing the door (for her modesty), armed. From Moll's point of view we can see only the chair back and his rather large weapon sticking out over the arm. Then, as Moll sets to work, that which ostensibly begins as a discussion of her fortune takes on an entirely different meaning in her hands. Moll comments that her fortune is 'but a small one', to which Mr Bland innocently replies 'A small one may grow and flourish, if it is handled in the right way, Ma'am'. Moll's response becomes more obvious: 'That's true. I mean ... I can't help wondering – do you not grow ... stiff, sitting up quite so long?' Finally, Mr Bland seems to have cottoned on, and responds correctly, 'I am a little stiff, Ma'am'. Within a couple of minutes, Moll and Mr Bland are under the bedcovers together (once Moll has checked that 'there's no chance they'll discharge spontaneously, is there?' – referring to the pistols, of course).

Moll Flanders is peppered with such innuendoes: when Moll and Roland attempt to have illicit sex on the stairs in the Richardsons' home, one of Roland's sisters calls Moll to ask her where she is; Moll's quick reply is 'I'm coming'. Though such humour could become tiresome, it is handled with such deftness of touch that it cannot help but raise a smile; it certainly confounds the expectations of those anticipating a traditionally restrained classic-novel adaptation. The serial's playfulness can also be viewed as indicative of its televisuality, for television itself has been characterised within these terms: 'the relationship between television programme and audience is also "playful"' (Wilson, 1993: 205).

Moll Flanders: a challenge to generic norms

Moll Flanders creates a fascinating challenge to generic conventions of content, form and mood. It complies with the aims of fidelity to period detail, offering as convincing a portrayal of eighteenth-century urban life as Austen adaptations offer of nineteenth-century rural upper-middle-class life. It reflects a wider generic shift in emphasis from upper/upper-middle-class heritage to middle/working-class history, attempting to render more accurately the social and physical conditions of the time. The programme certainly has the potential to establish in the audience a relationship with the past, but the nature of this relationship is not nostalgic. Instead, the different aspects of the past presented do not elicit a desire for a 'return' to the past. In addition, the lack of heritage content – few extant houses or estates, no true English landscapes, barely any period furnishings – means that any sense of continuity between past and present is undermined. We do not see the 'past' of *Moll Flanders* still extant around us; we are distanced from it.

The use of direct address also works to distance us from the past depicted on screen, calling as it does upon our cognitive faculties and contemporary understanding so that we may historicise Moll's actions and situation, recognising the differences between her limited choices and our own relative freedom. For, although direct address distances us from the past portrayed, reminding us of its nature as present performance, it simultaneously helps to bring us closer to Moll – emotionally and cognitively – allowing us critical distance yet sympathetic closeness. *Moll Flanders* therefore offers us an alternative relationship with the past: a cognitive and emotional understanding of particular aspects of it, based on imagination, rather than an emotional feeling of nostalgia for a mythical, generic past.

To those writers concerned with ideology and nostalgia, *Moll Flanders* is highly significant. Notions of genre and nostalgia are far less informative for our understanding of this programme than they were for previous adaptations, as the programme is defined almost negatively against these notions. Yet a conceptualisation of televisuality is absolutely vital to an interpretation of the programme's narrative and affective power. In particular, the form of the programme challenges generic convention through its constant assertion of its own performativity. We see performance in the programme (through Moll) and we see the programme as performance. This playful performativity undermines any traditional claims to serious literariness.

Mood, being established through content and form, will necessarily be altered when each of these other aspects is. The mood of *Moll Flanders*, despite its considerations of the problems of poverty in the 1700s, and despite its dark and gloomy settings, is overwhelmingly playful. Whilst wistful nostalgia defined *Brideshead* and *Pride and Prejudice*, it is playfulness that defines this adaptation. These features define the programme as 'postmodern', as does its representation of gender, which separates behaviour and performance from any underlying, determining force (of sex), allowing Moll's performed femininity to be constituted through 'detached, floating signifiers, free of content and reference' (Brooker and Brooker, 1997: 1). Yet despite its postmodern credentials, *Moll Flanders* is not an apolitical, meaningless spectacle; in fact, as I have argued, some elements are potentially radically progressive – they are ideologically significant. Most saliently here, *Moll Flanders* undermines almost every key feature of the genre that has concerned critics of classic-novel adaptations.

Notes

1 Hill's work is concerned with films of the 1980s, regarding which his observations are accurate. Yet his book was published in 1999, and he appears unaware of the changes that took place in the genre during the 1990s.

2 The stage show *Oliver!* was, of course, adapted in Carol Reed's famous film of the same name, in 1968.

3 Raphael Samuel, *Theatres of Memory: Volume I* (1994). Higson notes Samuel's arguments about the ambiguous political nature of heritage, but still argues that such 'heritage projects' are, in the main, nostalgic and reactionary; many film theorists have followed suit.

4 It might be suggested, in response to the above, that the differences in marketing between *Moll Flanders* and *Pride and Prejudice* (and their significant, stylistic differences) might be put down to differences in role and image between BBC and ITV. I would not dismiss this out of hand. *Moll Flanders* is more commercially marketed, with greater emphasis laid upon the cruder pleasures of the text (the noted seventeen sex scenes, for example) than on its artistic merits. This does not reflect any real differences in merit between the two adaptations: their filming, editing, acting, etc.; both were critically and popularly acclaimed.

I would be content to concede that the more contemporary, televisual style and the corresponding marketing of *Moll Flanders* might be in part due to the different image audiences have of ITV rather than BBC: more modern, less restrained, more 'mass-targeted'. However, I am not sure how useful (or accurate) it would be to take this comparison beyond this stage. No simplistic distinction is possible. Granada, the makers of *Moll Flanders*, were also responsible for *Brideshead Revisited*; Andrew Davies, the screenwriter of *Moll Flanders* and *Pride and Prejudice*, has been involved in both archetypal and radical classic-novel adaptations, for both BBC and ITV. Nor does the BBC still market its dramas (in particular, its literary adaptations) on the strength of their cultural and literary statuses – or, at least, not in Britain – as the cases of both *Pride and Prejudice* and the very different *The Tenant of Wildfell Hall* reveal.

5 The notion of 'performance' and the 'performative' nature of the television text is as I outlined in Chapter 4. However, I shall extend the idea of 'performance' in my analysis of *Moll Flanders*, for the programme demands that I do so. *Moll Flanders* actively manipulates (plays with) a range of 'performances': not just the 'performance' of the actors and the broadcast of the text, but also its performance of the past, of generic features and of gender.

6 Brecht's well-known notion of 'verfremdung' or 'estrangement' describes the relationship a viewer must establish with a dramatic performance in order to historicise the drama and become an active, critical respondent to the issues raised in it. A good introductory discussion of Brecht's work is offered in R. Williams, *Drama from Ibsen to Brecht* (1993), 277–90.

7 Those theorists who would characterise our filmic/televisual gaze as 'voyeuristic' would probably suggest that this aggressive use of direct address turns the conventional filmic gaze back on us, drawing attention to this gaze and making us feel uncomfortable. Yet we do not usually feel uncomfortable when addressed directly in other television programmes, despite the 'challenge' of the returned gaze. It is more likely, I would argue, that we feel uncomfortable here because of the particular diegetic situation and because of the noticeable similarity to other instances of 'real' television intrusion. Indeed, we would feel awkward in this situation were it to occur in real, everyday life.

8 Defoe's Moll overtly recognises her 'sinfulness', making it clear that she did not mend her ways even when she had enough money to do so (Defoe, 1722: 267–8).

9 Defoe aims to present the narrative as morally educative, but also exciting, responding to the Puritan context of 1722. For a good discussion of Defoe's novel as it relates to its historical context, see I. Watt, 'Defoe as Novelist: *Moll Flanders*', in *The Rise of the Novel* (1976), 104–51. The film *Moll Flanders* (1996) attempts to imitate the 'moral purpose' of Defoe's novel by constructing the narrative around Moll's daughter, to whom Moll's journal is being read, and who is warned to learn from Moll's mistakes, just as Defoe advises the readers of 'his' Moll's journal to do (Defoe, 1722: 38–40).

10 Jemmy is the spelling used in the programme credits, though in the source novel this name is spelled 'Jemy'. I have used names as they were spelled in the programme credits, not the source novel, throughout.

11 A form of direct address is also used in the film *Tom Jones* (1963), based on Henry Fielding's *Tom Jones* (1749). This earlier film is one of only a few eighteenth-century-novel adaptations that are well known, and viewers familiar with it will doubtless see resonances of it here. However, the use of direct glances to camera in *Tom Jones* is rare, happening only a few times during the film; in contrast, Moll maintains 'contact' with the camera, both through looking and speaking, throughout *Moll Flanders*, so that the use of direct address is foregrounded. I would suggest that the technique is appropriate (and successful) in *Moll Flanders* because it is a device we customarily associate with televisual (not filmic) presentation.

12 My use of the term 'role' here is deliberate, suggesting Moll's 'performance' within different roles throughout the serial.

13 Merchant Ivory's *The Remains of the Day* (1993) also focuses on the servant, rather than the served – namely, Mr Stevens, the butler of Darlington Hall – and utilises similar shot constructions to draw attention to Stevens as a person in his own right, even when he is excluded from the 'main' action on screen.

14 Postmodernity and postmodernism are said to be marked by plurality, eclecticism and fragmentation, which undermine previously accepted notions that people or things can be understood through reference to a fundamental 'essence' that is universal amongst members of the same group. Applying this idea to 'gender', Butler's argument denies that there is a female 'essence' which is inherent and universal in all women; in contrast,

'femininity' is perceived by Butler as a 'performance' which can be undertaken by anyone, or rejected by anyone. Thus to be female is not necessarily to 'act femininely', and to be male is not necessarily to be excluded from 'performing femininity' should one wish to. *Moll Flanders'* presentation of Butler-ian gender performance could thus position it as a postfeminist (or postmodern) adaptation. There is not the space here to consider this idea in detail, but it would appear to have much to commend it.

15 Unfortunately, I do not have the space here to expand on this suggestion. The sense that *Moll Flanders* exhibits an alternative 'Englishness' in the form of a bawdy, 'seaside' humour is a challenge to those that consider classic-novel adaptations to perpetuate only a certain type of upper-middle-class, reserved, 'serious' Englishness. Humour is, of course, one of the more positive and egalitarian traits traditionally associated with the English, and in certain forms can cut across class, regional and gender distinctions which are held in place by other national(istic) characteristics. An exploration of *Moll Flanders* in these terms would offer an illuminating comparison with more 'traditional' examples of the genre.

8

The Tenant of Wildfell Hall (1996)

In the context of the indisputable cultural importance of nostalgic films and television programmes, it is interesting that in 1991 Jameson observed the death of the 'nostalgia film' as he had defined it: 'the costume film ... has fallen into disrepute and infrequency, not merely because, in the postmodern age, we no longer tell ourselves our history in that fashion, but also because we no longer experience it that way, and, indeed, perhaps no longer experience it at all' (1991: 283–4). Ten years and many classic-novel adaptations later, one would be mistaken for thinking Jameson wrong in his prediction. The reasons for his claim lie in postmodern theorists' understanding of our modern-day relationship with the past, and in their conception of the 'nostalgia' film/programme.

Nostalgia is considered a postmodern phenomenon; so is television. Indeed, even adaptation itself can even be regarded as postmodern, if one considers the kind of claims made for postmodern texts:

> [They] have been identified, by Fredric Jameson and others, as exhibiting a formal self-consciousness, borrowing from other texts and styles in a meta-historical and cross-generic free-for-all which breaks down distinctions between high and low, Western and other cultures, or the past and the present. (Brooker and Brooker, 1997: 3)

The above description could be applied with ease to adaptations as conceptualised and discussed herein. Jameson's argument that the effects of our postmodern condition could be read within the nostalgic classic-novel adaptation (and our pleasure in it) is therefore understandable, and was groundbreaking at the time. Nevertheless, his characterisation of the genre was couched in strikingly familiar terms: 'the classical nostalgia film, while evading its present altogether, registered its historicist deficiency by losing itself in mesmerized fascination in lavish images of specific generational pasts' (Jameson, 1991: 296). There are echoes here of the traditional complaints levied at classic-novel adaptations since the 1960s:

frivolous, 'lavish' images which elicit 'mesmerized fascination' in the viewer. Jameson, however, does not dismiss these features within a simplistic criticism of the programmes' style, but instead explains them through his allusion to postmodernist aesthetics. Lynne Joyrich para-phrases Jameson: 'as even the illusion of a full or authentic relation of lived experience to history dissolves, we seem left with merely a random collection of images to which we turn in a frantic effort to appropriate a collective past' (1996: 57). Thus according to postmodernists our notions of the past become dependent upon a fragmented selection of 'images', which bear greater relation to our own lack of historicity than to the real-life past; 'the past is, now, inexorably bound with images of a constructed past: a confusing blur of "simulated" and "real"' (Friedburg, 1993: 6). This is why our (postmodern) desire for historicity, for a real relation to our past is, according to postmodern theorists, doomed to failure: 'the past is reproduced as flat, depthless pastiche, where the reference point is not the past itself, but other images, other texts. The past as referent is effaced, and all that remains is a self-referential intertextuality' (Higson, 1993: 112). The ideologically problematic nature of these texts is therefore clear: Jameson's, Higson's and others' own 'nostalgia' for a 'real', honest account of and relationship with the past – and the present – derives from their Marxist understanding that reality is being veiled by ideology.

Postmodernism, the past and television

By now the cultural and theoretical significance of television classic-novel adaptations is clear. Television has been described as 'the quintessence of postmodern culture' (Collins, 1992: 327): key features include its proli-feration of images, 'fragmentation', intertextuality, and overwhelming 'presentness'.[1] These are the same features that postmodernists ascribe to our attempts to represent and connect with the past. Classic-novel adapta-tions could therefore be regarded as the epitome of our postmodern quest for the past; in addition they, like our quest, are characterised by a prevailing nostalgic mood. Perhaps, then, it is surprising that I have employed postmodern theories only very cautiously in the analysis of this genre, yet others have shown a similar prudence in their explication and use of such theories (Smart, 1993; Collins, 1992; Kellner, 1994). The reason for such caution is that some postmodern theorists have a tendency to over-dramatise and exaggerate the changes in the state of contemporary Western culture and society. In the case of classic-novel adaptations, notions of a postmodern aesthetic are valuable, but the assumed effects of this aesthetic (confusion and disappointment in the viewer who attempts to extract some kind of firm 'vision' of the past) are unnecessarily fatalistic and reveal a lack of understanding of the genre.[2]

If we accept the usual postmodernist arguments, we are left with a depiction of the genre which appears to be at odds with the one we have seen so far. Postmodernism offers us a messy, fragmented, unstable parade of meaningless images of a fictional past, which we gaze upon in nostalgic longing. In comparison, *Brideshead* and *Pride and Prejudice* establish and consolidate a far more coherent, self-supporting, self-referential generic microcosm, a fictional world that (imaginatively) 'exists and is independent of the viewer, or so it appears. It was there before the viewer made their entrance, and it will continue to exist when the film [or programme] is over' (Tan, 1996: 54). Indeed, while many theorists conclude that the nostalgic project, an attempt to 'connect' with the past and reassure us of a concrete historical past, must ultimately fail, one could argue it is the genre's very postmodernity that helps it to succeed in these objectives.

Intertextuality is frequently cited as a postmodern feature.[3] An adaptation's intertextuality – in particular its reference to other adaptations' representations of the past – though a 'postmodern' feature, stabilises and does not fragment our imaginative images of the 'real past'. Far from displaying an 'array of *competing* signs' (Collins, 1992: 331) (my emphasis), the profusion and repetition of generic representations of the past reinforce each other, and the conformity to style across the genre concretises, confirms and perpetuates particular notions of past times. Though it is true that the images of the past presented are representations (and therefore, due to intertextuality, representations of representations), and bear only a passing resemblance to the 'real' past, there is a solidity and coherence to the (fictional) 'past world' they concretise, which is reassuring to the viewer. It is even possible that this concretisation of the generic microcosm works to bring order not only to the microcosm itself but also to our notions of the real past, with the result that we feel that 'orderliness is immanent to the [real] world, prior to its generic reconception'.[4] So our representations of the past may be 'postmodern', for they are self-validating, intertextual representations of representations, and our consequent understanding of and relationship to the real past may be 'postmodern' also, but there is greater order and reassurance to be found in these things than some postmodernists suggest.

A strongly postmodern view of the 'past' that adaptations depict, though accurate to a considerable degree, also runs the risk of denying the complexity of their potential links with the real past. Adaptations' representations of the past, while rooted in preceding generic images, are also based on their source novels; they thus present a past world that is doubly fictional (a fictional world adapted from another fictional world) – a more postmodern presentation is barely imaginable. Yet the source novels, though fictions, do hold real connections with the past because at the time they were written they were recording the present (or very recent past). This means that *Jude the Obscure* (1896) can be said to bear a greater existential link to the past than a modern-day costume drama set in the same period, even if the latter is based on a retrospective use of historical events and statistics.[5] So while it is true that in our postmodern culture our links with the past are tentatively made through a series of representations, or even representations of representations, the real past does not 'vanish' but only becomes (as must be expected) harder to reach. Material relics and primary sources still offer us tangible traces of the past: the *Jude* we read today is the same *Jude* Hardy's contemporaries read in 1896. The past that was Hardy's present can only be glimpsed through his representation of it in his writing; the same applies to adaptations of his work. This does not discount the possibility of either a 'real past' or a possible connection with it.

In a sense, then, the source novels for classic-novel adaptations perform the function of relics. But these are not the only relics used in classic-novel adaptations. Postmodernism is charged not only with conflating the real with simulacra (or, as Baudrillard (1988) argues, 'losing' the referent entirely) but also with recycling culture for the sake of consumption. This is clearly pertinent to the links between classic-novel adaptations and the relics upon which the heritage industry is built. The artefacts used in adaptations forge links between their nostalgic fictions and the real-life past: National Trust properties, land and furniture exist both in the fictional world and in our real-life present-day world; the consumerism which thrives on nostalgia (through organisations like the National Trust and English Heritage, and businesses such as Laura Ashley and Past Times) also allows people to 'buy' into, recreate their own piece of the past. The connections forged by consumerism, though perhaps lamentable, do however work to consolidate and confirm our tentative connection with a past world, however selective about the 'real-life' past it may be. Although Lowenthal states that 'the high visibility of relics, especially of old buildings, leads many to over-estimate – and over-value – the stability of the past' (1985: 243), he also argues convincingly for the importance of relics as material links between past and present.[6]

Thus, whilst postmodernism blurs the real past and the simulated past, real life and fiction, and whilst it recycles 'history' for the sake of consumption and profits, the net result might not be fragmentation and confusion but rather a consolidation of people's imaginative notions of what the past was like. Indeed, it is possible to theorise our contemporary relationship with the past, and to recognise the importance of some aspects of postmodernity, without rejecting notions of knowledge, 'history' and the 'real' as many postmodernists do.[7] Lowenthal's argument that 'every advance in our knowledge of the past paradoxically makes it more remote, less knowable' (1985: 258) might, at a glance, appear compatible with that of postmodern theorists, but his acknowledgement that knowledge is possible, and his subsequent argument that 'the sense of loss attending increased knowledge is an old story, however' (1985: 258), emphasise that our contemporary relationship with the past, while it may be more uncertain than ever before, exists on a continuum and does not reflect the sudden break postmodernists describe. Barry Smart, a critical (cautious) theorist of postmodernity, echoes this idea in his statement that postmodernity, 'rather than signifying a new period or epoch point[s] instead to the steady accretion, the increasing pervasiveness of a mood or condition, a response to modernity that is relatively long-standing, one that has been gathering momentum since the nineteenth century' (1993: 26).

However one conceptualises the issues at stake, what is undeniable is the importance of television classic-novel adaptations at the hub of these intertwining, often competing, discourses. Jameson's trumpeting of the death of nostalgic screen fictions appears somewhat precipitate, but instead of dismissing the genre as outdated and irrelevant, he qualified his initial assessment, suggesting that the 'postmodern age' would herald a new way of depicting and understanding the past:

> it is by way of so-called nostalgia films that some properly allegorical processing of the past becomes possible: it is because the formal apparatus of nostalgia films has trained us to consume the past in the form of glossy images that new and more complex 'postnostalgia' statements and form become possible. (1991: 287)

His prescience becomes clear when we look at recent adaptations that are indeed utilising the classic-novel adaptation's conventional representations of the past in order to create 'more complex "postnostalgia" statements and form[s]'.[8] *The Tenant of Wildfell Hall* is a prime example.

A unique locus

The television genre of classic-novel adaptations is a unique locus for the creation and perpetuation of nostalgia and/or 'postnostalgia' and for the encouragement of complex relationships with the past.[9] The reason that this is possible is that our potential responses to the genre's characteristic style and display of the past are not completely predetermined. We must not make the mistake of 'genre theorists [who] have typically assumed that texts with similar characteristics systematically generate similar readings, similar meanings, and similar uses' (Altman, 1999: 12). For instance, we can characterise the pleasure derived from watching traditional programmes of this genre without referring to nostalgia. Tan writes that

> spectacle in the film is, as the term implies, appealing, simply because it is largely divorced from the fate of the protagonists. And there is a great deal of spectacle in film because the medium itself is spectacular. Few film plots are set in a totally empty space, and there is always some aspect of the background to enjoy, from a breath-taking landscape to indoor spaces that most people have never been privileged to enter. (1996: 83)

Tan's explanation resonates with traditional descriptions of classic-novel adaptations. He suggests that shots of 'breath-taking landscape[s]' and exclusive 'indoor spaces' are often divorced from the development of the narrative; he also notes the 'spectacular' nature of these shots. His analysis can be extended – if the object of these spectacles is something that is 'past', perhaps our feelings of awe and satisfaction might become tainted with nostalgia. But this is by no means a necessary extension, just as nostalgia is not the only relationship we can hold with the past. As David Bordwell and Kristin Thompson write, 'the fact is that framings have no absolute or general meanings ... The context of the film will determine the function of the framings' (1993: 213–14). Although within the terms of generic conventions specific framings may tend to suggest specific (conventional) meanings, there is still the possibility that the expected meanings can be undermined by the narrative context. *Wildfell Hall* (BBC, 1996) offers a particularly good example of this.

Wildfell Hall renegotiates the accepted meanings of generic conventions through a process of (postmodern) detachment. Just as in the case of *Moll Flanders*, though, the result is not 'a pastiche of tropes' (Nelson, 1997: 14) but a knowing, self-conscious commentary on the classic-novel adaptation genre. Both adaptations, exhibiting as they do a focus on the generic and televisual worlds they inhabit, rather than the external, 'real' world, reflect what Robin Nelson describes as 'a new affective order, a distinctive postmodern experience – a consciousness even – increasingly disarticulated, if not quite detached, from the empirical world' (1997: 4).

Wildfell Hall's 'disarticulation' from the real world is partly achieved through its overt use of intertextuality. In addition to forming intertextual links with other classic-novel adaptations, the programme problematises its generic status through its intertextuality with different films. Most obviously, there are many foregrounded textual features which are strongly reminiscent of *The Piano* (1993): Tara Fitzgerald's costumes and appearance; a preponderance of bleak weather; and, most obviously, the desolate, windswept locations in place of green, lush landscapes. Ken Gelder, writing about *The Piano*, recognises the influence of the Brontës' novels *Wuthering Heights* and *Jane Eyre* on Jane Campion's visual landscape, but he fails to note the influence of *The Piano* on the Brontë adaptation *Wildfell Hall* (Gelder, 1999: 157–9). (In comparison, television reviewer Barbara Ellen writes of Helen as 'impersonating Holly Hunter in *The Piano* on the Yorkshire moors' (1996: 8)).

The Piano was critically acclaimed, and its use of setting, costume and mood was widely analysed (see, for example, Stella Bruzzi, Lynda Dyson and Sue Gillett in *Screen*, in 1995[10]); in being so overtly reminiscent of it, *Wildfell Hall* utilises intertextuality to recreate a similar tone. Thus, just as *The Piano* was characterised as an artistic, feminist, women-oriented film – 'the critical acclaim surrounding the film constructed *The Piano* as a feminist exploration of nineteenth-century sexuality' (Dyson, 1995: 267) – *Wildfell Hall* is perceived similarly, which suits the narrative thrust of the serial. *The Piano* is not the only text to which the programme refers: there is a notable sequence, for example, when Arthur (junior) is pedalling his tricycle around Grassdale, to find his father. The camera follows the tricycle at low level, swerving with it around corners, before coming to a halt at the foot of Arthur's father (Arthur senior) (figure 10). This use of camera angle and trajectory, and the sound of the cycle's squeaky wheels on the soundtrack, are clearly 'borrowed' from *The Shining* (1980), and serve to position Arthur senior in the place of the dreaded Room 237, emphasising him as a threat to the child. As with most instances of televisual intertextuality, this sequence is effective even if the viewer lacks knowledge of the film to which it refers, but it also reveals that *Wildfell Hall* is not afraid to utilise intertextual references that place the programme within a wider televisual/filmic framework. Even more important, though, is *Wildfell Hall*'s manipulation of expected generic conventions.

Revisiting genre

Moll Flanders challenged the type of perception we direct at traditional classic-novel adaptations, rejecting a detached, admiring gaze for an involved, acknowledged 'look'. As a result, *Moll Flanders'* radical form, in combination with its use of different 'content', almost entirely failed to establish nostalgic associations, instead relying for its appeal upon an overt recognition and playful use of its televisuality and, specifically, its performativity. Its rejection of conventional generic content and form was vital to its constitution of a different kind of relationship between the viewer and the text, and the viewer and the past depicted. Larsen, writing about literature, states that 'nostalgia ... is betokened by one kind or other of aesthetic or emotional conservatism, whether in form, tone, subject matter or attitude' (Larsen, 1983: 462). His suggestion that there are links between aesthetic conservatism and nostalgia is apt. In a sense, genre can be regarded as conservative in two senses: it is resistant to radical formal change, for to alter generic conventions too dramatically is to undermine a text's place within a genre, and it is conservative in the sense that it literally conserves (preserves) the generic microcosm upon which it relies. Because a generic text is expected to remain faithful to key tropes, to challenge generic norms is to alter the traditional cultural function and significance of that genre, as *Moll Flanders* shows so clearly.

Yet the choice for programme-makers working within a generic tradition is not simply one between wholesale acceptance and complete rejection of generic norms. There is no absolute set of generic rules with which 'conventional' adaptations entirely comply. In addition, any genre is constantly evolving, such as in the case of classic-novel adaptations increasingly admitting and utilising their televisual nature. Larsen recognises that the relationship between a conservative form (such as a traditionally generic one) and its consequent emotional valencies is an uncertain and ambiguous one. He notes that conservative aesthetic form 'becomes nostalgia at a certain very important point: it does so at the point when the artist ceases to be aware of that conservatism as a *tool* of his art' (italics in original) (Larsen, 1983: 463). We can thus distinguish between an active use of generic conventions as a 'tool' and an uncritical adherence to conventional norms. While *Moll Flanders* challenges and rejects many of the generic norms of the classic-novel adaptation, *Wildfell Hall* 'plays' with accepted form, sometimes altering generic content, sometimes not, but significantly reconfiguring the mode (if not the object) of our look. Instead of rejecting nostalgia, *Wildfell Hall* accepts its generic and cultural significance, but utilises it as a 'tool'; this programme plays with nostalgia. The serial exhibits a self-conscious use of generic tropes only possible (as Jameson suggests above) since these tropes have become firmly established. Without *Brideshead*, without *Pride and Prejudice*, there could be no *Wildfell Hall*.

Landscapes and country houses

Wildfell Hall relies heavily upon typical generic tropes of content, displaying exterior and interior settings associated with the genre; there is a particular reliance upon familiar country landscape long shots and, in the second and third episodes of the three, an equal dependence upon the lavish interior of Huntingdon's large country home, Grassdale, replete with furniture and props carefully arranged to reveal their ornate, period detail. Yet the programme reconfigures the objects of our gaze within a diegesis that forces us to regard these familiar sights in a new way. In addition, *Wildfell Hall* plays with the viewer's gaze with the result that the serial facilitates in the viewer a critical reflection upon the nostalgia of the classic-novel adaptation itself. The use of conventional generic tropes of content and form in *Wildfell Hall* is therefore such that we should not leap to conclusions regarding the reactionary nature of the 'heritage project' of which this programme is, on the face of it, a part.

The use of generic landscape shots in *Wildfell Hall* mirrors, in a sense, the changing use of historical detail seen in *Moll Flanders*. Thus the type of landscape used appears to the viewer to be less romanticised and more 'realistic' in the sense that it is duller, colder and starker than that used in traditional classic-novel adaptations and heritage films. The choice of alternative landscapes in *Wildfell Hall* is in great part due to the settings employed in Brontë's source book, and these settings bear different historical resonances from those used in traditional adaptations. That is, these landscapes do not 'mean' the same thing to the viewer; they do not elicit fond nostalgia for our national heritage. In addition, landscapes in *Wildfell Hall* function resolutely as a part of the narrative; they are not simply used as 'settings' that refine the mood of the diegesis. The landscapes themselves, the way in which they are filmed, and the characters' relations to them, supplement the explicit narrative with an implicit discourse about landscapes and their emotional importance to people.

The first episode is set almost entirely at Wildfell Hall and on the expansive Yorkshire moors that surround it. There are a few brief shots of Grassdale – an impressive country house – preceding the credit sequence in which, at dawn, Helen secretly absconds with her child, Arthur. However, the residence is purposefully obscured: the interior shots are too dark for us to see anything significant of Helen's surroundings, and the one exterior shot of the building is obstructed by a big close-up of half of Helen's face, in the foreground. This obstruction of our view of the house is exacerbated by the sharp focus upon Helen and the soft, blurred focus upon the background, and the corresponding narrative emphasis on Helen, which accords with our desire to see who she is. This deliberate impeding of our view of the house, and the fact that the entire first episode is set at Wildfell Hall, on the moors, has the desired effect of firmly establishing the latter location as the 'arena' for the drama: the background against which we become acquainted with the characters and the story.[11]

Wildfell Hall is not presented to us in any detail: the only rooms we see are the two main 'living' rooms, one an under-furnished kitchen, the other an almost empty drawing room, where Helen does her painting. Instead, Helen and Arthur's lives there seem to be lived outside – primarily on the moors, also in the village (in direct comparison with Helen's virtual imprisonment at Grassdale, where she rarely ventures outside). The moors are central, and although this country landscape is not 'pretty' in the Merchant Ivory sense, it is striking in itself, and it is perhaps tempting to see the oft-repeated shots of it as working in the same way as those much-maligned shots of rolling English countryside that acted as backdrops or 'fillers' in preceding traditional heritage films. But, as I implied above, the striking, rocky landscapes used here bear quite different cultural resonances to those borne by the traditional landscapes of classic-novel adaptations. 'Landscape' has been characterised in a particular way in previous chapters, roughly corresponding to David Crouch's argument:

> the idea of landscapes in western culture is centered around consumption rather than production ... It is read as an icon of what people stand for, but rarely of an ordinary everyday culture; rather as someone else's idea: an image of the countryside; of the past; of a nation; an idea of a region's identity and heritage. (Crouch, 1993: 27)

This is clearly applicable to the traditional, generic landscape shots for which classic-novel adaptations are well known. However, *Wildfell Hall* challenges the notion that 'visions of "Old England" are conservative and attempt to sell a lifestyle – and a landscape – that no longer exist (if they ever did)' (Ellington, 1998: 108).

In the first place, the type of landscape presented is significant; it contrasts with 'Austen's' landscape, described by Ellington as 'the landscape most easily recognisable as England, timeless and rustic' (1998: 93). Samuel writes enchantingly of his memories of a different kind of English landscape, 'one which, though by its own lights purist, was the very reverse of the Arcadian. Not buttercups and daisies but gorse and heather were its flora and fauna, not quiet meadows but rocky heights its *ultima Thule*' (1998: 132). Samuel relates how he inherited his mother's love of 'the spectacle of the untamed' (1998: 133), which landscapes like those used in *Wildfell Hall* exhibit: 'the countryside only became interesting when it was "hilly". It only qualified as scenery when it was bleak. Indeed the lonelier the aspect, the more sombre the setting, the more barren the landscape, the more authentic the view' (1998: 140). Whilst Samuel and his mother sought the freedom, openness and wildness of these 'primitive' landscapes (1998: 132), others enjoy this countryside for different cultural reasons. Just as Ellington draws attention to a long history of viewing landscapes, an article about the huge number of visitors flocking to the locations used in the serial *Wildfell Hall* notes that 'more than a century before, Brontë lovers were making pilgrimages to this bleak Pennine landscape' (Graham, 1996: 22). Once again the landscapes of the serial are historically significant, but here they clearly bear very different connotations from the 'pretty pretty' (Samuel, 1998: 133) ones that dominate traditional classic-novel adaptations.[12] They offer a different experience to the tourist and viewer, suggesting the impressive and expressive beauty of nature unrefined and uncultivated.

But the landscapes and locales of the serial *Wildfell Hall* are not just iconic – they are utilised not just as scenery but as parts of the narrative, so that these characteristic generic shots, aesthetically pleasing in themselves, take on an additional burden of meaning. Take, for example, the beautifully organised and framed shot of Helen who, having abandoned a picnic party, has found herself a viewing point from which to paint, has set up her easel and is busy sketching the view when Gilbert Markham joins her. There are certainly echoes here of the pictorialism that Higson noted (1993: 117): one of the ubiquitous bare and blackened trees, bent permanently horizontal by the wind, leans over Helen, framing her perfectly; her easel stands at an obtuse angle from her – a much more attractive position for the camera than if it faced her, and a positioning that necessitates her activity of sketching, as opposed to painting (figure 11). Yet this image is not a meaningless one, included for its aesthetic merits alone. The arched tree, with its strange shape that draws attention to its presence, the particular shot size (a medium-long to long shot) and the specific shot angle are all repeated twice more in the serial, and Helen appears beneath the tree each time. In Episode Two there appears a strikingly similar shot, but this time the tree is in the garden of Grassdale, and is in full bloom with white flowers, and Helen and her husband Arthur are beneath it; later in that episode the image is shown again, the tree now heavy with green leaves, and under it are Helen, her young son Arthur, and the baby's nanny. The state of the tree does not simply relay changes in season, for the seasons seem somewhat indeterminate throughout; instead its recurrence is employed to reflect the changes which are affecting Helen. In the first episode she feels isolated, bent over by the storm she has weathered – thin, angular and dressed in black, her appearance is comparable with that of the overarching tree; in the second episode (flashback) she is depicted as naïve, hopeful, still blinded by the memory of her white wedding (echoed in the flowers and her pale, overly 'frilly' dress), whilst the dialogue reveals the reality of the situation – Arthur's lack of thought and care for her; later in this episode she is a little older and wiser, the flowers of innocence gone, her dress more subdued, but the fresh, green leaves of the tree mirroring her hopes of the 'consolation' that she naïvely thinks her new-born son will provide (again, the dialogue reveals the truth of her husband's thoughtlessness).

It is important to note the (tele)visual nature of this repeated image: the particular image is not 'lifted' from the book – indeed, any attempt to 'describe' the artistic arrangement within the frame in words would ruin its simplicity and inhibit its instantaneous redeployment. Bruce Kawin writes of a similar use of repetition in literature, describing authors 'who draw contrasts and assume you will *remember* how a word was used last and will draw your own conclusions from the difference of context; who *emphasize*. Their art is primarily one of repetition with variation' (1972: 34) (italics in original). It is salient that Kawin refers to the repetition of single words, for the repetition of an entire description ('Helen sits under an overarching tree, to the left of its trunk as we look at it') would be clumsy, and would draw attention to the sentence's deliberate redeployment, undermining its effect. A repeated image, in comparison, works far more subtly, reinforcing Kawin's claim that 'repetition has the unique ability to bring us within reach of the nonverbal, even to generate nonverbal states of apprehension' (1972: 8).

Moreover, these shots, so important to the adaptation's narrative, are not explicable in terms of the book, but in terms of the adaptation text itself: they emphasise Helen's state of mind, they stress the disjunction between her view of each situation and the truth of the situation, and they are visually striking, too. Shots such as these expose the redundancy of the comparative approach: though they *may* accurately depict how Helen feels in the book, it is only important that they accurately portray how she feels in the adaptation. If they had failed in the latter, and had only been explicable with reference to the source book, then the adaptation would simply have failed to make sense, to express meaning. But they do not fail; they achieve their goal – the coherent communication of meaning. The source novel's account of each situation is, therefore, superfluous.

There are many traditional landscape long shots in this adaptation, but in each one the presence of a person (Helen, Gilbert, etc.) renders the landscape centrally important in diegetic terms, this role superseding its function as a striking, well-framed background for the action. Nicolson observes that 'people almost never appear in picture-England ... People are difficult; picture-England never can be' (1992: 28). His comments are certainly pertinent in terms of traditional classic-novel adaptations, where 'photographed England now looks as if a neutron bomb has hit it: no damage to buildings or landscapes but people have been utterly removed' (Nicolson, 1992: 28). The presence of actors/characters can endow these generic landscapes with narrative meanings which might clash with, even undermine, the meaning with which we as an audience wish to endow them. It is as if our own emotional connection with these views is the source of their affective power; ordinarily the appearance of other people threatens our direct relationship with 'the real star of the show, Old England, bucolic and gorgeous' (Ellington, 1998: 92). In *Wildfell Hall*, generic landscape shots frequently contain people, most often Helen. It is true that the size of the person in these shots is proportionately tiny – they appear to be overwhelmed by their surroundings – but far from ensuring that our attention is directed towards the landscape as 'scenery', this comparative proportion is used to enhance the diegesis.

One such shot is that of Helen as she waits for Gilbert, to hand him her diary and reveal the truth of her flight from Arthur. Unbeknownst to her, Gilbert has mistakenly assumed a relationship between her and her brother, Mr Lawrence, and so he fails to meet her. Her tiny frame, dressed in black, stands out in stark contrast to the vast, grey, rocky outcrop where she waits, highlighting her voluntary exposure to the hazards and isolation which she fears could result from her actions, the particular land-form metaphorically connoting the rocky path she treads and the state of her relationship with Gilbert at that time ('on the rocks') (figure 12). Landscape here plays a clear role in referring to and accentuating the diegesis. At other moments in the serial, in return, the placement of people within the landscape alters or enhances the feel of the landscape itself. A group takes a picnic out on the moors, but the composition and framing of the sequence suggests their insignificance and powerlessness in the face of nature, as they are filmed in long shot, tiny figures perched on a steep slope which cuts the frame with a diagonal line – it is almost as though the people might slide off the edge of the world (figure 13).

Yet the landscape is not depicted as being inherently linked to values such as harshness, coldness and danger. In contrast to its use in the above scene, the shots of desolate moorland are often juxtaposed with scenes from Helen's past life, scenes which emphasise the containment, enclosure and eventual claustrophobia which characterise her life with Arthur, thus allying a sense of space and freedom, and a lack societal strictures, with the sweeping, unpopulated Yorkshire moors. Here, again, Samuel's description of his mother's feelings for such a landscape echo those emotions we can ascribe to Helen: 'a woman in revolt against the servitudes of domestic life, ... she scorned comfort and revelled in the freedom of unruly open space' (1998: 132).

In this way the open, wild and often stark landscapes which characterise the programme seem to change with the narrative, at some times representing a place of unrestrained freedom and anonymity, at others emphasising Helen's diminutive size, physical abandonment and emotional solitude, at yet others simultaneously suggesting the possibility of both. The potentially contradictory nature of landscape in *Wildfell Hall* is heavily dependent upon the choice of countryside used in it. The ambivalence which characterises the programme's representations of the countryside is made manifest by Helen herself: whilst she is painting (in the picnic scene mentioned earlier), Gilbert comments upon the 'fine view', at which she looks up, smiling, to agree; at that moment, however, her face changes to show terror, as she sees her son Arthur take a forward nose-dive down a steep hill leading to the cliff-edge. All at once, the countryside, with its beauty, space and the possibility for a new and less confining romantic love (through Gilbert, a farmer, who thus holds a close relationship with the land), becomes a place of danger, of potential abandonment and isolation. How could this programme state more clearly that these landscape settings, though seemingly straightforward generic conventions, cannot be simply dismissed as 'views', for they can conceal a wealth of ambiguous and complex meaning?

Interior settings and generic scenes

Higson emphasises that 'it is the tension between visual splendour and narrative meaning in [heritage] films that makes them so fascinating' (1993: 110). Though Higson was referring to the kind of 'nostalgic' text of which *Pride and Prejudice* (1995) is an archetype, in fact his argument is even more applicable to a text like *Wildfell Hall*. I would argue that, rather than there being a '*tension*' between visual splendour and narrative meaning' in *Pride and Prejudice*, there is in fact an extraordinarily carefully constructed *congruence* between the two. The romanticised depiction of Austen's world is achieved through both narrative structure and a sentimental and admiring display of heritage. But in *Wildfell Hall* it is indeed the tension to which Higson refers that endows the programme with its fascinating qualities. These qualities include not just an alternative depiction of the past, but a complex reflection upon the classic-novel adaptation genre itself, and its customary mood of nostalgia. This is begun in the sequences described in the previous section, where generic landscapes are utilised with a sense of greater realistic and narrative purpose; however, the use of interior settings and generic scenes such as dining and ballroom scenes is even more interesting.

The generic country-house setting is one with which this programme is well endowed, and in the use of this locale the serial appears at first sight solidly conventional. The second and third episodes reveal to us Grassdale, Helen's home with her first husband, Arthur. As was mentioned above, this residence is filmed in a way that is typical of the genre: unlike the under-lighting that characterises the interiors at Wildfell Hall, these interiors are (at least, at first) well lit and tastefully furnished – each room is decorated immaculately and in an ornate fashion, and there is an abundance of furniture and props in each scene. The first couple of scenes from Helen's past take place in ballrooms, and the decor, costumes and finery present would seem to invite the misty-eyed gaze and impressed, satisfied appreciation with which we are ordinarily invited to respond to such displays. The light-hearted tone, restrained grace, and not inconsiderable beauty of Rupert Graves at his most charming are indeed pleasing to the eye. Yet, even at this point, the costumes and props are not used unambiguously, as part of a sumptuous pageant of a recreated elegant past. Helen's flouncy, pale dresses only emphasise her youth and girlish nature – the excessive, billowing, puffy sleeves serving to make the angular Fitzgerald look faintly ridiculous (for example, during the scene in which the buxom Annabella Wilmot is winning the attentions of Arthur, at the piano, and Helen looks on, downcast and uncertain). The elegant formal dances and the slow, 'ladylike' movements of the guests are what prevent Helen from reaching Arthur on the other side of the room – we take little pleasure in this graceful decadence when we experience, with Helen, her frustrated attempt to reach Arthur, now glimpsing him, now losing sight of him in the crowd of smiling faces. And when Helen finally espies him, the dreaded Annabella is already there and, using that most elegant and admired accessory of the nineteenth century 'lady', she hides her whispered sneers about Helen behind her genteel fan. Though the scene bears superficial resemblances in its deployment of 'heritage' props to the equivalent scenes in *Pride and Prejudice* where Elizabeth meets Darcy, the camerawork and direction used to present Helen's experience in that environment are likely to create a sense of frustration and dissatisfaction in the viewer, not wistful nostalgia.

Even inanimate objects such as the admired 'heritage' furniture play a divisive part in the narrative. From an early scene at a party, when a deep-focus, medium-long shot emphasises how Helen is divided from Arthur (and his lover, Annabella) by not only an immense floor space but also the obstacle of a huge sofa-back, which forms a wall between them, these heritage articles serve mostly to divide Helen and Arthur, to intrude into their relationship and enforce distance between them. At the end of the second episode, when Arthur returns from London, cantankerous, in need of alcohol, and irritated by the claustrophobia of his home life, the two sit down to a meal, one at each end of a huge table, laden with silverware. The usual sounds and sights of this familiar scene-type – the quiet clinking of crystal and silver; the gentle sound of wine being poured; the anonymous servants bowing and scraping, trying not to detract from the important action taking place at the table – are significantly re-cast in this particular rendering. The tension is already palpable due to Arthur's explosion of annoyance as he arrived at the house, and his second outburst, when a servant nervously drops a piece of silverware, does not encourage the viewer to wish for such splendid objects as adorn their table, but rather encourages feelings of sympathy for Helen, and relief that we in the modern world have dispensed with the formality, the silverware, the endless dishes and the omnipresent servants.

Similarly, the servants' presence is neither romanticised nor minimised – they are not simply 'standing around', forming part of the authentic period background; rather, they often intrude in the same way that the furniture and props do, again making the audience aware of the problems of the past, and not the ideal nature of it. When, at a dinner party, Helen gets up to comfort her son, whom Arthur has just pressed into drinking wine, her husband shouts at her to sit down. In the reverse shot of Helen's face we are aware of the presence of three servants standing behind her, looking on. Helen's humiliation in front of the guests, her acceptance of her subservience in front of her own servants, and her expected obedience to Arthur's command dispel any nostalgia that the female viewer, at least, may have been feeling for the 'good old days'. *Moll Flanders* utilised Moll's unique position in the household to reveal the injustices of the class system for the servant class, and allow a narrative focus upon them; *Wildfell Hall* utilises Helen's traditional generic role as one of the 'served' in order to expose the iniquities of the patriarchal structure vital to the maintenance of that hierarchical system. Both programmes depend for their critiques upon the generic conventions of classic-novel adaptations, and the audience's acquaintance with these conventions and their traditional valencies.

Nostalgia revisited

Wildfell Hall maintains its place within the genre of classic-novel adaptations through its use of recognisable generic tropes of content and style. Yet it also subtly undermines the cultural significance of these tropes, utilising our previous knowledge of them. In wider terms, whilst

Brideshead and *Pride and Prejudice* revelled in nostalgia, and *Moll Flanders* almost totally rejected it, *Wildfell Hall* actively engages itself in an examination of nostalgia as it is created through classic-novel adaptations. Nostalgia is, itself, a return – a return to an illusory past, for the purposes of escape and reassurance. Yet *Wildfell Hall* exists in a period when reflection upon nostalgia – its prevalence, importance and implications – is becoming common, and when in popular and mass culture nostalgia is openly acknowledged as a cultural force (evidenced by the growth in explicitly nostalgic products such as those sold by specialist retro shops and chains like Past Times). Thus, we can now return again – we can return to nostalgia itself.

I have described how *Wildfell Hall* undermines the audience's propensity to feel nostalgia for the past depicted, through its selection of certain aspects of that past and the tension it establishes between its generic portrayals of heritage and its narrative. One is tempted to assume that such a portrayal leaves the 'heritage project' out in the cold (on those rocky moors). Yet it does not – not quite. There is one scene in particular which lends itself readily to a nostalgic response, and that is the scene after Arthur's death, when Helen leaves Grassdale to return to the Yorkshire moors. Packed and ready to go, Helen takes one last walk through the pale lemon-coloured drawing room, yet the shot of this room is held for a few seconds after she has left it, allowing us to gaze upon it. The image is perfectly symmetrical: a sofa-back stands in the centre, and a chair stands each side of it. Each of the double doors through which we look has standing next to it a large urn, and the camera angle is completely centred. A shaft of sunlight falls through the left-hand window and gently lights the room (figure 14). It is a romantic picture, one that conjures up feelings of affection and mild desire for a time past – in other words, it elicits nostalgia. The following shot, taking the view of Arthur junior as he leans out of the window of the departing carriage, is the first and only clear, centred long shot of Grassdale we are offered – a long shot characteristic of the genre and usually employed more frequently. There is no formal subversion of the genre here – this shot is purely generic. Arthur is looking back with feelings that can be described as nostalgia, and it is his gaze that we follow.

In terms of nostalgia, though, these shots are two of the most polysemic and meaningful in the serial, and they work to complicate and subvert our relation to the past as it is usually constituted through this genre. First, on one level, both shots are narratively important. The first shot, seen through the eyes of Helen, serves to emphasise the lack of impression that she has made upon her surroundings: the striking order and symmetry of the room seem to suggest a lack of any human impact upon it, and highlight Helen's ultimate futility and irrelevance within the larger scheme of life in that particular class and at that specific time in history. The continuation of the shot after Helen has left the room, with the empty chair in which she sat central to the foreground, accentuates the contrast between Helen's short-lived and ineffectual existence and the lasting solidity of the place upon which she has barely left a mark. The second shot, seen through the eyes of Arthur, is not a generalised nostalgia, but is diegetically motivated; it is personalised. Arthur has lost his father in that house, and is leaving behind his childhood home. We understand the motivation behind his backward gaze.

However, our gaze cannot be just emotionally loaded, for we cannot put aside our knowledge about the places depicted. Even if we regard these two shots as wistfully nostalgic, we perceive them within the context of the story, and associate Grassdale with the same adverse experiences that Helen does, so our response to these shots is not unproblematically favourable. We gaze at Grassdale knowing the true nature (within the terms of the story) of the past that has been lived out there. The programme relies upon a knowingness for its effect; as viewers, we must be both aware of generic conventions and their emotional connotations, and conscious of what the programme is doing with them, in order to appreciate its 'ironic self-referentiality' (Brooker and Brooker, 1997: 1). That is why *Wildfell Hall* is both firmly within the genre (it contains such generic shots) and yet subverts it (through the use it makes of the shots). In this serial one can see the rapid development of a long-standing television genre which has moved far away from its filmic progenitors and is becoming sophisticated in its own right.

At the level of cognitive and emotional engagement, the development and subversion of the genre as seen in this sequence are even more complex, precisely because the shots do not produce a simple, rational response in the viewer. The viewer is placed in a curiously ambivalent, almost self-contradictory position: although we see these shots within the context of the narrative, we also respond emotionally in the way in which we are expected to when confronted by such generic moments. So the moment elicits nostalgia that is complicated by our 'knowledge' that that past may have been composed of events like those in the story we have just seen. Davis (1979) postulates three forms of nostalgic response, where the first is a simple nostalgia for times past – the type of nostalgia with which Higson *et al.* are concerned – and the other two types exhibit increasing levels of epistemological and emotional sophistication. In a sense, through our combined emotional and cognitive response to *Wildfell Hall*, we experience what Fred Davis defines as 'second order' or 'reflexive' nostalgia, whereupon we summon 'to feeling and thought certain empirically oriented questions concerning the truth, accuracy, complete- ness, or representativeness of the nostalgic claim' (1979: 21).

Yet *Wildfell Hall*, because of its clear connections with a genre that is so strongly concerned with nostalgia, is also able to elicit in the viewer Davis's 'third order or interpreted nostalgia, which causes the viewer to consider "analytically oriented questions concerning its sources, typical character, significance and psychological purpose"' (1979: 24). That is, we are able to reflect not just on the unrealistic nature of a romanticised nostalgia for the past, but also on the way in which the genre of classic- novel adaptations utilises our emotional responses to the past in order to elicit nostalgia from us. Thus *Wildfell Hall* also encourages us as viewers to reflect upon the affective significance of generic tropes, in order to place the genre and our responses to it within a clearer analytical frame- work. As Morris B. Holbrook accurately sums up reflexive nostalgia, 'Such an analytic "framing of the nostalgic response" involves a "stepping outside ... of its givenness" in ways that raise searching questions' (1993: 105).[13]

The reflexive challenge to unquestioning nostalgia that *Wildfell Hall* encourages has the potential to impact upon our cultural lives beyond our viewing of the programme, to subtly alter our relationship with the past. Dramas like this help to forge an important emotional link between our modern-day selves and our 'heritage', a link that can be felt when we visit 'heritage locations' and utilise our memories of such representations to make sense of, and imagine, the past times of which these buildings are an extant part. By problematising the nostalgic nature of this 'heritage representation', *Wildfell Hall* works extra-textually, complicating this emotional link with our inherited past – not destroying it, but questioning it and putting it in an appropriate perspective. It is also significant that the second shot discussed above (Arthur's backward gaze upon Grassdale, as his carriage leaves) inverts the traditional shot sequence as employed so frequently in *Pride and Prejudice*: the long shot is offered as a point-of-view shot, but it is the point of view of someone *leaving* the house, travelling away from their past. The house, with its heritage interiors and its identity as a locus of the past, is left behind; casting back our gaze, we feel a complex affection for it, but we travel forward, knowing that what lies behind us is as flawed and abstruse as that which lies ahead. Larsen defines nostalgia: 'it tends to look only backward. It is a closing up and a withdrawal from the probabilities of the future, rather than a long glance backward before a releasing step forward' (1983: 464). *Wildfell Hall* leaves us with an exact visualisation of the latter response to our past, rather than the former (nostalgic) one.

Notes

1 The televisual was elucidated in Chapter 4.
2 I put aside the problematic question of whether a postmodern aesthetic determines, or is determined by, the socio-cultural milieu of postmodernity. For my purposes here, it is sufficient to tentatively assume that postmodern aesthetics both reflect and exacerbate the 'postmodern condition'. My arguments do not stand or fall on the basis of the reader's acceptance of this connection.
3 It is salient to reiterate the oft-quoted difference between 'traditional' intertextuality and postmodern intertextuality: that the former aims to express or enhance meaning, whereas the latter is merely a superficial pastiche of images and references. I should also repeat my doubts about such a stark differentiation: the former kind of intertextuality is still apparent, even in 'postmodern' classic-novel adaptations.
4 This apt quote, which sums up my point so accurately, is taken from an unpublished research paper, '"You Cannot Look at This": Thresholds of Unrepresentability in Holocaust Film' (on genre and representations of the Holocaust) given by Barry Langford at Royal Holloway College, 1999.
5 These examples clearly exist on a continuum. A fictional book based in history and written by a scholar (e.g. *The Name of the Rose* (1980), by Umberto Eco – a specialist in mediaeval history) would, I contend, bear a greater relation to the 'real' past than a romantic fiction that uses a specific period merely as a backdrop. Again we must recognise that all these texts are representations of the past; whilst a dyed-in-the-wool postmodernist might argue that none (therefore) bears a closer relationship to the 'real past' than any other, I would argue for the possibility of differentiation as I have suggested.
6 One might have to concede that 'postmodern cultural analysis' is better placed than Lowenthal's more traditional historical analysis to explain the 'impact of consumerism on social life' (Collins, 1992: 339) evident in the heritage industry that has grown up around many historical relics.
7 A 'postmodern' approach to history (as opposed to a postmodern view of the past) incorporates echoes of the same instability and insecurity that Jameson notes, as it 'problematizes the entire notion of historical knowledge' (Rosenstone, 1996: 203). However, as Rosenstone points out, postmodern history does not mark a complete break with traditional history. He offers a valuable discussion of 'postmodernist history', revealing several flaws, anomalies and contradictions in such an approach, whilst noting its value to minorities previously under- or mis-represented in 'traditional history'. Baudrillard (1988) appears to reject the notion of the 'real' when he argues that the proliferation of simulacra leads to the loss of the 'referent' – the 'real' to which the images refer.
8 An example of a postnostalgic point of view might be one that reflects upon nostalgia itself, or one that is nostalgic for a state of simple nostalgia itself.
9 This relationship may be nostalgic, but may also or instead be 'postnostalgic'; it is possible that the adaptation might permit several different relationships with its viewers, thus being characteristically 'postmodern' in its address to multiple simultaneous audiences.
10 The section 'Reports and Debates' featured essays by each of these theorists in *Screen*, 36: 3, Autumn 1995.
11 Comparative theorists might like to note that this use of location to 'centre' the drama on the moors has the added effect of making Helen's settlement there and her attachment to Gilbert Markham more credible than they seem in the book.
12 David Crouch offers an interesting discussion on what different types of landscape 'mean' to different people, in 'Representing Ourselves in the Landscape: Cultural Meanings in Everyday Landscape' (1993).
13 Holbrook utilises Davis's categories in his own exploration of nostalgia. Here he draws from Davis (1979: 25).

9

Reconfiguring the genre

Wildfell Hall overtly positions itself within the generic microcosm of classic-novel adaptations, through its use of traditional tropes of content, style, even mood. Unlike *Moll Flanders*, therefore, *Wildfell Hall* perpetuates conventions of the genre; unlike *Brideshead* and *Pride and Prejudice*, it actively uses our expectations to alter their traditional affectiveness. Through its 'lifting out' of generic tropes, which are then re-presented within a reflective, reflexive presentation, *Wildfell Hall* could be considered typically postmodern, but as Brooker and Brooker argue, 'instead of pastiche, we might think of "re-writing" or "re-viewing" and, in terms of the spectator's experience, of the "re-activation" and "re-configuration" of a given generational "structure of feeling" within a more dynamic and varied set of histories' (1997: 7).

To an extent, all generic texts 're-write, re-view, re-activate and re-configure'; certainly all four of the adaptations considered in this book do so. *Brideshead Revisited*, a traditional, 'faithful' adaptation, rewrote and reviewed its source text and thus reactivated and reconfigured its nostalgia in televisual terms. *Pride and Prejudice* revisits the classic-novel adaptation's recognisable tropes in order to consolidate a generic archetype rooted in a nostalgic mood that is derived from previous adaptations, not from its source novel. *Moll Flanders* dramatically rewrites the rule book, using expectations of the genre to reactivate and reconfigure the audience's relationship with the past, with the genre, and with the televisual. *Wildfell Hall* offers a reflexive return to the genre and to nostalgia through its reworking of generic tropes.

Just as adaptations have moved away from their source books, so too must the approach through which we consider them. I hope to have shown that novel-adaptation comparison is an inadequate starting point for the interpretation, analysis and evaluation of individual adaptations. Instead, we ought to begin from what the programmes themselves offer us – from their aesthetic and generic particularities, and from their televisuality. Each of the programmes discussed here has extended television's possibilities and the realm of the classic-novel adaptation; analyses of particular texts should recognise this, and assess each one's individual qualities and its broader contribution to the genre.

The question of evaluation

Adaptations have, perhaps more consistently than other films and tele-vision programmes, been subject to criticism, assessment and evaluation as well as interpretation and theorising. In the past, evaluation has been carried out according to prevailing criteria such as fidelity to the source novel or ideological or political 'correctness'. Evaluation – a judgement about how 'good' an artwork is – is an important part of critical discourse, yet has been mostly avoided in television studies, as Brunsdon has noted (1990a). The question of how we might construct more reasonable, useful and rigorous criteria for the evaluation of a classic-novel adaptation has not been explicitly addressed in this book, but lies beneath the surface. Concepts utilised herein include those that problematise the question of assessment and those that may open up further avenues for setting evaluative criteria.

The references made in this book to postmodern theories complicate the question of evaluation. Classic-novel adaptations have not been fully reconsidered in postmodern terms, probably as a result of the still-prevalent characterisation of them as different from the rest of television. Yet there is a movement towards a more 'postmodern' aesthetic style in adaptations, as classic-novel adaptations appear to become more visually sophisticated, intertextual, contemporaneous, consumerist, performative, playful and internally reflexive. They also blur the boundaries between text and context, past and present. This makes theories of the postmodern doubly relevant to the genre.

However, it is difficult to avoid the evaluative presumptions implicit in postmodernists' writing. There is a certain absolutism glimpsed in Jameson:

> the distinctive features attributed by Jameson to postmodernism include the following: a new depthlessness and a consequent weakening of historicity; the waning of affect; a fragmentation of the subject; the omnipresence of pastiche and prevalence of a 'nostalgia mode'; and the breakdown of the signifying chain following the collapse of the referent and associated crisis of representation. (Smart, 1993: 17)

Though it may be hotly denied, there is an underlying sense of condemnation, or at least admonition, in postmodernists' talk of depthlessness, fragmentation, crises, breakdown and collapse. Yet within the framework of a postmodern (con)text there is the possibility of historicism (as *Moll Flanders* and *Wildfell Hall* reveal); textuality is often demarcated as distinct from reality (through the foregrounding of performance or genre, for example); and adaptations can have a potential impact on real life, and on our understanding of 'history', through the links they forge with extant artefacts, literature, and so on. My position is closer to that of Corner and Harvey, as they warn, '[postmodern] theory seems to us to be at its weakest in those variants which reject or ignore the possibility of historical analysis' (1991: 18).

Thus while accepting the validity and interpretative usefulness of notions of the postmodern, I would reject their implicit evaluation of texts. It is not the postmodern nature of texts that determines whether or not they are 'good' or 'bad'; whether they permit considered, critical responses or encourage a 'loss of affect'; or whether they enforce, blur or destroy the line between 'reality' and 'simulation'. It is the way in which the texts themselves manipulate the often competing discourses within which they are sited, and through which they are constituted, that determines their value.

This book raises another concept that may prove to be of use in evaluation: the televisual. Throughout, it considers the televisual in terms of its value as a conceptual framework and an interpretative tool, but avoids addressing the question of whether the televisual is of any use as an evaluative category. If there are certain textual features, modes of address, etc., that are televisual, and others that are not, are some television texts therefore 'more televisual' than others, and does this make them better television? Early, traditional classic-novel adaptations held a strange contradictory position in these terms: they were 'good television' because they rejected the televisual. Later adaptations have embraced the televisual – does this make them better television than their predecessors? The repetition of specific images in *Wildfell Hall*, and the interplay of direct address and voice-over in *Moll Flanders*, utilise specifically audiovisual characteristics inaccessible to the novelist; should then these programmes be praised for their recognition of the potential of the televisual medium? I have implied that recent adaptations are more inventive, varied, thoughtful and engaging, but I leave open the question of to what extent these traits arise from an increased emphasis on televisuality. The problematic notion of medium essentialism, and the relation between the 'essence' of a medium and the evaluation of its 'texts' is an ancient one (as Carroll notes, 1996), but it is a notion that has not yet been overtly or fully considered in terms of television aesthetics. I hope its implicit presence within this book will encourage greater scholarship on the subject.

Perhaps the simplest criteria one might begin with are those of coherence and 'depth'. An adaptation is based on a novel, but it cannot be regarded as successful if it is wholly explicable only with reference to that source. Watching *Jude* (1996), I found myself explaining details of plot, characterisation and chronology to my friend, who was unfamiliar with the book. The film seemed to give rise to confusion through gaps in plot and inconsistencies in character; this could be overcome only with reference to the source novel. It thus appeared to be incoherent as an artwork, incapable of standing alone, incomplete. In comparison, each of the adaptations considered in detail in this book is comprehensible and coherent as an entity in its own right, needing no input from a viewer with knowledge of the source novel.

Beyond this, some adaptations allow engagement on many levels. This is not to be confused with the polysemy or pluralism lauded by cultural-studies theorists; I am not proposing that we value a text for its potential provision of a plethora of (subversive) interpretations. Rather, we have seen that, particularly in the examples of *Moll Flanders* and *Wildfell Hall*, the viewer may engage in a variety of ways, on a number of levels, allowing movement beyond enjoyable emotional engagement to greater cognitive, reflective and reflexive awareness. This is possible because of features contained within the adaptations themselves. In the sense then that adaptations like these repay repeated viewings, offering more to the viewer on each subsequent occasion, they can be regarded as having depth.

Most importantly, though, whatever criteria one decides upon, I hope to have indicated the importance of aesthetic evaluation on two levels: in appreciating and critiquing the more particular qualities of individual adaptations, and in developing an awareness of wider movements within a genre.

Looking ahead

At the beginning of the twenty-first century, the general move towards eclecticism in the genre is sustained. Whilst Dickens remains popular with adapters, there is a continuation of the tendency away from Austen, primarily because many of her novels have been adapted fairly recently; even when Austen is adapted, it is in a way radically different from previous adaptations. For example, Fay Weldon is planning a new, 'updated' adaptation of *Pride and Prejudice*, which features men, not women, in the key roles of the Bennet siblings, reflecting changes in society that see more men than women living at home until they move in with a long-term partner.

Increasingly, adaptations make use of their televisuality, moving further away from slow-paced literariness. Adaptations of British 'classics' range from the hard-hitting *Oliver Twist* (1999, ITV), scripted by Alan Bleasdale, to the raucous *Vanity Fair* (1998, BBC), another Andrew Davies adaptation. In terms of mood, many of these programmes shift the focus from nostalgia to suspense, humour, romance and other variations. *Gormenghast* (2000, BBC), an extravagant adaptation of Mervyn Peake's fantastical trilogy, was literally a world removed from the traditional generic microcosm of classic-novel adaptations. Tellingly, though, the series was neither critically nor commercially popular. It is clear that conventional adaptations are still valued, for while big-budget adaptations have become increasingly innovative and varied, generic nostalgic features remain central to adaptations of novels such as Elizabeth Gaskell's *Wives and Daughters* (1999, BBC), Stella Tillyard's *Aristocrats* (1999, BBC) and Anthony Trollope's *The Way We Live Now* (2001, BBC), adapted by the prolific Andrew Davies. Nostalgic representations of the more recent past are apparent in the adaptations of Kingsley Amis's *Take a Girl Like You* (2000, BBC) and Nancy Mitford's *Love in a Cold Climate* (2001, BBC). And high-profile adaptations of non-British novels such as *Madame Bovary* (2000, BBC) and *Anna Karenina* (2000, Channel Four) have provided new stories and exotic settings combined with all the splendours of traditional adaptations: fine frocks, beautiful scenery and exquisite interiors. Though the range of novels chosen for high-budget adaptations is broadening, it is notable that the 'traditional' classic-novel adaptation continues to hold its treasured place in television: the BBC web-page for Spring 1999 advertised forthcoming adaptations as a group, but singled out *Great Expectations*, placing it in a separate category of 'Event Television'.[1]

Perhaps the genre's evident eclecticism and variety is rooted in a desire for life: whilst this genre is alive and flourishing, so too is television, and so too our desire to forge new connections with the past. The latter does not have to be configured as a need to escape or reject the present, but can be understood as a singularly 'un-postmodern' desire for historicism – a determination to understand the present as it relates to the past, or 'a perception of the present as history' (Jameson, 1991: 284). To appreciate the genre of classic-novel adaptations is thus to value the present for the potential it holds for enjoyment, entertainment and the development of an emotional and cognitive understanding of past and present. As Kawin writes:

> That we are always dying is the tyranny of the present tense. Personal memory does not, any more than art or children, keep *us* alive. The answer

time offers us, and the gift of the present tense, is that we are always living. It is entirely up to us whether our time is always ending or always beginning. (1972: 33) (italics in original)

Note

1   See http://www.bbc.co.uk/info/news161.htm (accessed August 2001).

Bibliography

Adams, P. (1993) 'In TV: On "Nearness", on Heidegger and on Television', in T. Fry (ed.), *RUA TV?: Heidegger and the Televisual*, Sydney, Power Institute of Fine Arts, 45–66.

Agger, G. and J. F. Jensen (eds) (forthcoming) *The Aesthetics of Television*, Aalborg, Aalborg University Press.

Allen, B. (1990) 'A Study of Evelyn Waugh's *Brideshead Revisited* as compared to the Telefilm version', unpub. PhD thesis, East Texas State University.

Allen, R. and M. Smith (eds) (1997) *Film Theory and Philosophy: Aesthetics and the Analytical Tradition*, Oxford, Oxford University Press.

Allen, R. C. (1992) 'Audience-Oriented Criticism and Television', in R. C. Allen (ed.), *Channels of Discourse, Reassembled*, 2nd edn, London, Routledge, 101–37.

Allen, R. C. (ed.) (1992) *Channels of Discourse, Reassembled*, 2nd edn, London, Routledge.

Altman, R. (1999) *Film/Genre*, London, British Film Institute.

Amis, K. (1981) 'How I Lived in Very Big House and Found God', *Times Literary Supplement*, 20 November, 1352.

Anderson, B. (1993) *Imagined Communities: Reflections on the Origin and Spread of Nationalism*, London, Verso.

Andrew, D. (1984) *Concepts in Film Theory*, Oxford, Oxford University Press.

Andrew, D. (1980) 'The Well-Worn Muse: Adaptation in Film History and Theory', in S. Conger and J. Welsh (eds), *Narrative Strategies*, Macomb, West Illinois University Press, 9–17.

Anon. (1998) 'The Little Brother with a Big Future', *The Sunday Times*, 26 April, 6.

Anon. (1998) 'Easy Sits the Crown', *The Sunday Times*, 20 September, 4.

Asheim, L. (1951) 'From Book to Film: Simplification', *Film Quarterly*, 5, 289–304.

Asheim, L. (1949) 'From Book to Film', unpub. PhD thesis, University of Chicago.

Atkins, E. (1993) '*Jane Eyre* Transformed', *Literature Film Quarterly*, 21: 1, 54–60.

Austin, J. L. (1971) *How To Do Things with Words (The William James Lectures Delivered at Harvard University in 1955)*, London, Oxford University Press.

Aycock, W. and M. Schoenecke (eds) (1988) *Film and Literature: A Comparative Approach to Adaptation*, Texas, Texas University Press.

Baker, N. (1996) *The Size of Thoughts*, London, Chatto and Windus.

Balázs, B. (1972) *Theory of the Film: Character and Growth of a New Art*, New York, Arno.

Barker, S. (1994) '"Period" Detective Drama and the Limits of Contemporary Nostalgia: *Inspector Morse* and the Strange Case of a Lost England', *Critical Survey (Oxford)*, 6: 2, 234–42.

Barry, P. (1995) *Beginning Theory: An Introduction to Literary and Cultural Theory*, Manchester, Manchester University Press.

Barthes, R. (1971) 'From Work to Text', ed. and trans. R. Howard, in *The Rustle of Language*, Oxford, Basil Blackwell, 1986, 57–64.

Barthes, R. (1968) 'The Death of the Author', ed. and trans. R. Howard, in *The Rustle of Language*, Oxford, Basil Blackwell, 1986, 49–56.

Barthes, R. (1964) 'Rhetoric of the Image', ed. and trans. S. Heath, in *Image, Music, Text*, London, Fontana, 1977, 32–51.

Battestin, M. C. (1967) 'Osborne's Tom Jones: Adapting a Classic', in J. Harrington (ed.), *Film And/As Literature*, Englewood Cliffs, NJ, Prentice-Hall, 1977, 38–44.

Baudrillard, J. (1988) *The Evil Demon of Images*, Sydney, Power Institute Publications.

Baudrillard, J. (1981) *Simulacres et simulation*, repr. as 'The Precession of Simulacra' and 'The Orders of Simulacra', in P. Foss, P. Patton and P. Bleitchman (trans.), *Simulations*, New York, Semiotext(e), 1983, 1–79.

Bazin, A. (1958) *What is Cinema?: Volume I*, trans. H. Gray, Berkeley, University of California Press.

Beard, M. and J. Henderson (1995) *Classics: A Very Short Introduction*, Oxford, Oxford University Press.

Beja, M. (1979) *Film and Literature*, New York, Longman.

Benjamin, W. (1936) 'The Work of Art in the Age of Mechanical Reproduction', ed. H. Arendt, trans. H. Zohn, *Illuminations*, London, Fontana, 1992, 211–44.

Bentley, H. (1996) 'Televising a Classic Novel for Students', *Contemporary Review*, 268: 1562, 141–3.

Blair, J. G. (1996) 'American Drama: Text and Video', *American Studies International*, 34: 1 (April), 1–17.

Blewett, D. (1989) 'Introduction' to Daniel Defoe, *Moll Flanders* (1722), Harmondsworth, Penguin.

Bluestone, G. (1957) *Novels into Film*, Berkeley, University of California Press.

Blythe, R. (1985) 'Introduction' to Thomas Hardy, *Far from the Madding Crowd* (1874), Harmondsworth, Penguin.

Bordwell, D. and N. Carroll (eds) (1996) *Post-Theory: Reconstructing Film Studies*, Madison, University of Wisconsin Press.

Bordwell, D. and Kristin Thompson (1993) *Film Art: An Introduction*, 4th edn, New York, McGraw Hill.

Bourdieu, P. (1979) *Distinction: A Social Critique of the Judgement of Taste*, trans. Richard Nice, London, Routledge and Kegan Paul, 1984.

Boyd, W. (1982a) 'Back to *Brideshead*', *New Statesman*, 1 January, 23–4.

Boyd, W. (1982b) 'Faithful to a Fault', *New Statesman*, 9 October, 25–6.

Branigan, E. (1997) 'Sound, Epistemology, Film', in R. Allen and M. Smith (eds), *Film Theory and Philosophy: Aesthetics and the Analytical Tradition*, Oxford, Oxford University Press, 95–125.

Branigan, E. (1992) *Narrative Comprehension and Film*, London, Routledge.

Bromley, R. (1999) 'Imagining the Puritan Body: The 1995 Cinematic Version of Nathaniel Hawthorne's *The Scarlet Letter*', in D. Cartmell and I. Whelehan (eds), *Adaptations: From Text to Screen, Screen to Text*, London, Routledge, 63–80.

Brooker, P. and W. Brooker (eds) (1997) *Postmodern After-images*, London, Arnold.

Browne, R. B. and R. J. Ambrosetti (eds) (1993) *Continuities in Popular Culture: The Present in the Past and the Past in the Present and Future*, London, Routledge.

Brownstein, R. M. (1998) 'Out of the Drawing Room, Onto the Lawn', in L. Troost and S. Green-field (eds), *Jane Austen in Hollywood*, Kentucky, The University Press of Kentucky, 13–21.

Brunette, P. and D. Wills (1989) *Screen/Play: Derrida and Film Theory*, Princeton, NJ.

Brunsdon, C. (1998) 'Structure of Anxiety: Recent British Television Crime Fiction', *Screen*, 39: 3, 223–42.

Brunsdon, C. (1990a) 'Problems with Quality', *Screen*, 31: 1 (Spring), 67–90.

Brunsdon, C. (1990b) 'Television: Aesthetics and Audiences', in P. Mellencamp (ed.), *Logics of Television: Essays in Cultural Criticism*, Bloomington and Indianapolis, Indiana University Press, 59–72.

Bruzzi, S. (1995) 'Tempestuous Petticoats: Costume and Desire in *The Piano*', *Screen*, 36: 3 (Autumn), 257–67.

Bullen, B. (1990) 'Is Hardy a "Cinematic Novelist"?: The Problem of Adaptation', *Yearbook of English Studies*, 20, 48–59.

Bullough, G. (1957–75) *Narrative and Dramatic Sources of Shakespeare*, London, Routledge and Kegan Paul.

Bundey, A. B. (1986) 'The Adaptation of the Novel for Television (The Process and the Educational Implications)', unpub. MA thesis, University of Exeter.

Burke, S. (ed.) (1995) *Authorship: From Plato to the Postmodern*, Edinburgh, Edinburgh University Press.

Butler, J. (1990), *Gender Trouble: Feminism and the Subversion of Identity*, New York, Routledge.

Caldwell, J. T. (1995) *Televisuality: Style, Crisis and Authority in American Television*, Piscataway, NJ, Rutgers University Press.

Cardwell, S. (2000a) 'Present(ing) Tense: Temporality and Tense in Comparative Theories of Literature-Film Adaptation', *Scope (Film Studies)* 1: 2 (July), www.nottingham.ac.uk/ film/journal/index/htm.

Cardwell, S. (2000b) 'Darcy's Escape: An Icon in the Making', in S. Bruzzi and P. Church Gibson (eds), *Fashion Cultures*, London, Routledge.

Carroll, N. (1999) 'Film, Emotion, and Genre', in C. Plantinga and G. M. Smith (eds), *Passionate Views: Film, Cognition and Emotion*, Baltimore, The Johns Hopkins University Press, 21–47.

Carroll, N. (1996) *Theorizing the Moving Image*, Cambridge, Cambridge University Press.

Carroll, N. (1988) *Mystifying Movies: Fads and Fallacies in Contemporary Film Theory*, New York, Columbia University Press.

Cartmell, D. (1999) 'Introduction', in D. Cartmell and I. Whelehan (eds), *Adaptations: From Text to Screen, Screen to Text*, London, Routledge, 23–8.

Cartmell, D. and I. Whelehan (eds) (1999) *Adaptations: From Text to Screen, Screen to Text*, London, Routledge.

Cartmell, D. (1996) 'Introduction', in D. Cartmell, I. Q. Hunter, H. Kaye and I. Whelehan (eds), *Pulping Fictions: Consuming Culture Across the Literature/Media Divide*, London, Pluto Press.

Cartmell, D., I. Q. Hunter, H. Kaye and I. Whelehan (eds) (1996) *Pulping Fictions: Consuming Culture Across the Literature/Media Divide*, London, Pluto Press.

Caughie, J. (2000) *Television Drama: Realism, Modernism, and British Culture*, Oxford, Oxford University Press.

Caughie, J. (ed.) (1981) *Theories of Authorship*, London, British Film Institute.

Cavell, S. (1971) *The World Viewed: Reflections on the Ontology of Film*, New York, Viking Press.

Cohen, A. J.-J. (1999) 'Three *Madame Bovarys*: Renoir, Minnelli, Chabrol', in J. Bignell (ed.) *Writing and Cinema*, Harlow, Essex, Pearson Education, 119–33.

Collins, J. (1992) 'Postmodernism and Television', in R. Allen (ed.), *Channels of Discourse, Reassembled*, 2nd edn, London, Routledge, 327–53.

Comrie, B. (1986) 'Tense and Time Reference: From Meaning to Interpretation in the Chronological Structure of a Text', *Journal of Literary Semantics*, 15: 1 (April), 12–22.

Conger, S. and J. Welsh (eds) (1980) *Narrative Strategies*, Macomb, West Illinois University Press.

Connor, S. (1989) *Postmodernist Culture: An Introduction to Theories of the Contemporary*, Oxford, Basil Blackwell.

Cook, A.-M. (1998) 'Parallels to the Past: The Political Critique of Thatcherism in adaptations of E.M. Forster's novels', conference paper, University of East Anglia, June.

Cook, P. (1996) 'Neither Here nor There: National Identity in Gainsborough Costume Drama', in A. Higson (ed.), *Dissolving Views: Key Writings on British Cinema*, London, Cassell, 51–65.

Corner, J. (1999) *Critical Ideas in Television Studies*, Oxford, Oxford University Press.

Corner, J. and S. Harvey (1991) *Enterprise and Heritage: Crosscurrents of National Culture*, London, Routledge.

Craig, A. (1996) 'Television Review [adaptations]', *Observer*, 24 November, 92.

Craig, S. (1983) 'Daughter of Brideshead', *Listener*, 40: 2831, 20 October, 31.

Crouch, D. (1993) 'Representing Ourselves in the Landscape: Cultural Meanings in Everyday Landscape', in R. B. Browne and R. J. Ambrosetti (eds), *Continuities in Popular Culture*, London, Routledge, 26–48.

Currie, G. (1995) *Image and Mind: Film, Philosophy and Cognitive Science*, Cambridge, Cambridge University Press.

Dagle, J. (1980) 'The Question of the Present Tense', in S. Conger and J. Welsh (eds), *Narrative Strategies*, Macomb, West Illinois University Press, 47–59.

Davis, F. (1979) *Yearning for Yesterday: A Sociology of Nostalgia*, New York, Free Press.

Davis, R. M. (1990) 'Review of Boo Allen's Doctoral Thesis: A Study of Evelyn Waugh's *Brideshead Revisited* as Compared to the Telefilm Version', *Evelyn Waugh Newsletter and Studies*, 32: 2 (Autumn), 8.

Dickson, R. (1998) 'Misrepresenting Jane Austen's Ladies: Revising Texts (and History) to Sell Films', in L. Troost and S. Greenfield (eds), *Jane Austen in Hollywood*, Kentucky, The University Press of Kentucky, 44–57.

Dienst, R. (1994) *Still Life in Real Time: Theory after Television*, Durham, NC, Duke University Press.

Dittmar, L. (1983) 'Fashioning and Re-fashioning: Framing Narratives in the Novel and Film', *Mosaic*, 16: 1–2, 189–203.

Doane, M. A. (1990) 'Information, Crisis, Catastrophe', in P. Mellencamp (ed.), *Logics of Television: Essays in Cultural Criticism*, Bloomington and Indianapolis, Indiana University Press, 222–39.

Docker, J. (1994) *Postmodernism and Popular Culture: A Cultural History*, Cambridge, Cambridge University Press.

Doyle, P. A. (1982) 'The Year's Work in Waugh Studies', *Evelyn Waugh Newsletter*, 16: 1 (Spring), 1–2.

Durgnat, R. (1971) 'The Mongrel Muse', in F. H. Marcus (ed.), *Film and Literature: Contrasts in Media*, Seranton, Chandler, 71–82.

Dyson, L. (1995) 'The Return of the Repressed? Whiteness, Femininity and Colonialism in *The Piano*', *Screen*, 36: 3 (Autumn), 267–77.

Eagleton, T. (1983) *Literary Theory: An Introduction*, Oxford, Basil Blackwell.

Easthope, A. (1991) *Literary into Cultural Studies*, London, Routledge.

Edel, L. (1974) 'Novel and Camera', in J. Halperin (ed.), *The Theory of the Novel*, Oxford, Oxford University Press, 176–95.

Edgar, D. (1982) *Ah! Mischief: The Writer and Television*, London, Faber.

Eidsvik, C. (1977) 'Toward a "Politique des Adaptations"' in J. Harrington (ed.), *Film And/As Literature*, Englewood Cliffs, NJ, Prentice-Hall, 27–37.

Eisenstein, S. (1949) *Film Form*, trans. J. Leyda, Florida, Harcourt Brace, 1977.

Ellen, B. (1996) 'I Bet They Outdrink Carling', *Observer*, 24 November, 8.

Ellington, E. H. (1998) '"A Correct Taste in Landscape": Pemberley as Fetish and Commodity', in L. Troost and S. Greenfield (eds), *Jane Austen in Hollywood*, Kentucky, The University Press of Kentucky, 90–110.

Ellis, J. (1992) *Visible Fictions*, London, Routledge.

Ellis, J. (1990) 'What Does a Script Do?', *Yearbook of English Studies*, 20, 60–4.

Ellis, J. (1982) 'The Literary Adaptation', *Screen*, 23: 1, 6–19.

Enright, D. J. (1988) *Fields of Vision: Essays on Literature, Language and Television*, Oxford, Oxford University Press.

Ferris, S. (1998) 'Emma Becomes Clueless', in L. Troost and S. Greenfield (eds), *Jane Austen in Hollywood*, Kentucky, The University Press of Kentucky, 122–9.

Feuer, J. (1992) 'Genre Study and Television', in R. Allen (ed.), *Channels of Discourse, Reassembled*, 2nd edn, London, Routledge, 138–60.

Feuer, J. (1983) 'The Concept of Live Television: Ontology as Ideology', in Ann E. Kaplan (ed.), *Regarding Television: Critical Approaches – An Anthology*, Los Angeles, University Publications of America, 12–22.

Fiske, J. (1989a) *Reading the Popular*, London, Routledge.

Fiske, J. (1989b) *Understanding Popular Culture*, London, Routledge.

Ford, G. H. (1987) 'Dickens' *Hard Times* on Television – Problems of Adaptation', *Papers on Language and Literature*, 23: 3, 319–31.

Friedburg, A. (1993) *Window Shopping: Cinema and the Postmodern*, London, University of California Press.

Fry, T. (1993a) 'Introduction', in T. Fry, *RUA TV? Heidegger and the Televisual*, Sydney, Power Institute of Fine Arts, 11–23.

Fry, T. (1993b) *RUA TV? Heidegger and the Televisual*, Sydney, Power Institute of Fine Arts.

Fulton, A. R. (1977) 'From Novel to Film', in J. Harrington (ed.), *Film And/As Literature*, Englewood Cliffs, NJ, Prentice-Hall, 151–5.

Garvin, P. L. (ed. and trans.) (1964) *A Prague School Reader on Aesthetics, Literary Structure and Style*, Washington, Georgetown University Press.

Gaut, B. (1997) 'Film Authorship and Collaboration', in R. Allen and M. Smith (eds), *Film Theory and Philosophy: Aesthetics and the Analytical Tradition*, Oxford, Oxford University Press, 149–72.

Gelder, K. (1999) 'Jane Campion and the Limits of Literary Cinema', in D. Cartmell and I. Whelehan (eds), *Adaptations: From Text to Screen, Screen to Text*, London, Routledge, 157–71.

Gelion, G. (1988) 'The Plight of Film Adaptation in France: Toward Dialogic Process in the Auteur Film', in Aycock and Schoenecke, *Film and Literature: A Comparative Approach to Adaptation*, Texas, Texas University Press, 135–48.

Geraghty, C. and D. Lusted (eds) (1997), *The Television Studies Book*, London, Arnold.

Gervais, D. (1994) 'Televising *Middlemarch*', *English: The Journal of the English Association*, 43: 175 (Spring), 59–64.

Giddings, R., K. Selby and C. Wensley (1990) *Screening the Novel: The Theory and Practice of Literary Dramatization*, Basingstoke, Hampshire, Macmillan Press.

Giddings, R. (1983) 'Recycling the Classics', *Listener*, 40: 2836, 8 December, 42.

Gillett, S. (1995) 'Lips and Fingers: Jane Campion's *The Piano*', *Screen*, 36: 3 (Autumn), 277–87.

Golub, S. (1993) 'Spies in the House of Quality', in P. Reynolds (ed.), *Novel Images: Literature in Performance*, London, Routledge, 139–56.

Goodman, N. (1976) *Languages of Art: An Approach to a Theory of Symbols*, 2nd edn, Indianapolis, Hackett.

Gould, S. J. (1980) *Ever Since Darwin: Reflections in Natural History*, Harmondsworth, Penguin.

Graham, A. (1997a) 'My Goodness, How They've Changed', *Radio Times*, 12–18 July, 22–3.

Graham, A. (1997b) 'Confessions of a Belated Darcy Fan', *Radio Times*, 26 July–1 August, 122.

Graham, A. (1996) 'The Brontë Business', *Radio Times*, 16–22 November, 22.

Greenblatt, S. and G. Gunn (eds) (1992) *Redrawing the Boundaries (The Transformation of English and American Literary Studies)*, New York, The Modern Language Association of America.

Gripsrud, J. (1997) 'Television, Broadcasting, Flow: Key Metaphors in TV Theory', in C. Geraghty and D. Lusted (eds), *The Television Studies Book*, London, Arnold, 17–32.

Grodal, T. (1997) *Moving Pictures: A New Theory of Film Genres, Feelings and Cognition*, Oxford, Clarendon Press.

Grossberg, L. (1987) 'The In-Difference of Television: TV's Affective Economy', *Screen*, 28: 2 (Spring), 28–45.

Guillery, J. (1993) *Cultural Capital: The Problem of Literary Canon Formation*, London, University of Chicago Press.

Gwozdz, A. (1999) 'On Some Aspects of Television Temporality', *Kinema: A Journal for Film and Audiovisual Media* (Fall). Republished at http://www.arts.uwaterloo.ca/FINE/ juhde/ gwoz992.htm.

Harper, H. M. and C. Edge (eds) (1977) *The Classic British Novel*, Athens, University of Georgia Press.

Harrington, J. (ed.) (1977) *Film And/As Literature*, Englewood Cliffs, NJ, Prentice-Hall.

Harris, M. (1995) 'Whose *Middlemarch?* The 1994 British Broadcasting Corporation's Television Production', *Sydney Studies in English*, 21, 95–102.

Hawkins, H. (1990) *Classics and Trash: Traditions and Taboos in High Literature and Popular Modern Genres*, London, Harvester Wheatsheaf.

Heath, S. (1990) 'Representing Television', in P. Mellencamp (ed.), *Logics of Television: Essays in Cultural Criticism*, Bloomington and Indianapolis, Indiana University Press, 267–302.

Heath, S. and G. Skirrow (1977), 'Television: A World in Action', *Screen*, 18: 2, 7–59.

Helman, A. and W. M. Osadnik (1996) 'Film and Literature: Historical Models of Film Adaptation and a Proposal for a (Poly)System Approach', *Canadian Review of Comparative Literature*, 23: 2 (September), 645–58.

Henderson, B. (1983) 'Tense, Mood, and Voice in Film (Notes after Genette)', *Film Quarterly*, 36: 3 (Summer), 4–17.

Hewison, R. (1987) *The Heritage Industry: Britain in a Climate of Decline*, London, Methuen.

Higson, A. (1996) 'The Heritage Film and British Cinema', in A. Higson (ed.), *Dissolving Views: Key Writings on British Cinema*, London, Cassell, 232–49.

Higson, A. (1995) *Waving the Flag: Constructing a National Cinema in Britain*, Oxford, Clarendon Press.

Higson, A. (1993) 'Re-presenting the National Past: Nostalgia and Pastiche in the Heritage Film', in L. Friedman (ed.), *British Cinema and Thatcherism: Fires Were Started*, London, University College London Press, 109–29.

Hill, J. (1999) *British Cinema in the 1980s: Issues and Themes*, Oxford, Oxford University Press.

Hill, J. (1999) 'The Heritage Film: Issues and Debates', in J. Hill, *British Cinema in the 1980s*, Oxford, Oxford University Press, 73–98.

Hipsky, M. A. (1994) 'Anglophil(m)ia: Why Does America Watch Merchant-Ivory Movies?', *Journal of Popular Film and Television*, 22: 3 (Fall), 98–107.

Holbrook, M. B. (1993) 'On the New Nostalgia: "These Foolish Things" and Echoes of the Dear Departed Past', in R. B. Browne and R. J. Ambrosetti (eds), *Continuities in Popular Culture: The Present in the Past and the Past in the Present and Future*, London, Routledge, 74–120.

Hopkins, L. (1998) 'Mr. Darcy's Body: Privileging the Female Gaze', in L. Troost and S. Greenfield, *Jane Austen in Hollywood*, Kentucky, The University Press of Kentucky, 111–21.

Ingarden, R. (1965) *The Literary Work of Art*, trans. G. G. Grabowicz, Evanston, Northwestern University Press, 1973.

Jameson, F. (1991) *Postmodernism; Or, the Cultural Logic of Late Capitalism*, Durham, NC, Duke University Press.

Jarvie, I. (1987) *Philosophy of the Film: Epistemology, Ontology and Aesthetics*, London, Routledge and Kegan Paul.

Jinks, W. (1971) *The Celluloid Literature*, Los Angeles, Glencoe Press.

Jones, J. C. (1992) *The Novel on the Screen (W. D. Thomas Memorial Lecture, University College of Swansea, 20 January)*, Swansea, University College of Swansea Press.

Jordan, M. (1981) 'A Study of the Relationship between the Novel and the Film (for Cinema or Television), with Special Reference to the Novels of Henry James', unpub. Master's thesis, University of Warwick.

Joyrich, L. (1996) *Re-viewing Reception: Television, Gender, and Postmodern Culture*, Bloomington and Indianapolis, Indiana University Press.

BIBLIOGRAPHY 217

Kaplan, D. (1998) 'Mass Marketing Jane Austen: Men, Women and Courtship in Two Film Adaptations', in L. Troost and S. Greenfield (eds), *Jane Austen in Hollywood*, Kentucky, The University Press of Kentucky, 177–87.

Kaplan, E. A. (1987) *Rocking Around the Clock: Music Television, Postmodernism and Consumer Culture*, London, Methuen.

Kawin, B. (1972) *Telling it Again and Again: Repetition in Literature and Film*, London, Cornell University Press.

Kearney, R. (1982) 'Revisualizing Times Past', *Studies: An Irish Quarterly Review*, 71: 281 (Spring), 85–93.

Kellner, D. (1994) 'Introduction: Jean Baudrillard in the Fin-de-Millenium', in D. Kellner (ed.), *Baudrillard: A Critical Reader*, Oxford, Basil Blackwell, 1–23.

Kerr, P. (1982) 'Classic Serials To-Be-Continued', *Screen*, 23: 1, 6–19.

Kivy, P. (1997) 'Music in the Movies: A Philosophical Enquiry', in R. Allen and M. Smith, *Film Theory and Philosophy: Aesthetics and the Analytical Tradition*, Oxford, Oxford University Press, 308–28.

Klein, M. and G. Parker (eds) (1981) *The English Novel and the Movies*, New York, Frederick Ungar Publishing.

Kline, K. E. (1996) '*The Accidental Tourist* On Page and On Screen: Interrogating Normative Theories About Film Adaptation', *Literature Film Quarterly*, 24: 1, 70–82.

Lamarque, P. (1990) 'The Death of the Author: An Analytical Autopsy', *British Journal of Aesthetics*, 30: 4, 319–31.

Langford, B. (1999) '"You Cannot Look at This": Thresholds of Unrepresentability in Holocaust Film', research seminar paper, Royal Holloway College, University of London, March.

Larsen, E. (1983) 'Writing and Nostalgia: Hiding in the Past', *New England Review and Bread Loaf Quarterly*, 5: 4, 461–77.

Lauritzen, M. (1981) *Jane Austen's 'Emma' on Television: A Study of a BBC Classic Serial*, Goteburg, Acto Universitatis Gothoburgensis.

Linden, G. (1971) 'The Storied World', in F. H. Marcus, *Film and Literature: Contrasts in Media*, Seranton, Chandler, 157–63.

Lindley, A. (1992) 'Raj as Romance, Raj as Parody: Lean's and Forster's *Passage to India*', *Literature Film Quarterly*, 20: 1, 61–7.

Livingston, P. (1997) 'Cinematic Authorship', in R. Allen and M. Smith, *Film Theory and Philosophy: Aesthetics and the Analytical Tradition*, Oxford, Oxford University Press, 132–48.

Lock, K. (1996a) 'It's Austenmania', *Radio Times*, 13–19 July, 66–7.

Lock, K. (1996b) 'Wicked Lady', *Radio Times*, 30 November–6 December, 41.

Lodge, D. (1981) 'Thomas Hardy as a Cinematic Novelist', in D. Lodge, *Working with Structuralism: Essays and Reviews on Nineteenth- and Twentieth-century Literature*, London, Routledge and Kegan Paul, 95–105.

Long, R. E. (1997) *The Films of Merchant Ivory*, New York, Abrams.

Looser, D. (1998) 'Feminist Implications of the Silver Screen Austen', in L. Troost and S. Greenfield, *Jane Austen in Hollywood*, Kentucky, The University Press of Kentucky, 159–76.

Lowenthal, D. (1985) *The Past is a Foreign Country*, Cambridge, Cambridge University Press.

Luhr, W. and P. Lehman (1977) *Authorship and Narrative in the Cinema: Issues in Contemporary Aesthetics and Criticism*, New York, Capricorn Books.

MacCormac, E. R. (1985) *A Cognitive Theory of Metaphor*, Cambridge, MA, MIT Press.

Malor, D. (1993) 'Touch TV: Finding Out What Is at Hand in the Televisual Environment', in T. Fry, *RUA TV? Heidegger and the Televisual*, Sydney, Power Institute of Fine Arts, 67–84.

Marcus, F. H. (ed.) (1971) *Film and Literature: Contrasts in Media*, Seranton, Chandler.

Marcus, M. (1993) *Filmmaking by the Book: Italian Cinema and Literary Adaptation*, Baltimore, The Johns Hopkins University Press.

Mayer, P. C. (1980) 'Film Ontology and the Structure of a Novel', *Literature Film Quarterly*, 8: 3, 204–8.

McArthur, C. (1978) *Television and History*, London, British Film Institute.

McDougal, S. Y. (1985) *Made into Movies: From Literature to Film*, New York, Holt, Rinehart and Winston.

McFarlane, B. (1996) *Novel to Film: An Introduction to the Theory of Adaptation*, Oxford, Clarendon Press.

McFarlane, B. (1987) 'Novel into Film', PhD thesis, University of East Anglia.

McLuhan, M. (1964) *Understanding Media: The Extensions of Man*, London, Routledge and Kegan Paul.

Mellencamp, P. (ed.) (1990) *Logics of Television: Essays in Cultural Criticism*, Bloomington and Indianapolis, Indiana University Press.

Metallinos, Nikos, *Television Aesthetics: Perceptual, Cognitive and Compositional Bases*, Mahwah, NJ, Lawrence Erlbaum Associates, 1996.

Metz, C. (1977) *The Imaginary Signifier*, trans. Celia Britton, London, Macmillan, 1982.

Metz, C. (1974) *Film Language: A Semiotics of the Cinema*, trans. Michael Taylor, New York, Oxford University Press.

Miller, J. (1986) *Subsequent Performances*, London, Faber and Faber.

Miller, J. (1983) 'The James McTaggart Memorial Lecture', Eighth Edinburgh International Television Festival.

Mitry, J. (1971) 'Remarks on the Problem of Cinematic Adaptation', *Bulletin of Midwest Modern Language Association*, 1, 1–7.

Morse, M. (1990) 'An Ontology of Everyday Distraction', in P. Mellencamp (ed.), *Logics of Television Essays in Cultural Criticism*, Bloomington and Indianapolis, Indiana University Press, 193–221.

Moynahan, J. (1981) 'Great Expectations: Seeing the Book, Reading the Movie', in M. Klein and G. Parker, *The English Novel and the Movies*, New York, Frederick Ungar Publishing, 143–54.

Muir, K. (1986) *King Lear*, Harmondsworth, Penguin.

Muir, K. (1977) *The Sources of Shakespeare's Plays*, London, Methuen.

Murray, E. (1972) *The Cinematic Imagination: Writers and the Motion Pictures*, New York, Frederick Ungar Publishing.

Neale, S. (1980) *Genre*, London, British Film Institute.

Nelson, R. (1997) *TV Drama in Transition: Forms, Values and Cultural Change*, Basingstoke, Hampshire, Macmillan Press.

Nicolson, A. (1992) 'Introduction', in A. Nicolson (text) and N. Meers (photographs) *Panoramas of England*, London, Phoenix Illustrated, 14–28.

North, J. (1999) 'Conservative Austen, Radical Austen: *Sense and Sensibility* from Text to Screen', in D. Cartmell and I. Whelehan, *Adaptations: From Text to Screen, Screen to Text*, London, Routledge, 38–50.

O'Connor, J. E. (1988) 'History in Images/Images in History: Reflections on the Importance of Film and Television Study for an Understanding of the Past', *American Historical Review*, 94: 5, 1200–9.

Olsen, S. H. (1976) 'Defining A Literary Work', *British Journal of Aesthetics*, 35, 133–42.

Orr, C. (1984) 'The Discourse on Adaptation', *Wide Angle*, 6: 2, 72–6.

Parker, A. and E. K. Sedgwick (1995) 'Introduction: Performativity and Performance', in A. Parker and E. K. Sedgwick (eds), *Performativity and Performance*, London, Routledge, 1–18.

Pearce, E. (1982) '*Brideshead Revisited*', *Quadrant*, 26: 7, 59–61.

Peary, G. and R. Shatzkin (eds) (1977) *The Classic American Novel and the Movies*, New York, Frederick Ungar Publishing.

Perkins, V. (1972) *Film as Film*, Harmondsworth, Penguin.

Phillips, G. D. (1980) *Hemmingway and Film*, New York, Frederick Ungar Publishing.

Pidduck, J. (1998) 'Of Windows and Country Walks: Frames of Space and Movement in 1990s Austen Adaptations', *Screen*, 39: 4, 381–400.

Pilkington, A. G. (1990) 'Shakespeare on the Big Screen, the Small Box, and in Between', *Yearbook of English Studies*, 20, 65–81.

Plantinga, C. (1997) *Rhetoric and Representation in Nonfiction Film*, Cambridge, Cambridge University Press.

Plantinga, C. and G. M. Smith (eds) (1999) *Passionate Views: Film, Cognition and Emotion*, Baltimore, The Johns Hopkins University Press.

Ratcliffe, M. (1982) 'Drama on Television: *Brideshead Revisited*', *Drama*, 143, 52–5.

Rector, M. (1991) 'Transmutation: From the Written Literary text to the Video Narrative', *Romance Languages Annual*, 3, 578–82.

Reynolds, P. (1993) *Novel Images: Literature in Performance*, London, Routledge.

Richards, J. (ed.) (1997) *Films and British National Identity: From Dickens to 'Dad's Army'*, Manchester, Manchester University Press.

Richardson, R. (1969) 'Verbal and Visual Languages', in F. H. Marcus, *Film and Literature: Contrasts in Media*, Seranton, Chandler, 1971, 115–26.

Robbe-Grillet, A. (1962) 'Introduction' to *Last Year at Marienbad*, trans. Richard Howard, New York, Grove.

Robyns, C. (1988) 'The Camera Eye – Between Film and Novel', *Poetics Today*, 9: 3, 675–6.

Roddick, N. (1982) '*Brideshead Revisited*', *Sight and Sound*, 51: 1, 58–60.

Roemer, M. (1971) 'The Surfaces of Reality', in F. H. Marcus, *Film and Literature: Contrasts in Media*, Seranton, Chandler, 41–52.

Rosenstone, R. A. (1996) 'The Future of the Past: Film and the Beginnings of Postmodern History', in V. Sobchack (ed.), *The Persistence of History*, London, Routledge, 201–18.

Rosenstone, R. A. (1995), *Visions of the Past: The Challenge of Film to Our Idea of History*, Cambridge, MA, Harvard University Press.

Rosenstone, R. A. (1988) 'History in Images/Images in History: Reflections on the Possibility of Really Putting History onto Film', *American Historical Review*, 94: 5, 1173–85.

Ruhe, E. L. (1973) 'Film: The "Literary" Approach', *Literature Film Quarterly*, 1: 1 (Winter/ January), 76–83.

Ruthven, K. K. (1979) *Critical Assumptions*, Cambridge, Cambridge University Press.

Samuel, R. (1998) *Island Stories: Unravelling Britain (Theatres of Memory: Volume II)*, London, Verso.

Samuel, R. (1994) *Theatres of Memory: Volume I*, London, Verso.

Sargeant, A., (1998) 'The Darcy Effect', conference paper given at 'Cinema, Identity, History', University of East Anglia, 10–12 July.

Saynor, J. (1982) '*Brideshead Revisited*', *Stills*, 1: 4, 56–9.

Scholes, R. (1976) 'Narration and Narrativity in Film', *Quarterly Review of Film Studies*, 1: 3, 283–96.

Schutz, A. (1962) 'On Multiple Realities', in A. Schutz, *Collected Papers, Volume 1: The Problem of Social Reality*, The Hague, Martinus Nijhoff, 207–59.

Sheen, E. (2000) 'Introduction', in R. Giddings and E. Sheen (eds), *The Classic Novel: From Page to Screen*, Manchester, Manchester University Press, 1–13.

Silverstone, R. (1993) 'Television, Ontological Security and the Transitional Object', *Media, Culture and Society*, 15: 4, 573–98.

Sinyard, N. (1986) *Filming Literature: The Art of Screen Adaptation*, London, Croom Helm.

Slater, T. J. (1988) '*One Flew Over the Cuckoo's Nest*: A Tale of Two Decades', in W. Aycock and M. Schoenecke (eds) (1988) *Film and Literature: A Comparative Approach to Adaptation*, Texas, Texas University Press, 45–58.

Smart, B. (1993) *Postmodernity: Key Ideas*, London, Routledge.

Smith, G. (1990) 'Novel into Film: The Case of *Little Dorrit*', *Yearbook of English Studies*, 20, 33–47.

Smith, G. M. (1999) 'Local Emotions, Global Moods, and Film Structure', in C. Plantinga and G. M. Smith (eds), *Passionate Views: Film, Cognition and Emotion*, 103–26.

Smith, M. (1995) *Engaging Characters: Fiction, Emotion, and the Cinema*, Oxford, Clarendon Press.

Sparks, R. (1993) '*Inspector Morse*: "The Last Enemy"', in G. W. Brandt (ed.), *British Television Drama in the 1980s*, Cambridge, Cambridge University Press, 86–102.

Sutrop, M. (1994) 'The Death of the Literary Work', *Philosophy and Literature*, 18, 38–49.

Tan, E. S. (1996) *Emotion and the Structure of Narrative Film: Film as an Emotion Machine*, trans. Barbara Fasting, Mahwah, NJ, Lawrence Erlbaum Associates.

Taylor, J. (1994) *A Dream of England: Landscape, Photography and the Tourist's Imagination*, Manchester, Manchester University Press.

Thomson, D. (1981) 'Big Books, Small Screens (Television Adaptations)', *American Film*, 6: 4, 16.

Thompson, J. O. (1996) '"Vanishing" Worlds: Film Adaptation and the Mystery of the Original', in D. Cartmell, I. Q. Hunter, H. Kaye and I. Whelehan (eds), *Pulping Fictions: Consuming Culture Across the Literature/Media Divide*, London, Pluto Press, 11–28.

Tomashevsky, B. (1929) 'Thematics', in L. T. Lemon and M. J. Reis (eds), *Russian Formalist Criticism: Four Essays*, Lincoln, University of Nebraska Press, 1965, 61–95.

Toplin, R. B. (1988) 'The Filmmaker as Historian', *American Historical Review*, 94: 5, 1210–27.

Toynton, E. (1998) 'Rereading: Revisiting *Brideshead*', *The American Scholar*, 67: 4 (Autumn), 134–7.

Troost, L. and S. Greenfield (1998) *Jane Austen in Hollywood*, Kentucky, The University Press of Kentucky.

Troost, L. (1998) 'Watching Ourselves Watching', in L. Troost and S. Greenfield, *Jane Austen in Hollywood*, Kentucky, The University Press of Kentucky, 1–12.

Wagner, G. (1975) *The Novel and the Cinema*, Rutherford, NJ, Fairleigh Dickinson University Press.

Watt, I. (1976) *The Rise of the Novel*, Harmondsworth, Penguin.

Waugh, E. (1962) 'Preface to 1960 Edition', in E. Waugh, *Brideshead Revisited*, Harmondsworth, Penguin, 1945, 7–8.

Way, E. C. (1994) *Knowledge, Representation and Metaphor*, Oxford, Intellect.

Webster, R. (1993) 'Reproducing Hardy: Familiar and Unfamiliar Versions of *Far from the Madding Crowd* and *Tess of the d'Urbervilles*', *Critical Survey*, 5: 2, 143–51.

Whelehan, I. (1999) 'Adaptations: The Contemporary Dilemmas', in D. Cartmell and I. Whelehan, *Adaptations: From Text to Screen, Screen to Text*, London, Routledge, 3–20.

Whelehan, I. and D. Cartmell (1996) 'Introduction', in D. Cartmell, I. Q. Hunter, H. Kaye and I. Whelehan (eds), *Pulping Fictions: Consuming Culture Across the Literature/Media Divide*, London, Pluto Press, 1–10.

White, H. (1988) 'Historiography and Historiophoty', *American Historical Review*, 94: 5, 1193–9.

White, P. (1985) *On Living in an Old Country: The National Past in Contemporary Britain*, London, Verso.

White, P. (1982) 'Remembrance of Things Past: Nostalgia in Recent American Films', *New Orleans Review*, 9: 1, 5–11.

Williams, R. (1993) 'Bertolt Brecht', in R. Williams, *Drama from Ibsen to Brecht*, London, Hogarth Press, 277–90.

Williams, R. (1975) *Television: Technology and Cultural Form*, London, Routledge.

Wilsmore, S. (1987) 'The Literary Work is not its Text', *Philosophy and Literature*, 11, 307–16.

Wilson, J. (1997) 'Adapting Jane Austen? The Battle for Jane Austen', conference paper, Centre for Extra-Mural Studies, Birkbeck College, University of London, April.

Wilson, T. (1993) *Watching Television: Hermeneutics, Reception and Popular Culture*, Cambridge, Polity Press.

Wimsatt Jr., W. K. and M. C. Beardsley (1995) 'The Intentional Fallacy', in S. Burke (ed.), *Authorship: From Plato to the Postmodern*, Edinburgh, Edinburgh University Press, 90–100.

Wollen, T. (1991) 'Over our Shoulders: Nostalgic Screen Fictions for the 1980s', in J. Corner and S. Harvey (eds), *Enterprise and Heritage: Crosscurrents of National Culture*, London, Routledge, 178–93.

Yakir, D. (1982) 'Waugh Revisited', *Horizon*, 25: 1, 58–9.

Zettl, H. (1978) 'The Rare Case of Television Aesthetics', *Journal of the University Film Association*, 2 (Spring), 1–12.

Electronic sources

BBC website
www.bbc.co.uk (accessed March 2000)

'*Brideshead*' website
www.geocities.com/Athens/Parthenon/6588/tv.htm (accessed October 1998)

'Republic of Pemberley' website
www.pemberley.com/janeinfo/janeinfo.html#janetoc (accessed March 2000)

Key source novels

Austen, J. ([1813] 1994) *Pride and Prejudice*, Harmondsworth, Penguin.

Bronte, A. ([1848] 1996) *The Tenant of Wildfell Hall*, Harmondsworth, Penguin.

Defoe, D. ([1722] 1989) *The Fortunes and Misfortunes of the Famous Moll Flanders*, Harmondsworth, Penguin.

Waugh, E. ([1945] 1962) *Brideshead Revisited*, Harmondsworth, Penguin.

Filmography

Classic-novel adaptations (television and film)

Anna Karenina, Channel Four (Company Productions), 2000.
Screenplay Allan Cubitt; dir. David Blair.
Based on the novel *Anna Karenina* (1877) by Leo Tolstoy.

Brideshead Revisited, ITV (Granada), 1981.
Screenplay John Mortimer; dir. Charles Sturridge and Michael Lindsay-Hogg.
Based on the novel *Brideshead Revisited* (1945) by Evelyn Waugh.

Clueless, cinema release, Paramount, 1995.
Screenplay and dir. Amy Heckerling.
Based on the novel *Emma* (1816) by Jane Austen.

David Copperfield, BBC (BBB/WGBH Boston), 1999.
Screenplay Adrian Hodges; dir Simon Curtis.
Based on the novel *David Copperfield* (1850) by Charles Dickens.

Elizabeth, cinema release, Channel Four Films/PolyGram/Working Title, 1998.
Screenplay Michael Hirst; dir. Shekar Kapur.

Emma, cinema release, Miramax, 1996.
Screenplay and dir. Douglas McGrath.
Based on the novel *Emma* (1816) by Jane Austen.

Emma, ITV (Meridian/A&E), 1996.
Screenplay Andrew Davies; dir. Diarmuid Lawrence.
Based on the novel *Emma* (1816) by Jane Austen.

Far from the Madding Crowd, ITV (Granada/WGBH Boston/Mobil Masterpiece Theatre), 1998.
Screenplay Philomena McDonagh; dir. Nicholas Renton.
Based on the novel *Far from the Madding Crowd* (1874) by Thomas Hardy.

Great Expectations, BBC (BBC/WGBH Boston), 1999.
Screenplay Tony Marchant; Dir. Julian Jarrold.
Based on the novel *Great Expectations* (1861) by Charles Dickens.

Great Expectations, cinema release, Cineguild, 1946.
Screenplay Ronald Neame, David Lean and Anthony Havelock Allen; dir. David Lean.
Based on the novel *Great Expectations* (1861) by Charles Dickens.

Hard Times, ITV (Granada/WNET Channel 13 New York), 1977.
Screenplay Arthur Hopcraft; dir. John Irvin.
Based on the novel *Hard Times* (1854) by Charles Dickens.

Howards End, cinema release, Merchant Ivory Productions, 1992.
Screenplay Ruth Prawer Jhabvala; dir. James Ivory.
Based on the novel *Howards End* (1910) by E. M. Forster.

Jane Eyre, ITV (A&E/LWT), 1997.
Screenplay Richard Hawley, Kay Mellor, Peter Wright; dir. Robert Young.
Based on the novel *Jane Eyre* (1847) by Charlotte Brontë.

Jane Eyre, cinema release, 20th Century Fox, 1943.
Screenplay John Houseman and Aldous Huxley; dir. Robert Stevenson.
Based on the novel *Jane Eyre* (1847) by Charlotte Brontë.

Jewel in the Crown, The, ITV (Granada), 1984.
Screenplay Ken Taylor; dir. Christopher Morahan.
Based on the series of novels 'The Raj Quartet' by Paul Scott (1966–75).

Jude, cinema release, Revolution Films, 1996.
Screenplay Hossein Amini; dir. Michael Winterbottom.
Based on the novel *Jude the Obscure* (1895) by Thomas Hardy.

Little Dorrit (*Nobody's Fault* and *Little Dorrit's Story*), cinema release, Cannon Street
    Entertainment, 1987.
Screenplay and dir. Christine Edzard.
Based on the novel *Little Dorrit* (1857) by Charles Dickens.

Madame Bovary, BBC (BBC/WGBH Boston), 2000.
Screenplay Heidi Thomas; dir. Tim Fywell.
Based on the novel *Madame Bovary* (1857) by Gustave Flaubert.

Martin Chuzzlewit, BBC (BBC/WGBH Boston), 1994.
Screenplay David Lodge; dir. Pedr James
Based on the novel *Martin Chuzzlewit* (1843–44) by Charles Dickens

Maurice, cinema release, Merchant Ivory Productions, 1987.
Screenplay Kit Hesketh-Harvey and James Ivory; dir. James Ivory.
Based on the novel *Maurice* (completed 1914; revised 1960; first published 1971) by E. M.
    Forster.

Mayor of Casterbridge, The, BBC (BBC/Time-Life Television), 1991.
Screenplay Dennis Potter; dir. David Giles.
Based on the novel *The Mayor of Casterbridge* (1886) by Thomas Hardy.

Middlemarch, BBC (BBC), 1994.
Screenplay Andrew Davies; dir. Anthony Page.
Based on the novel *Middlemarch* (1872) by George Eliot.

Moll Flanders, The Fortunes and Misfortunes of, ITV (Granada Television/WGBH Boston),
    1996.
Screenplay Andrew Davies; dir. David Attwood.
Based on the novel *Moll Flanders* (1722) by Daniel Defoe.

Moll Flanders, cinema release, MGM, 1996.
Screenplay and dir. Pen Densham.
Based on the novel *Moll Flanders* (1722) by Daniel Defoe.

Oliver!, cinema release, Warwick/Romulus Productions, 1968.
Screenplay Lionel Bart; dir. Carol Reed.
Based on the novel *Oliver Twist* (1837–39) by Charles Dickens.

Oliver Twist, ITV (ITV/Meridian Broadcasting), 1999.
Screenplay Alan Bleasdale; dir. Renny Rye.
Based on the novel *Oliver Twist* (1837–39) by Charles Dickens.

Our Mutual Friend, BBC (BBC), 1998.
Screenplay Sandy Welch; dir. Julian Farino.
Based on the novel *Our Mutual Friend* (1864–65) by Charles Dickens.

Passage to India, A, cinema release, EMI Films, 1984.
Screenplay and dir. David Lean.
Based on the novel *A Passage to India* (1924) by E. M. Forster.

Persuasion, BBC (BBC/WGBH Boston), 1995.
Screenplay Nick Dear; dir. Roger Michell.
Based on the novel *Persuasion* (1818) by Jane Austen.

Persuasion, ITV (Granada), 1971.
Screenplay Julian Mitchell; dir. Howard Baker.
Based on the novel *Persuasion* (1818) by Jane Austen.

Pride and Prejudice, BBC (BBC/A&E), 1995.
Screenplay Andrew Davies; dir. Simon Langton.
Based on the novel *Pride and Prejudice* (1813) by Jane Austen.

Pride and Prejudice, BBC (BBC/A&E), 1980.
Screenplay Fay Weldon; dir. Cyril Coke.
Based on the novel *Pride and Prejudice* (1813) by Jane Austen.

Pride and Prejudice, cinema release, MGM, 1940
Screenplay Aldous Huxley, Helen Jerome, Jane Murfin; dir. Robert Z. Leonard.
Based on the novel *Pride and Prejudice* (1813) by Jane Austen.

Room with a View, A, cinema release, Merchant Ivory Productions, 1985.
Screenplay Ruth Prawer Jhabvala; dir. James Ivory.
Based on the novel *A Room with a View* (1908) by E. M. Forster.

Sense and Sensibility, cinema release, Mirage/Columbia, 1995.
Screenplay Emma Thompson; dir. Ang Lee.
Based on the novel *Sense and Sensibility* (1811) by Jane Austen.

Sense and Sensibility, BBC (BBC), 1985.
Screenplay Alexander Baron; dir. Rodney Bennett.
Based on the novel *Sense and Sensibility* (1811) by Jane Austen.

Tenant of Wildfell Hall, The, BBC (BBC), 1996.
Screenplay David Nokes and Janet Barron; dir. Mike Barker.
Based on the novel *The Tenant of Wildfell Hall* (1848) by Anne Brontë.

Tess of the D'Urbervilles, ITV (LWT/A&E), 1998.
Screenplay Ted Whitehead; dir. Ian Sharp.
Based on the novel *Tess of the D'Urbervilles* (1891) by Thomas Hardy.

Tom Jones, cinema release, Woodfall Film Productions, 1963.
Screenplay John Osborne; dir. Tony Richardson.
Based on the novel *The History of Tom Jones, a Foundling* (1749) by Henry Fielding.

Turn of Screw, The, ITV (United Productions/WGBH Boston), 1999.
Screenplay Nick Dear; dir. Ben Bolt.
Based on the novel *The Turn of the Screw* (1898) by Henry James.

Vanity Fair, BBC (BBC/A&E), 1998.
Screenplay Andrew Davies; dir. Marc Munden.
Based on the novel *Vanity Fair* (1847–48) by William M. Thackeray.

Where Angels Fear to Tread, cinema release, Stagescreen Productions/LWT/Sovereign Pictures, 1991.
Screenplay Tim Sullivan, Derek Granger, Charles Sturridge; dir. Charles Sturridge.
Based on the novel *Where Angels Fear to Tread* (1905) by E. M. Forster.

Wives and Daughters, BBC (BBC/WGBH Boston), 1999.
Screenplay Andrew Davies, dir. Nicholas Renton.
Based on the novel *Wives and Daughters* (1865) by Elizabeth Gaskell.

Wuthering Heights, ITV (LWT/WGBH Boston), 1999.
Screenplay Neil McKay; dir. David Skynner.
Based on the novel *Wuthering Heights* (1847) by Emily Brontë.

Other programmes and films

Alan Partridge, BBC (Talk Back Productions), 1997.
Creators Peter Baynham and Steve Coogan; dir. Dominic Brigstocke.

Aristocrats, BBC (BBC/Irish Screen/WGBH Boston), 1999.
Screenplay Harriet O'Carroll ; dir. David Caffrey.
Based on the novel *Aristocrats* (1994) by Stella Tillyard.

Forsyte Saga, The, BBC (BBC), 1967.
Screenplay Lennox Philips and others; dir. David Giles and James Cellan Jones.
Based on the series of novels (1906–28) by John Galsworthy.

Gormenghast, BBC (BBC/WGBH Boston), 2000.
Screenplay Malcolm McKay; dir. Andy Wilson.
Based on the Gormenghast trilogy of novels (1946–59) by Mervyn Peake.

Hamlet, cinema release, Castle Rock Entertainment/Fishmonger Films, 1989.
Screenplay and dir. Kenneth Branagh.
Based on the play *Hamlet* (1603) by William Shakespeare.

House of Eliott, The, BBC (BBC), 1991–94.
Screenplay Eileen Atkins and Jean Marsh; dir. Jeremy Silberston.

Inspector Morse, ITV (Central TV/Zenith), 1987–93
(Followed by several 'one-off' films 1995–2000).
Screenplay various (including Julian Mitchell, Daniel Boyle, Alma Cullen and Anthony Minghella); dir. various.
Based on the series of 'Morse' novels (1975–99) by Colin Dexter.

Knock, The, ITV (Bronson Knight Productions), 1994–2000.
Creators Paul Knight and Anita Bronson; dir. various

Let Them Eat Cake, BBC (Tiger Aspect Productions), 1999.
Screenplay Peter Learmouth; dir. Christine Gernon.

Love in a Cold Climate, BBC (BBC), 2001.
Screenplay Deborah Moggach; dir. Tom Hooper.
Based on the novel *Love in a Cold Climate* (1948) by Nancy Mitford.

Lovejoy, BBC (BBC), 1986–94.
Screenplay various; dir. various
Based on a series of novels (1977–) by Jonathan Gash (John Grant).

Piano, The, cinema release, Entertainment/CIBY, 1993.
Screenplay and dir. Jane Campion.

Pride and Prejudice: From Page to Screen, BBC (BBC), 1995.
Producer Sarah Feilden.

Remains of the Day, The, cinema release, Merchant Ivory Productions, 1993.
Screenplay Ruth Prawer Jhabvala; dir. James Ivory.
Based on the novel *The Remains of the Day* (1989) by Kazuo Ishiguro.

Shadowlands, cinema release, Shadowlands Productions, 1993.
Screenplay William Nicholson; dir. Richard Attenborough.
Based on the play *Shadowlands* (1990) by William Nicholson.

Shining, The, cinema release, Peregrine/Warner Bros./Hawk Films, 1980.
Screenplay Diane Johnson and Stanley Kubrick; dir. Stanley Kubrick.

Sirens, The, cinema release, WMG Film/British Screen Finance/Australian Film Finance/
    Samson Productions/Sarah Radclyffe Productions, 1994.
Screenplay and dir. John Duigan.

Take a Girl Like You, BBC (BBC/WGBH Boston), 2000.
Screenplay Andrew Davies; dir. Nick Hurran.
Based on the novel *Take a Girl Like You* (1960) by Kingsley Amis.

Index